Exile and the Writer

EXILE AND THE WRITER

Exoteric and Esoteric Experiences
A Jungian Approach

BETTINA L. KNAPP

The Pennsylvania State University Press
University Park, Pennsylvania

This publication has been supported by the National Endowment for the Humanities, a federal agency which supports the study of such fields as history, philosophy, literature, and languages.

Library of Congress Cataloging-in-Publication Data

Knapp, Bettina Liebowitz, 1926–
    Exile and the writer : exoteric and esoteric experiences : a
  Jungian approach / Bettina L. Knapp

        p.   cm.
    Includes bibliographical references (p.   ).
    ISBN 0-271-00710-9
    1. Exiles' writings—Psychological aspects.   2. Authors,
  Exiled.   3. Jung, C. G. (Carl Gustav), 1875–1961—Influence.
  4. Psychoanalysis and literature.   I. Title.
  PN495.K58   1991
  809'.8920694—dc20   90–6867

It is the policy of The Pennsylvania State University Press to use
acid-free paper for the first printing of all clothbound books.
Publications on uncoated stock satisfy the minimum requirements
of American National Standard for Information Sciences—Permanence
of Paper for Printed Library Materials, ANSI Z39.48–1984.

*To Professor Salo W. Baron
and
Jeanette M. Baron
for their nobility of spirit
and
for being inspirational forces
in my life*

Contents

Introduction

Exile may be involuntary (one is banished or expelled from one's native land by authoritative decree), or voluntary (one escapes persecution, evades punishment or stressful circumstances, or carves out a new existence for oneself). The fact or state of being deported, expelled, proscribed, expatriated, or simply freely leaving one's homeland implies prolonged separation from one's native country.

Exoteric exile, permanent physical departure from the land and banishment to areas outside of the boundaries of the country, was the penalty meted out in ancient Greece to murderers; ostracism, temporary banishment lasting up to ten years, was imposed on perpetrators of political crimes. A citizen of ancient Rome who had received the death penalty had the choice of execution or exile. During the time of the Roman Empire, criminals were frequently deported to distant islands. The ancient Hebrews allowed those who committed homicide to take refuge in specific cities of sanctuary. Prior to the American Revolution, certain English criminals were sent to the colonies in the New World as punishment; after 1853 they were removed to penal areas in Australia. In Nazi Germany, those who were not considered sufficiently Aryan were imprisoned and/or killed in concentration camps and crematoriums. In imperial and Communist Russia, enemies of the state were banished to Siberia. Prior to, during, and after the Cultural Revolution in Communist China, the reeducational process required that individuals and groups be forcibly exiled from their native cities to the country to work the land.

Exoteric exile, whether voluntary or involuntary, may be identified, though not always necessarily so, with extraverted behavioral patterns.

Discussing such patterns, C. G. Jung wrote: "When the orientation to the object and to objective facts is so predominant that the most frequent and essential decisions and actions are determined, not by subjective values but by objective relations, one speaks of an extraverted attitude" (*Collected Works*, 6:416). An extraverted mode of psychic functioning implies that meaning, value, and interest are applied mostly to external objects rather than to inner subjective matters.

Esoteric or private exile suggests a withdrawal on the part of individuals from the empirical realm and a desire or need to live predominantly in their inner world. Such an inward thrust implies, psychologically, an emptying of the conscious mind of activity related to the external world and its channeling into subliminal realms. C. G. Jung noted that the introverted mode of psychic functioning indicates

> a turning inwards of the libido. . . . Interest does not move towards the object, but recedes towards the subject. Everyone whose attitude is introverted thinks, feels, and acts in a way that clearly demonstrates that the subject is the chief factor of motivation while the object at most receives only a secondary value. Introversion may possess either a more intellectual or more emotional character, just as it can be characterized by either intuition or sensation. Introversion is *active*, when the subject *wills* a certain seclusion in face of the object; it is *passive* when the subject is unable to restore again to the object the libido which is streaming back from it. (*Collected Works*, 6:567)

To live inwardly, for whatever reason, is to exile oneself from outside forces, events, or relationships that one might find repugnant (as in the case of Socrates); or difficult (as was the case for Novalis). One might also choose introversion in order to enrich one's understanding of the world and deepen one's spiritual development, as Marsilio Ficino did.

The concept of exile, be it exoteric or esoteric, extraverted or introverted, may be explored with regard to human development only after nomadism gave way to a sedentary mode of life. Prior to the birth of the city, state, or nation, when Neanderthal and Cro-Magnon men roamed about vast expanses of land, hunting for food, seasonal encampments depended upon climate and the bounties of nature. The sedentary life-style of the Sumerians (peoples in southern Mesopotamia who may have come from Iran or India around 3000 B.C.E.) led to the forming of the first city-states and future empires. Ourouk is mentioned in connection with Gilgamesh, one of a dynasty of "heroized" kings and the protagonist of the Babylonian epic named after him. Menes (3400 B.C.E.), the first Egyptian pharaoh, took up residence in what was to be known as Memphis. As nations grew, conquests and invasions multiplied, and new kingdoms came into being while others vanished into oblivion: the Hittites in Anatolia, the Assyrians in the north of Mesopotamia, and the Medes in Persia. The word *exile* now took on meaning.

In biblical literature, Cain is given credit for the forming of the first city-state: "And Cain knew his wife; and she conceived, and bare Enoch: and he builded a city, and called the name of the city, after the name of his son, Enoch" (Gen. 4:17). Was the Hebrews' newly acquired sedentary way an ironic premonition of the continuous exiles this group was to experience throughout the centuries? Abraham, at the age of seventy-five, was instructed by God to leave his native Ur of the Chaldees and proceed to an unknown destination, later called Canaan. Moses led his people out of bondage from Egypt into exile in the wilderness which lasted forty years. Torture and deportation by the Assyrian ruler and conqueror Sargon II (722 B.C.E.) was also the lot of the ancient Hebrews. In 587, the destruction of Jerusalem by Nebuchadnezzar was followed by the forcible exile of the Hebrews to Babylonia, their displacement ending officially in 539, when the Persian monarch Cyrus the Great conquered Babylonia and opened wide for them the gates of freedom. The psalms of King David convey the feelings of grief and sadness experienced during the Hebrews' captivity.

> By the rivers of Babylon, there we sat down, yea, we wept, when we remembered Zion.
> We hanged our harps upon the willows in the midst thereof
> For there they that carried us away captive required of us a song; and they that wasted us required of us mirth, saying, Sing us one of the songs of Zion.
> How shall we sing the Lord's song in a strange land?
> If I forget thee, O Jerusalem, let my right hand forget her cunning. (Psalms 138:1–5)

Emigrations and exiles were frequent with the advent of Cretan, Hellenic, and Phoenician civilizations. Homer tells us that Odysseus spent ten years fighting the Trojans and another ten wandering about the seas, undergoing many trials in his attempt to return to his wife and son in his homeland of Ithaca: "So surely is there nought sweeter than a man's own country and his parents, even though he dwell far off in a rich home, in a strange land, away from them that begat him" (*Odyssey*, IX, 109).

In Aeschylus's *Agamemnon*, we read: "Ah, well I know how exiles feed on hopes of their return" (224). And does not Euripides' Medea, an alien in her land, also speak out her torment when Jason condemns her to exile? "Insult me. You have a refuge, but I am helpless, faced with exile" (45).

Intent upon creating a climate of moral austerity, the Roman emperor Augustus reacted negatively to *The Art of Love* by the Latin poet Ovid (43 B.C.E.–18 C.E.), a "scandalously" erotic work which praised adultery. Its author, therefore, was expelled to Tomis, a Black Sea outpost, until his death. Ovid's poems of exile, *Sorrows*, and his *Letters from the Black Sea* convey his despair and his supplication for mercy.

The notion of esoteric exile is implicit in many faiths. According to the Vedic Aryans, the creation of the universe, human procreation, and the birth of the arts all resulted from a primeval sacrifice: the self-immolation, or exile from the world, of the cosmic being Purusha: "With the sacrifice the gods sacrificed to the sacrifice. These were the first ritual laws. These very powers reached the dome of the sky where dwell the Sadhyas, the ancient gods."[1]

In the Hindu *Chandogya Upanishad*, many sages contend that salvation may be obtained through mental and physical disciplines, frequently culminating in extreme asceticism requiring physical and spiritual exile from the material world. Indeed, in the well-known parable concerning the nature of the real Self, that Self is identified with neither body nor mind nor a complete negation of consciousness: it is conscious of nothing else but itself.

> There is a Spirit which is pure and which is beyond old age and death; and beyond hunger and thirst and sorrow. This is Atman, the Spirit in man. All the desires of this Spirit are Truth. It is this Spirit that we must find and know: man must find his own Soul. He who has found and knows his Soul has found all the worlds, has achieved all his desires. (*Upanishads*, 121)

After the Buddha had successfully divested himself of most of his earthly desires and needs as well as his individuality, he reached the state of Nirvana, thus exiling himself so completely from the world of contingencies that he no longer existed as a human being.

> The Lord has passed completely away in Nirvana, so that nothing is left which could lead to the formation of another being. And so he cannot be pointed out as being here or there. . . . He can only be

---

[1] *The Rig Veda*, 31. The Sadhyas are "a class of demi-gods or saints, whose name literally means 'those who are not yet to be fulfilled.' " Ibid., 32.

pointed out in the body of his doctrine, for it was he who taught it. (Bary, *Sources of Indian Tradition*, I, 111)

In Valmiki's epic, *The Ramayana* (fourth cent. B.C.E.), the protagonist, Rama (accompanied by his wife and his brother), is banished to the forests for fourteen years.

> When Rama's exile became known, the kings and commoners assembled at the hall broke down and wept; so did the religious heads and ascetics. Men and women wept aloud; the parrots in their cages wept, the cats in people's homes; the infants in their cradles, the cows and calves. Flowers that had just bloomed wilted away. The water birds, the elephants, the charges that drew chariots—all broke down and lamented like Dsaratha [Rama's father] himself, unable to bear the pang of separation from Rama. What a moment ago had been a world of festivities had become one of mourning. (Narayan, *Ramayana*, 53)

Thrust upon his own devices, however, Rama was strengthened physically as well as spiritually by his years of trial and anguish and thus was made worthy of the kingship awaiting him.

Many Christian mystics practiced esoteric exile—introversion, martyrdom, self-abasement—in an attempt to reject the ephemeral joys of the here-and-now, thus making them worthy of eternal beatitude in the world to come. St. Paul, in an *imitatio Christi*, withdrew into the solitude of the wilderness:

> In journeyings often, in perils of waters, in perils of robbers, in perils of mine own countrymen, in perils by the heathen, in perils in the city, in perils in the wilderness, in perils in the sea, in perils among false brethren;
>
> In weariness and painfulness, in watchings often, in hunger and thirst, in fastings often, in cold and nakedness. (2 Cor. 11:26–27)
>
> Therefore I take pleasure in infirmities, in reproaches, in necessities, in persecutions, in distresses for Christ's sake: for when I am weak, then I am strong. (2 Cor. 12:10)

St. Paul's words had an enormous influence on the early church fathers. They encouraged St. Anthony, among many others, to withdraw into the desert. Significant as well was the role they played in the development of the concepts of monasticism, hermitism, asceticism, self-flagellation, and suffering. The continuous deprecation of earthly life enhanced the notion of salvation in celestial spheres. St. Augustine's *Confessions* is a case in point, revealing his need for exile and renunciation of the finite sphere in an attempt to *know* God. In the centuries following Augustine, the spirit of withdrawal from the material world increased in power, as exemplified by Dionysius the Areopagite, Meister Eckehart, St. Hildegarde, St. Benedict, Bernard of Clairvaux, St. Mechthild of Magdeburg, St. Gertrude the Great, St. Ignatius Loyola, and others (see Underhill).

Unlike many Christian mystics, who lived their exiles esoterically, most of the Crusaders experienced their exiles exoterically. They left their native lands after Pope Urban II proclaimed the First Crusade (1095), ostensibly to "liberate" the Holy Land from the Turkish "infidels." Such a lofty aim disintegrated in time into political and economic power struggles. The killings and pillagings of the "holy" Crusaders reached untold proportions during the Fourth Crusade in 1204. Serving the material and political greed of Venice and the pope, the Crusaders' obsessive need for lucre and conquest drove them on to sack Constantinople, burning this extraordinary city, killing and raping many of its citizens, and carrying back with them nine hundred years of accumulated treasure.

The exoteric exile—flight, or *Hegira*—of Muhammad (570–632), the last of the Prophets, from Mecca to Yathrib (later named Medina) led to the founding of his model theocratic state. Islam dates its birth from the time of Muhammad's exile, 622 years after the birth of Jesus Christ, whom the Muslims look upon as a previous "Prophet."

Many Islamic mystics preached an esoteric "secret doctrine" which demanded spiritual and emotional exile from the empirical world. Nezami (d. 1209), the Persian Sufi, wrote: "Under the poet's tongue lies the key of the treasury." Ibn al-'Arabi (1165–1240), a Spanish Arab from Murcia, considered by the Sufis to be their Master Poet, experienced the revelation of God out of pure being, in a condition of absolute inwardness: "We ourselves are the attributes by which we describe God our existence is merely an objectification of His existence. God is necessary to us in order that we may exist, while we are necessary to Him in order that He may be manifested to Himself" (Schimmel, 266). In "The Song of the Reed," Jalal ad-Din Rumi (d. 1273), the *Mevelana*, or Master, and founder of the Whirling Dervishes, revealed the soul's longing during its earthly trajectory for deliverance from the world where it is a stranger in exile.

> The secret of my song, though near
> None can see and none can hear.
> Oh, for a friend to know the sign
> And mingle all his soul with mine!
>
> (*Rumi Poet and Mystic*, 31)

Examples of exoteric as opposed to esoteric exile are plentiful throughout history. Religious persecutions were frequent throughout the ages. Many exiles, be they Catholic, Protestant, Jew, Muslim, Hindu, Buddhist, or of any other faith, left their native lands to escape death or mutilation, or to preach new and "heretical" doctrines.

Political exile was forever sought during periods of revolution, insurrection, anarchy, unrest, colonial conquest, and periods of governmental change, reform, or regression. Madame de Staël was a case in point. She fled during the French Revolution, during the Reign of Terror, and was later expelled from France under Napoleon. Her unfinished work, *Ten Years of Exile*, depicts her peregrinations and the thoughts and feelings involved during that period of turmoil.

> So I spent my life studying the map of Europe in order to escape.
> For active and sensitive temperaments, exile is sometimes a more
> cruel torment than death.
>
> (Staël, 370)

Ironically, some of the world's most successful conquerors were exiles themselves. None better, perhaps, could exemplify the compulsion for conquest than Genghis Khan (1167–1227). Ruler of a Mongol confederacy, he left his homeland to subjugate an empire that included northern China, Turkestan, Transoxiania, and Afghanistan, raiding Persia and eastern Europe to the Dnieper River. He succeeded and became the ruler of one of the greatest land empires the world has ever known. Upon his death in exile, his empire extended from the Pacific to the Black Sea, from northern China to Siberia and Iran. His descendent Tamerlane (1336–1405), likewise a fierce and audacious conqueror, also died in exile. The poem by Edgar Allan Poe that bears the same name as this Asian despot begins as the dying Tamerlane, looking back upon his lost youth and his lost love, blames his need for exile on his "Unearthly pride" and his wild ambition to dominate the world. His departure from home and from his beloved caused him the deepest of sorrow.

> What was there left for me *now?—despair—*
> A kingdom for a broken-heart.

Unlike conqueror-exiles such as Tamerlane, who devoted their lives to the acquisition of material goods and power, Chinese philosophers, deeply influenced by Confucianism, Taoism, and Buddhism, pursued a life of esoterism. In his *Analects*, Confucius (551–479 B.C.E.) encourages exile in a life of inwardness and meditation rather than a life devoted to the acquisition of material goods and power:

> The Master said, "In the eating of coarse rice and the drinking of water, the using of one's elbow for a pillow, joy is to be found. Wealth and rank attained through immoral means have as much to do with me as passing clouds." (*Analects*, 88, 16)

Exile to the transcendental world of the spirit is of utmost importance to the Taoist. According to the teachings of the "unknown" philosopher-recluse, Lao-tzu (c. 604 B.C.E.) and the historical Chuang-tzu (c. 369–286 B.C.E.), to experience the great underlying eternal and nameless principle of Tao, or the Way, the origin of all being, requires detachment—exile—from the empirical world.

> The Tao [Way] that can be told of
> Is not the eternal Tao;
> The name that can be named
> Is not the eternal name.
> Nameless, it is the origin of Heaven and earth;
> Nameable, it is the mother of all things.
> Always nonexistent,
> That we may apprehend its inner secret.
> (Bary, *Sources of Chinese Tradition*, 1:51)

Chinese Buddhism, with its emphasis on concentration and meditation, rejects the illusion that individuality and permanence exist in the phenomenological domain. Because there is no eternal Self or soul, no individuality, there is no craving for permanence in any form; thus the human being is relieved from suffering. By adopting the right views about life, by adhering to a disciplined and controlled system of moral conduct that stresses inwardness and exile from the workaday world, an individual may stop the process of rebirth and achieve the condition of Nirvana. In the words of Mou-tzu (470–391 B.C.E.), who is believed to be the author of *The Disposition of Error*, we read: "The spirit never perishes. Only the body decays. The body is like the roots and leaves of the five grains, the spirit is like the seeds and kernels of the five grains. When the roots and leaves come forth they inevitably die. But do the seeds and kernels perish? Only the body of one who has achieved the Way perishes" (Bary, *Sources of Chinese Tradition*, 1:277).

Among the many esoteric Japanese Buddhist philosophers, Kukai (774–835) is known for his syncretistic work *Indications to the Teachings of the*

Three Religions (Confucianism, Taoism, and Buddhism). Upon his return from China, he brought back what has been called "True Words" (*Shingon*), underscoring the significance of the mysteries residing in the hiddenness of body, speech, and mind, by means of which one may attain Buddhahood.

> The ocean of the Law is one, but sometimes it is shallow and sometimes deep, according to the capacity of the believer. Five vehicles have been distinguished, sudden or gradual according to the vessel. Even among the teachings of sudden enlightenment, some are exoteric and some esoteric. In Esotericism itself, some doctrines represent the source while others are tributary. The masters of the Law of former times swam in the tributary waters and plucked at leaves, but the teachings I now bring back reach down to the sources and pull at the roots. (Bary, *Sources of Japanese Tradition*, 1:143)

Basho (1644–94), the author of esoteric Japanese haiku (seventeen-syllable poetry), belonged to no group and to no class. A free soul in perpetual exile, he spent his life continually journeying around Japan. Being "neither priest nor layman, bird nor rat, but something in between," Basho compared himself to a bat (Bary, *Sources of Japanese Tradition*, 1:451).

Another poet of exile from the French Renaissance was Joachim du Bellay, who experienced great sorrow during his four-year stay in Italy when he accompanied his uncle, a cardinal, to the Holy See. He continually suffered from homesickness and loneliness, and his series of poems *Regrets* (1553) convey his profound nostalgia for his beautiful Anjou in France. They also express his outrage and disgust at the intrigue, materialism, and carryings-on within the papal court.

Montaigne (1533–92) chose another form of exile. At the age of thirty-seven, unwilling to participate in the religious and civil wars rampant in his land, he decided to withdraw into his castle, eschewing active political and social life. Within its walls, which housed his extraordinary library, he spent his time in "worthwhile" pursuits: study, reflection, and the composition of his *Essays*. Montaigne's willed introversion strengthened his character and enriched his mind, leading him to achieve the independence of thought and spirit for which he longed. Using the analogy of a store to point up the psychological necessity of the formation of a personality, he speaks of it as having two parts: a front room, where the wares are displayed and outsiders congregate; and a back room, which is private and to which only the owner has access.

We must reserve a back shop all our own, entirely free, in which to
establish our real liberty and our principal retreat and solitude.
Here our ordinary conversation must be between us and ourselves,
and so private that no outside association or communication can
find a place; here we must talk and laugh as if without wife,
without children, without possessions, without retinue and servants, so that when the time comes to lose them, it will be nothing
new to us to do without them. We have a soul that can be turned
upon itself; it can keep itself company; it has the means to attack
and the means to defend, the means to receive and the means to
give; let us not fear that in this solitude we shall stagnate in tedious
idleness. (*Essays*, 177)

Montaigne articulated his voluntary exile clearly and explicitly. A different kind of esoteric exile was implicit in much of the poetry of the Romantics.
Because the Romantics saw God as inhabiting inaccessible climes, his isolation from them accentuated the impact of their already well developed
feelings of exile. A sense of solitude and abandonment pervades the writings
of such poets as Lamartine, Vigny, Wordsworth, Hölderlin, and Nerval.
Daily existence was so painful for the early Romantic German poet Novalis
that in *Hymns to the Night* he viewed his descent or exile into death as a
liberation from the suffering he knew in the circumscribed land of the living.

> Down to the sweet bride come away,
> To Jesus whom we love!
> Good cheer! The evening dawn shows gray
> On them who grieve and love.
> Dream bursts our bonds and sinks us free
> To our Father's arms eternally.
>
> (Novalis, *Hymns to the Night*, 15)

For many Romantics, their sojourn on earth meant foregoing any and all
temptation, basking in suffering, as a kind of *imitatio Christi*. Feelings of
dissatisfaction and of alienation, however, had a catalytic effect on the
creative life of such writers as Keats, Coleridge, and Byron. Exile for Shelley
became a positive experience: it afforded him great contentment by divesting him of the excessive constraints plaguing him in England. In "Julian
and Maddalo" he uses the phrase "Paradise of exiles, Italy!"

By glimpsing the ineffable and infinite realm through the creative process, Symbolists such as Baudelaire suffered less poignantly from feelings
of exile and alienation in the everyday world. Through the realm of *correspondences*, that is, affinities experienced between the macrocosm and the

microcosm, Baudelaire could *know* reality, if only ephemerally; he could enjoy a reconciliation between worlds in opposition, a dichotomy that tore at him powerfully. Balzac, Nerval, Dickinson, Melville, Sand, Mallarmé, Rimbaud, Flaubert, and the Brontë sisters, to mention but a few, experienced such co-relationships and were thus enabled to link mortal to cosmic spheres.

Political dissidents such as Voltaire, Heine, and Hugo exiled themselves from their native land. During Hugo's eighteen-year exile (1851–70) from France to the islands of Jersey and Guernsey, he wrote some of his greatest poems (*Chastisements, Contemplations, Legend of the Centuries*), their apocalyptic images remaining indelibly engraved in the minds and psyches of his readers.

For certain writers, such as Proust, who considered true life (the only one worthy of being lived) to exist only in the creative process, esoteric exile became a way of life. The creative act culminating in his monumental *Remembrance of Things Past*, required him to abstract or exile himself from the everyday world, while paradoxically, remaining in his own home surrounded by familiar objects and people.

The great traveler Joseph Conrad knew both exoteric and esoteric exile, voicing his thoughts on the theme in *Lord Jim:* "Each blade of grass has its spot on earth whence it draws its life, its strength; and so is man rooted to the land from which he draws his faith together with his life" (21).

James Joyce chose exile from the intellectually and emotionally stifling conditions of his native Ireland. Only by leaving his country could he grow and survive as a writer. Although he exiled himself from it physically, its presence was deeply embedded in his soul and psyche, forming the stuff out of which he molded his *Dubliners, Portrait of the Artist, Ulysses,* and other works.

Displacement from their native lands was a sine qua non for Henry James, Edith Wharton, Gertrude Stein, Ezra Pound, Henry Miller, T. S. Eliot, Ernest Hemingway, John Dos Passos, e. e. cummings, F. Scott Fitzgerald, W. H. Auden, Aldous Huxley, Christopher Isherwood. Willa Cather speaks of exile in *Shadows on the Rock:* "Only solitary men know the full joys of friendship. Others have their family; but to a solitary and an exile his friends are everything" (*Collected Works*, 10, Book 3, chap. 5).

Exoteric and esoteric exiles from Germany prior to and during World War II included such names as Vicky Baum, Lion Feuchtwanger, Thomas and Heinrich Mann, Nelly Sachs, Walter Benjamin, Ernst Toller, Stefan Zweig, Franz Werfel. Mention must also be made of the massive exodus of writers from Franco's Spain, during and after its civil war: Rafael Alberti, Jorge Guillén, Vicente Aleixandre, Fernando Arrabal. Russian dissident writers during and following the Stalinist era were plentiful: Anna

Akhmatova, Andrey Sinyavsky, Osip Mandelstam, Joseph Brodsky, Aleksandr Solzhenitsyn, Nina Berberova, and others.

Latin American novelists are, understandably (since many consider their ancestors as émigrés from Spain), inextricably associated with the notion of displacement: from Mexico, Carlos Fuentes; from Chile, José Donoso; from Argentina, Jorge Luis Borges, Julio Cortázar, Mario Goloboff, and Mario Satz; from Guatemala, Miguel Ángel Asturias; from Colombia, Gabriel García Márquez; from Paraguay, Augusto Roa Bastos; from Peru, Mario Vargas Llosa; from Cuba, Guillermo Cabrera Infante, Reinaldo Arenas, Severo Sarduy, Heberto Padilla, José Lezama Lima, Edmondo Desnoes, and others.

The list of exiles—exoteric and/or esoteric, voluntary or involuntary—is virtually infinite.

Not yet mentioned is the extraordinary, even revolutionary, concept of exile, conceived by the Hebrew Kabbalist Isaac Luria (1534–72). An unconscious compensatory means of dealing with the nearly universal persecution meted out to the Jews since time immemorial, Luria's concept posits the astonishing view that God's creation of the world resulted from his exile or withdrawal into himself. Traditional theologians viewed the cosmic drama of Creation as a *creatio ex nihilo* (creation out of nothingness); that is, an emanation, externalization, unfolding, projection, or outflowing of God's divine energy from himself into space.

According to Luria's concept of *tsimtsum*, God's act of withdrawal, contraction, or concentration into himself—his essence becoming increasingly hidden in the process—led to the liberation of primordial or pneumatic space, from which the manifest world came into being (Scholem, *Kabbalah and Its Symbolism*, 110).

> Know that before all the emanations were emanated and the creations were created, the simple supernal light filled all existence and there was no empty space in the sense of vacant air or void, but everything was filled by this undifferentiated infinite light. [This light] had neither beginning nor end but was rather undifferentiated light that was entirely homogeneous and it was called the infinite light.
>
> And when it arose in His undifferentiated will to create the worlds. . . . He contracted himself at the center-most point that was within Him and the light was contracted and withdrew towards the sides surrounding the central point, thus leaving an empty space, a vacuum, an empty void [where] the central point [had been]. (Sarmach, 323)

For Luria and his disciples, the myth of the *tsimtsum*, Divinity's exile into himself, was a theological answer to a historical experience: the "catastrophe" of the Inquisition and the expulsion of the Jews from Spain in 1492 was looked upon by those forced to flee as a soul in exile. The association made between God's exile within himself and the sufferings of the displaced Spanish Jews, indeed, of all exiles from earliest times to the victims of the twentieth-century Holocaust and thereafter, may also be applied to the creative person in general, and to the writer in particular.

Paralleling the human act of creation with Divinity's theogonic process in the *tsimtsum*, one might suggest that just as Divinity relinquished a space within himself, making room for the "mystical primordial space" to come into being, thus paving the way for the return of his essence in less concentrated form in his Creation, so the writer makes accessible his work through a retreat within his infinite and boundless subliminal realm (Scholem, *Major Trends in Jewish Mysticism*, 261).

Like God's self-imposed exile, contraction, or retreat into his absoluteness, and return into his depths, the writer's movement is inward. After his exile into his hidden, impersonal, and unfathomable depths during the precreative period, he liberates himself from outerworldly entanglements, thus activating, like God during his withdrawal into himself, the creative process. What the writer then makes manifest, be it in the form of a novel, poem, play, or essay, is a finite concreting of an infinite and ineffable essence. Only after the work has been brought forth, like God's Creation, does it take on personal value for both author and reader (Scholem, *Kabbalah and Its Symbolism*, 110, 129).

The concept of *tsimtsum*, or internalization, exiles the creative individual from the everyday world, while also drawing him into an undifferentiated and utterly dark inner dominion. During the writer's period of withdrawal, tension is aroused by the inflow of *libido* (psychic energy) previously expended on external matters. The once-nebulous idea, feeling, or sensation, like the seed implanted in the darkness of the earth, is nurtured by the nutrients all around. It gestates.

Many, but not all, writers attempting to realize a novel, poem, play, or essay feel it imperative to exile themselves from the workaday world so as to channel and concentrate their energies. To retreat into the transpersonal inner recesses of the psyche, defined by C. G. Jung, as the *collective unconscious* (also called the *objective psyche*), is to penetrate a world inaccessible for the most part to conscious understanding. This suprapersonal, undifferentiated, and nonindividual inner ocean is regarded as the deepest layer within the subliminal world. Archetypes and their symbolic representations in archetypal images make up the contents of the collective unconscious. It is from these mythical layers that great writers draw their material.

Unlike the collective unconscious, within which exist universal and transpersonal contents, the components of the personal unconscious are related to and may be made manifest to the individual. With proper "enlightenment" or understanding, certain subliminal factors may be integrated into the individual's *ego* (conscious personality), thereby enriching the person as a whole. *Archetypes*, an elusive concept put forward by Jung, cannot be fully defined. They are, as previously mentioned, contained within the collective unconscious, and are made manifest to conscious awareness in *archetypal images*. To clarify what is complex, the notion of the archetype has been related to that of the instinct.

> An instinct is a pattern of behavior which is inborn and characteristic for a certain species. . . . The instincts are the unknown motivating dynamisms that determine an animal's behavior on the biological level. An archetype is to the psyche what an instinct is to the body. The existence of archetypes is inferred by the same process as that by which we infer the existence of instincts. Just as instincts common to a species are postulated by observing the uniformities in biological behavior, so archetypes are inferred by observing the uniformities in psychic phenomena. Just as instincts are unknown motivating dynamisms of biological behavior, archetypes are unknown motivating dynamisms of the psyche. Archetypes are the psychic instincts of the human species. (Edinger, "An Outline of Analytical Psychology," 12)

Perceived in the form of primordial images, archetypes are present in dreams, legends, fairy tales, myths, religious and cultural notions, and modes of behavior the world over. They are energy centers, elements in perpetually mobile psychic structures, which, until manifested in events, patternings, and configurations, are nonperceptible, existing *in potentia* in their dormant state in the depths of the collective unconscious. Archetypal images are many and varied: they include, for example, the archetype of Transformation, as in growth and decay; the Great Mother in her nourishing and destructive aspects; the Spiritual or Monstrous Father; the Child, as harbinger of things to come; the Wise Old Man. The archetype of the Self, defined by Jung as the central one and identified with God in the religious sphere, conveys wholeness or totality, representing both "the center and circumference of the psyche. It incorporates within its paradoxical unity all the opposites embodied in the masculine and feminine archetypes. Since it is a borderline concept referring to an entity which transcends and encompasses the individual ego, we can only allude to it and not encompass it by a definition (Edinger, "An Outline of Analytical Psychology," 15).

To choose a Jungian approach in an exploration of the notion of exile in ten works by authors from diverse backgrounds, nationalities, socioeconomic levels, and religious preferences may help us understand the psychological patternings of the creative works under scrutiny. It also serves to illustrate the diversity and universality of Jungian analysis and criticism. The probings offered in this book take the literary work out of its individual and conventional context and relate it to humanity in general. In so doing, the Jungian approach lifts readers out of their specific and perhaps isolated worlds and allows them to expand their vision, and thus relate more easily to issues whose reality is part of an ongoing and cyclical world.

Each chapter deals with a single work to flesh out a variety of psychological types, traits, and aesthetic and creative fashionings. Such a route, it is hoped, will broaden the reader's understanding of the work under scrutiny and the culture from which it emerged, and also lead to a deeper understanding of human nature with regard to the implications of exile. The psychological, spiritual, physical, and sociological reactions of the fictional characters investigated in the literary works explored may encourage readers to analyze the characters in a new way and to contribute their own ideas and insights. The identification, projection, or confrontation that ensues with such an exploration may bring to light certain new values and points of view, fresh emotions and feelings, that could help harmonize or unify what has been severely polarized and compartmentalized. Probings of, and encounters with, creatures of fantasy or those stemming from the empirical world, as will be undertaken in the chapters to come, may serve to flesh out certain unconscious and conscious needs within readers of disparate cultures and faiths, inviting them to sound out their own souls, minds, senses, intuitive faculties, and visceral reactions in more universal, analogical, and syncretistic ways.

Jung has suggested time and time again that psychic life is a dynamic: uninterrupted permutations between the conscious and the unconscious. Such an interchange can, if properly realized, lead toward the process of *individuation* or psychic differentiation or wholeness of the Self (total personality). Individuation, which distinguishes each individual as unique and separate from the collective, is developed in terms of the personalities, actions, and events surrounding the lives of the characters focused upon in the works analyzed. The inner life of the characters may then be experienced by the reader as a living entity, provoking reflection upon the characters as well as a desire to assess the play, novel, poem, or essay in terms of the reader's own existential condition, or with regard to its aesthetic value. To do so may develop readers' analytical faculties, making individuals increasingly aware of their attributes and deficiencies, and in so doing, helping them remain open to new enrichment and greater fulfillment in their lives.

The choice of ten authors—Dostoevsky, Conrad, Huysmans, Malraux, Agnon, Kawabata, Levi, Garro, Beckett, Cheng—whose single works I explore here is purely subjective. My priorities were universality, quality, interest, and a variety in the approaches to the theme of exile.

The opening chapter, an example of both exoteric and esoteric exile, explores Fyodor Dostoevsky's Siberian imprisonment as depicted in *The House of the Dead*. This seminal work lays bare a soul corroded with affliction. Because Dostoevsky's account of his incarceration in the fortress at Omsk dismembers events, feelings, and ideations, it may be considered the source of his future works in embryonic form. His flaying insights into both conscious and unconscious realms expose networks of raw nerves to abrasive elements in the outside world. His exile denuded him of the protective emotional vestments he had worn as a youthful idealist. What was revealed was a blood-soaked soul.

Joseph Conrad's *Heart of Darkness*, written after his journey/exile to Central Africa, combines both exoteric and esoteric displacement. His work, psychologically speaking, may be viewed as a search for an exiled *shadow:* unconscious personality traits the individual considers inferior and does not accept as his own. That Conrad should have noted, upon his return to England, "Before the Congo I was just a mere animal" suggests the profundity of his psychological upheaval during the trip.

Joris-Karl Huysmans's *Against the Grain* analyzes the sensations aroused by the willed exile of his deeply introverted antihero, Duke Jean des Esseintes. Unable to face and live in reality, filled with uncontrollable ennui and with hatred for a society he sees as superficial, banal, vulgar, and materialistic, des Esseintes withdraws from the world and experiences extreme alienation from himself as well as his fellow beings.

André Malraux's view of his three heroes in *The Royal Way* is antithetical to Huysmans's inner trajectory. Exoteric exiles, these heroes leave Western Europe and struggle through life-threatening situations in their attempt to carve out their destinies in the forests of Cambodia. The periods of crisis, personal suffering, and loss they undergo drive them on to find fulfillment. Only one, however, succeeds in strengthening his ego and expanding his vision, thus building a new and strong structure upon what had once been a faulty foundation.

"Edo and Enam," by the Nobel Prize–winner S. Y. Agnon, narrates the spiritual and psychological drama confronting a young bride after leaving the land of her ancestors to follow her husband to Jerusalem. A descendent of the ancient tribe of Gad, one of the ten lost tribes of Israel, she feels displaced and alienated in her new environment. On a mystical level, Agnon's tale discloses another kind of crisis: a playing-out in an earthly sphere of a condition of uneasiness and disorientation experienced by God himself.

The Master of Go, by the Japanese Nobel Prize–winner Yasunari Kawabata, presents a view of the withdrawal process that is esoteric for the Westerner but in keeping with the Japanese culture and psyche. Kawabata's protagonist applies his intense powers of inner concentration to each of his moves in his game of Go, a most complex game, somewhat reminiscent of chess. The protagonist, a hitherto "invincible" but now ailing Go Master, who is also a Zen Master, plays in such a way that each successive move increases his ritualized sense of exile. After losing his championship match, he ceases to exist and dies. Psychologically, we may say that during each of his ritualized plays his libido (psychic energy), like blood, is being withdrawn from his body and poured into the stones moved about on the Go board.

Primo Levi's *Survival in Auschwitz* is a factual account of his abduction from his native city of Turin and his ten-month exile in a Nazi death camp. His memoir may be viewed as a testament to his heroic capacity for endurance when "crushed against the bottom" in the face of death. Although anguish accompanied him during all of his days at Auschwitz, his virtually unique conclusion to his ordeal reveals the depth of his understanding of human nature: "No human experience is without meaning or unworthy of analysis, and . . . fundamental values, even if they are not positive, can be deduced from this particular world."

Elena Garro's *Recollections of Things to Come*, a surrealistic work, sketches specific events in the lives of a community of Mexicans—"exiles from happiness"—during the politically troubled 1920s. Not only are the families involved cloistered in their small town of Ixtepec, and therefore exiled from the rest of their country, but they are cut off from the other members of their group and from themselves. In keeping with surrealistic dictates, Garro explores hidden and neglected areas of the psyche in poetic images that seem to have been molded from the very substance of her native Mexican landscape.

In Samuel Beckett's *That Time*, the "double-headed monster of damnation and salvation—Time" is the antagonist (Samuel Beckett, *Proust*, 1). The mutant and miscreant Time is the enemy that forces the protagonist's exile from life and his slow deterioration. Time, unceasingly and eternally, eats voraciously into every second, hour, day, year, decade, century. Past, present, and future in *That Time*, like three black holes in the heavens, expand when called upon to articulate thoughts and feelings, only to contract seconds later, in what becomes a final gravitational collapse at the play's conclusion.

A. Cheng's novella, "The King of the Trees," narrates the experiences of a group of Chinese city-bred high school students, referred to as "intellectuals," who are exiled by their government to a remote forested region for reeducational purposes. Virtually unique in contemporary Chinese literature is Cheng's manner of fusing Taoist, Buddhist, Confucian, and shamanist concepts with the modern Communist credo. That a tree is the protagonist of Cheng's tale suggests not only a poetic responsiveness to transpersonal powers governing the universe, but a concomitant unwillingness to reduce the tangible and intangible world to the mechanistic laws of science alone.

As the great variety of the literature to be discussed here suggests, exile is so fundamental a condition to humanity, so eternal and universal, that it takes on archetypal stature. As Jung noted:

> The unconscious, as the totality of all archetypes, is the deposit of all human experience right back to its remotest beginnings. Not, indeed, a dead deposit, a sort of abandoned rubbish heap, but a living system of reactions and aptitudes that determine the individual's life in invisible ways—all the more effective because invisible. It is not just a gigantic historical prejudice, so to speak, an *a priori* historical condition; but it is also the source of the instincts, for the archetypes are simply the forms which the instincts assume. (*Collected Works*, 8:157)

Let us now examine the living dispositions, dynamisms, thoughts, and images depicted in the works of Dostoevsky, Conrad, Huysmans, Malraux, Agnon, Kawabata, Levi, Garro, Beckett, and Cheng and see their impact on the behavioral patterns of their protagonists and our own ideas, feelings, actions—in exile! But before doing so, let us listen to the full-throated cry of one of the greatest exiles of all time: Prometheus, nailed to a rocky mountain peak in the wilderness of Scythia as punishment for having stolen fire from God in order to help humanity.

> O Earth, mother of all life!
> On you, and on the all-seeing circle of the sun, I call:
> See what is done by gods to me, a god!
> See with what outrage
> Racked and tortured
> I am to agonize

For a thousand years!
See this shameful prison
Invented for me
By the new master of the gods!
I groan in anguish
For pain present and pain to come:
Where shall I see rise
The star of my deliverance?

(Aeschylus, *Prometheus Bound*, 24)

1 Dostoevsky's *The House of the Dead:* Siberian Exile

The events depicted in Fyodor Dostoevsky's[1] *The House of the Dead* (1860) are based on his incarceration (23 January 1850–15 February 1854) in the prison fortress at Omsk, in Western Siberia. Because the account of his exile dismembers events, feelings, and ideations, laying bare a soul corroded with afflictions, *The House of the Dead* may be considered Dostoevsky's future works in embryonic form. His flaying insights into both conscious and unconscious realms expose networks of raw nerves to abrasive elements in the outside world. Dostoevsky's straightforward, objective, and restrained style serves to heighten the impression of solitude to which his displacement gave rise. His reactions at having been cut off from his family and from the St. Petersburg intelligentsia that had meant so much to him, and being forced to live with the most sordid of criminals and in the most depraved of atmospheres, are always understated. Circumspect as well are his reactions to the prison guards, who took pleasure in enforcing their ritualized corporal punishments. Nonetheless, the torment Dostoevsky sustained during his years of imprisonment was incalculable. The lack of privacy in his barracks existence was, paradoxically, the most arduous trial to bear: "The society of people acts like a poison or an infection, and from this insufferable torment I have suffered more than

---

[1]The literary career of Fyodor Mikhailovich Dostoevsky (1821–81), although beginning before his exile (*Poor Folk, The Double,* etc.), achieved greatness in the years following his return to society (*Notes from the Underground, Crime and Punishment, The Possessed, The Idiot, The Devils, The Brothers Karamazov,* etc.). He married Marya Dmitreyvna Isayeva (1857); after she died of consumption he married Anna Grigoryevna Snitkina (1867), living most of the time abroad to escape the bills from his frequent and uncontrollable gambling sprees.

from anything these four years. There have even been moments when I hated everyone who crossed my path, blameless or guilty, and looked on them as thieves who were stealing away my life with impunity" (Carr, 60).

Antinomy was implicit in Dostoevsky's psyche. There was hate, yes; but also love; ugliness, juxtaposed with beauty; evil, with goodness; the fettered, with the liberated. Facets of his psyche were rendered concrete in events and people during his exile, which stretched before him "like an immense tablecloth" in the seemingly infinite expanse of the desolate Siberian landscape.

The reasons for Dostoevsky's exile and imprisonment were political. Although he had not been an active agitator during the repressive and autocratic rule of Nicholas I (1796–1855), anyone even suspected of harboring liberal views concerning freedom, justice, and the separation of church and state was imprisoned. So fearful had the czar become of any soupçon of "revolutionary" ideas, any incursion of European thought into his land, that censorship was ruthlessly enforced. Critics and journalists, such as the socialist and atheist Grigorievich Belinski (1811–48), whose ideas Dostoevsky shared for a time, and political activists, such as Mikhail Petrashevsky, whose circle he joined, were closely watched by the secret police.

Petrashevsky, idealist and disciple of the economic reformer Charles Fourier (1772–1837), was not a revolutionary, and his group did not go underground. Talkers rather than doers, the members spent long hours in endless analytical and theoretical discussions. Some in the Petrashevsky circle, however, considering such evening get-togethers futile, founded their own group, called Palm-Durov. Most of its members, interested in the arts, were considered harmless when investigated by the Commission of Inquiry (1849). Not so, however, for one of them: Nikolay Speshnyov, a revolutionary terrorist and atheist accused of having established a secret printing press to disseminate works encouraging the overthrow of the government. Whether Dostoevsky took part in printing such dangerous documents is not known. That he shared many of Speshnyov's ideas and knew about the plot is quite possible. Dostoevsky, along with others of this group, was arrested and sent to the Peter and Paul (Petropavlovsky) Fortress in St. Petersburg.

Dostoevsky experienced "sickening boredom" during his ten-month stay in the Peter and Paul Fortress. He was tense, unable to sleep, a victim of "ugly dreams" and "hypochondria." Nevertheless, the writer's incarceration had a positive effect in that he became aware of many aspects of human nature which he might otherwise never have noticed and which, in time, he would discover in himself. In a letter of 18 July 1849, he could write that "man has infinite reserves of toughness and vitality" (Coulson,

52). Dostoevsky did experience pleasurable, albeit brief, moments during his incarceration. When, for example, permission to walk in the prison's garden was finally granted him after two months, the seventeen trees he observed filled him with wonderment and "complete happiness," as he wrote to his older brother, Mikhail (Coulson, 53). Melancholia, nevertheless, coupled with a sense of morbidity, marred his first "difficult autumn," a time when even "the sky began to scowl." Adding to his agony were those days of

> endless thinking and nothing but thinking, without any external stimulus to renew and support the thought. . . . It is like being under a vacuum pump which is always sucking away the air. Everything in me has been drawn into my head and from my head into my ideas, absolutely everything, and yet, in spite of this, work grows harder every day. (Coulson, 54)

A sense of inadequacy combined with guilt accentuated the torture of his enforced isolation, but he struggled valiantly to keep from being destroyed by his despair.

> How little I valued it [life], how often I sinned against my own heart and mind—my heart bleeds. Life is a gift, life is happiness, every minute might have been a century of happiness. *Si jeunesse savait!* Now my life changes, I am born again in a new mould. I swear to you, brother, that I will not lose hope and that I will keep my body and mind pure! I shall be born again to better things. This is my one hope, my one consolation! (Coulson, 58)

The most abrasive of experiences, however, was yet to follow. Dostoevsky, along with the twenty-one other men of his group found guilty by the military tribunal of crimes committed against the czar, was informed that he was to be executed by shooting. He was accused of having read and reproduced the "criminal" letter sent to the influential radical critic Visarion Belinsky by the poet Sergey Pleshcheev (one of the accused), and was also charged with having been present at Speshnyov's home during "the reading of Lieutenant Grigoryev's seditious work under the title of *A Soldier's Talk*" (Magarshack, 121. See also Yarmolinsky). On 22 December, Dostoevsky and his friends were driven to Semenovsky Square in St. Petersburg.

> There they read out the death-sentences to us, made us kiss the cross, broke sabers over our heads and put death garments (white shirts).

> Then three of us were tied to posts to be executed. They had called
> out three men. I was therefore next to be called and I had no more
> than a minute to live. I remembered you, Mikhail, and all yours; at
> the last moment you, you alone, were in my mind and it was only
> then that I realized how much I loved you, dear brother. I also had
> time to embrace Pleshcheev and Durov, who stood beside me, and
> say good bye to them. Finally, the retreat was beaten, those who had
> been tied to the posts were led back, and they read out to us that His
> Imperial Majesty granted us our lives. (Magarshack, 121)

Dostoevsky received, instead of the death penalty, an eight-year sentence to
a Siberian prison, which, because the czar had seemingly become interested in the affair, was commuted to four years, to be followed by four
years of army service as a private in the Seventh Siberian line regiment at
Semipalatinsk, a fortress town near the border of China, on the bank of the
Irtysh.

When Mikhail, Dostoevsky's older brother, visited the prisoner prior to
his departure for Siberia, Mikhail's "eyes were filled with tears, his lips
trembled." In sharp contrast was the behavior of the future exile, who
remained "calm, and consoled him," ready for his departure (Coulson,
60).

> Exactly at twelve o'clock, that is, exactly on Christmas day [1849], I
> put on fetters for the first time. They weighed ten pounds and they
> made walking extremely uncomfortable. Then they put us in open
> sledges, each one of us separately, with a gendarme, and, preceded
> by a sledge in which a government courier was traveling, we left
> Petersburg. I felt sick at heart, and confused in mind from the
> many different sensations of that day. My heart seemed to be "fidg-
> ety" and for that reason it moped and ached dully. But the fresh air
> revived me, and as one usually feels a kind of animation and excite-
> ment before every new step in life, I was actually quite self-
> composed and looked intently at Petersburg. (Magarshack, 128)

The journey lasted seven weeks.

We turn now to study of *The House of the Dead.* Dostoevsky referred to
the prison/fortress at Omsk as a "House of the Dead," a type of necropolis:
"I consider those four years as a time during which I was buried alive and
shut up in a coffin. Just how horrible that time was I have not the strength
to tell you . . . it was an indescribable, unending agony, because each
hour, each minute weighed upon my soul like a stone" (Dostoevsky, 7).
The "House," like a microcosm, represents Dostoevsky's universe. Its dor-

mitories and public rooms, so different from the living quarters to which he had been accustomed, mirror the lobes of his brain: dead to outside forces, but not to inner pulsations. A world turned upside down, it functioned as had the Serapeum for the ancient Egyptians, with one difference: rather than venerating Apis the bull, the authorities in the Siberian fortress directed their rituals toward the desiccation of this elemental power within the human being.

Death, then, was paradoxically very much alive in Dostoevsky's House. It was here that his former self, the "raw youth," would die. Here, too, the future writer of *The Possessed* and *The Brothers Karamazov* would be born. This circumscribed area, with all of its locked doors and barricades and its rigid disciplines, implanted in "the remote regions of Siberia, amidst endless steppes, mountains, and impassable forests," was to become that sacred ground leading to Dostoevsky's progressive discovery of self: his underground. His already highly introverted personality isolated him even more from the prison community. Self-absorbed, despondent, and taciturn, he most frequently walked with his eyes glued to the floor, unwilling or unable to relate to others. Yet he sensed, and had his narrator state in *The House of the Dead*, describing his prison experience, that something incredible was taking place within the House and in his brain and psyche: "My new life was only just beginning."

Psychologically, Dostoevsky's reference to death parallels the descent into the collective unconscious (the deepest layer of the unconscious) by the ego (center of consciousness). C. G. Jung also underwent such a trajectory, about which he writes:

> From that time on, the dead have become even more distinct for me as the voices of the Unanswered, Unresolved, and Unredeemed. . . . These conversations with the dead formed a kind of prelude to what I had to communicate to the world about the unconscious. . . . It was then that I ceased to belong to myself alone, ceased to have the right to do so. From then on my life belonged to the generality. (Edinger, *The Christian Archetype*, 112. See Jung, *Memories, Dreams, Reflections*, 191f.)

The same may be said of Dostoevsky. To belong exclusively to himself was a thing of the past. With the relativization of his ego, he became linked with the "generality," or "infinite."

Although the narrator in *The House of the Dead*, Aleksandr Petrovich Goryanchikov, is fictitious, he is modeled on the author and is his sounding board, as are also, to some extent, the prisoners and guards. About thirty-five years old, learned, "unsociable," considered a kind of "madman" because he hides from everyone, Aleksandr has been sentenced to ten years of hard labor for murdering his wife. As a projection of the author, Aleksandr also experiences a double exile: he is cut off from St. Petersburg and also alienated from the world of the convicts within the fortress. So accentuated has his sense of aloneness become that much of his time is spent probing his reactions to the psychological and spiritual world of the other inmates. Instincts, needs, loves, hates, and relationships are, thereby, continuously brought to light, first from a distance and then, as he grows to know his fellow inmates better and accept his surroundings, at close range and more empathetically.

Because the narrator's understanding of exile prior to his incarceration has been developed only intellectually, as an abstract principle or theory that he and his friends could debate, he has never really felt its sting. Only during his prison experience does he begin to absorb its devastating impact on his body and psyche. Alone, having to submit to the humiliation of fetters, to the shaving of his head on one side, to donning a black and gray tunic with a large yellow diamond-shaped piece of material sewn on the back, he is pierced by the acuteness of his plight. A desperate yearning for freedom lacerates him, bloodying him ever more deeply each time he looks through the cracks in the rampart to "God's world" outside and to "a corner of the sky, not the sky that stood above the prison, but another, distant and free." He becomes obsessed by the inaccessible.

> Beyond the gate was the bright world of freedom where people lived like everyone else. But to those on this side of the enclosure that world seemed like some unattainable fairyland. Here was our own world, unlike anything else; here were our own laws, our own dress, our own manners and customs, here was the house of the living dead, a life like none other upon earth, and people were special, set apart.

The "House of the Dead," he realized, was to be his "refuge," his "corner" of the earth, that sacred space where he would have to live out his feelings of "pain and mistrust" in the terror of a hostile environment. That he looked upon the other inmates in the early days of his incarceration as enemies added to his feelings of alienation. He describes

> The savage curiosity with which my new companions, my fellow-convicts, looked me all over, their extra severity with a novice from the nobility who had suddenly appeared in their brotherhood, a severity which almost became hatred.

Work, to some extent, was considered positive by the narrator. Not only did it help him escape his unflagging wretchedness, but it was a means of approaching the other convicts by living out their routine, that is, by getting "into the same rut as everybody else." During his periods of labor, he was less self-absorbed, even observing some kind and friendly faces among the convicts: "There are bad people everywhere, but among the bad there are some good ones." And, he added, "Perhaps these people are in no way worse than those *outsiders*, those people *outside* the prison."

The early days and months of the narrator's incarceration were spent trying to create a modus vivendi and to learn ways and means of comporting himself with his new "family." Why, he questioned, could he never refuse money to a prisoner who ruefully asked for some, though he had so little himself? Why was he so passive? Why could he not take a negative stand? Did his acquiescence reveal an intent to please others? to play the saintly figure? to earn their respect? After much self-probing, he realized that the best way of comporting himself was to be direct and act "as my inner feelings and my conscience dictated."

Nevertheless, harrowing distress permeated his world. Rather than allow himself to be devoured by the formidable pulsations emerging from his world of the dead (subliminal sphere), he decided to approach his situation in a more reasoned way. By studying the faces and personalities of the other inmates and by learning their stories, the narrator would be, in effect, exploring his reactions to them through projection. Not only would the convicts become his teachers; they would also help him enlarge his views concerning human nature in general, and himself in particular.

Not withdrawal, but confrontation, would be the narrator's choice. His line of conduct would forbid him ever to become overinvolved or over-intimate with any inmate; to do so would make it all the more difficult to maintain his independence. "To be fully accepted by them as one of their companions" would not only defeat the narrator's purpose, but would jeopardize his status as a free observer. He would never show fear of their violence, their threats, their hatreds. He would not curry favor with them; they might in time resent such deviousness on his part. Nor would he remain cold, inaccessible, or overcourteous, as was the custom of the Polish nobles imprisoned in the "House of the Dead." Nor, as a nobleman, would he attempt to become a role model, thus playing into their stereotypic image of what they considered a disdainful and arrogant type. By the same token, "I promised myself never by any action of mine to debase in their eyes either my education or my way of thinking."

Although the narrator never reconciled himself to his fate, he "accepted" his existence in the "House of the Dead" as a fact of life. Thus did he begin to enter into the routine of things, walking about the prison's corridors, courtyards, and maze of rooms, eating watered-down cabbage soup with its incredible number of cockroaches, submitting to having his head shaven with blunt razors: "The memory of this torture still gives me goose flesh." Only after having conformed to the prison routine did the narrator begin to understand the meaning of freedom. No longer only an intellectual concept to be bandied about, it had now branded him for life.

> The hope of a prisoner who has been deprived of freedom differs completely from that of a man who is living a normal life. The free man hopes, of course (for a change in his fortunes, for example, or for the success of some undertaking), but he lives, he acts; he is carried along entirely in the whirl of real life. Not so the convict. He also has a kind of life, it is true—that of a prisoner, a convict. But whoever a convict is and whatever the term of his sentence, he is emphatically, instinctively unable to accept his fate as something positive and final, as a part of real life. No convict feels *at home* in prison, but rather as if he were on a visit there.

Convict/Minotaur

"The house of the living dead," like the Cretan labyrinth, incarcerated the Convict/Minotaur within its depths. Unlike the Centaur, who had the head of a man (order and consciousness) and the body of a horse (instinct) and, symbolically speaking, behaved in a normal way (that is, in keeping with Western tradition), the Minotaur was an aberration of this stereotype. The head of a bull and the body of a man indicated a reversal of what was socially acceptable. Instinct (body), not reason (head), directed the Minotaur's acts. His deeds were uncontrollable and monstrous in their cruelty: he fed on the Athenian maidens and youths.

It was not a question of killing the Convict/Minotaur in Dostoevsky's *The House of the Dead*, but of living with this monstrous power within a complex network of interconnecting alleys and paths, kitchens, granaries, storage sheds, cellars, and barracks. The narrator had to wrestle with the problem of accommodating his principles and temperament and allowing himself to evolve spiritually and psychologically, amid so many members of a primitive species.

How did the narrator depict the Convict/Minotaur's personality? As "coarse, ill-natured, cross-grained," filled with hatred and hostility for "gentlemen," and reveling with "malicious joy" in their troubles. "They [the inmates] would have devoured us, given the chance." The acts of violence, thefts, and brawls that frequently occurred, along with the seeming delight the convicts took in "persecuting" their "enemies," the nobles, was in keeping with the instinctual behavior of the archetype (Coulson, 64).

Eruptions of primary emotions such as anger, fear, disgust, jealousy, hatred, and love are manifestations of some purposeful striving toward an end or goal that a Convict/Minotaur type is unable to articulate. His primitive psyche makes objective thinking virtually impossible, so he resorts to brute force, wish fulfillment, or magical/religious thinking. Excitation is substituted for mentation. The Convict/Minotaur, reduced to a state of archaic intellectual activity, seems to bear out the belief that ontogeny replicates phylogeny. Since reasoning in such anthropoid psyches has never evolved, the ability to differentiate has been blocked and the capacity to abstract is simply nonexistent. The Convict/Minotaur can be very much aware of his lot, but his awareness of the events he lives through is limited by the framework of the laws ruling his undeveloped mentality and psyche.

In the Omsk prison, the Convict/Minotaur's personality was governed directly by his amoral and recidivist impulses and desires. Translated into religious terms, he was a paradigm of sin. Whereas the human sacrifices offered to the Cretan Minotaur were intended only to assuage his insatiable hunger, the convict's life was structured by prison officials with the goal not only of dulling his desires and diminishing his murderous intent, but also of rehabilitating him. Yet his destructive energies, like those of the Minotaur, the narrator contended, were rarely diminished in the prison atmosphere; instead, they intensified.

Although the head, since Plato's time, had been associated with mentation, which was to control the individual, and the body with instinct, which was to obey the head, the reverse condition prevailed in the prison fortress at Omsk. Turbulence, either overt or latent, was the order of the day. Despite the fact that the narrator, an intellectual, found the upside-down world of the Convict/Minotaur chaotic, such imbalance had its positive side: with the exception of the nobles and some intellectuals, the inmates acted openly, unhypocritically. The narrator, perhaps for the first time, faced raw truth. Whereas rage, hatred, violence were outwardly controlled in the so-called "civilized" world, within the prison/labyrinth these emotions were given free reign. No longer were pulsations and pressures hidden or repressed, as among the "well-bred." They were enacted, opening up the narrator to a terrifying inner world: theirs, and his own through projection. No longer were actions evil, good, or stilled, as they were in the real world, under pretense of obedience to the czar's well-ordered government or submission to the Russian Orthodox Church.

Within the labyrinthian House there existed a society which, unlike the one that thrives under the nurturing care of a parent, displayed another pattern of behavior and a different mode of psychic functioning. The patriarchal and strictly regimented domain in which the Convict/Minotaur had been enclosed functioned in stench-filled and airless barracks and according to its own codes and etiquette. "No one dared to rebel against the endogenous and accepted rules of the prison."

Not only was forced labor required, but to discourage idleness and to supplement the Convict/Minotaur's virtually nonexistent income, trades were allowed to be practiced during spare hours: tailoring, carpentry, lock-repairing, engraving, shoe-making. Thus were the convicts able to buy liquor, tobacco, or food. Although life within the prison/labyrinth was structured, nothing could prevent an illicit underworld from flourishing. The Convict/Minotaur not only stole from other convicts, but smuggled into the "House" forbidden items such as sharp instruments, despite frequent searches and the constant threat of confiscation and floggings. The playing of games and gambling allowed merriment to enter an otherwise lugubrious and cloistered existence.

The regimented world of the Convict/Minotaur was physically traumatic: he shivered in the winter and burned in the summer. Another source of physical torment was the ever-present "fleas, lice and black beetles by the bushel" (Coulson, 64).

Because he was unable to articulate his gnawing sense of mortification, the Convict/Minotaur's emotions burst forth frequently, taking the form of frenzied, uncontrollable, and frequently destructive rage. Since, the narrator notes, "almost every self-willed manifestation of the convict's personality is considered to be a crime," no value judgments concerning the extent and deeper meaning of his offense were taken into account by the prison authorities. The authorities did not care to consider what the narrator came to understand: "So, perhaps, a man who has been buried alive in his coffin and who has woken up in it hammers on its lid and struggles to throw it open, although of course his reason tells him that all his efforts will be in vain."

Categories of Convicts

Although the Convict/Minotaur type prevailed in *The House of the Dead*, other personality groups were represented in this necropolis. The narrator, for example, in contrast to the powerful physical specimens making up the majority, considered himself a "weak, pathetic, submissive creature." At night, when lying on his three planks, restless and unable to sleep, he wondered whether he would have the stamina to exist in this awful place. Representatives of many nationalities and of many religious denominations were found in the prison: although antagonisms were rampant, particularly vicious was the animosity existing between the Old Believers (Schismatics), a sect of Russian Orthodoxy, and their enemies, those who had accepted the liturgical reforms promulgated in the seventeenth century by the Patriarch Nikon. One man in particular attracted the narrator's attention: a sixty-year-old, grey-haired man who radiated calm, peace, and kindness. The Convict/Minotaurs as a whole looked up to him and treated him with respect and admiration. They believed in his integrity, called him "granddad," even entrusted their most precious possessions and their money to him for safekeeping. Why had he been incarcerated? As a member of a group of "fanatics," he had set fire to a newly built church, to be used by the theocratic government, partisans of Nikon, to encourage converts. This "noble" soul was a believer in the efficacy of "martyrdom," particularly "for a noble cause." Exploring the intricacies of this dual-natured man, so meek, gentle, and childlike on the outside, yet capable of such a destructive act, the narrator concluded that the intensity of his struggle, evident in the "incurable sadness" written on his face, must have been excoriating.

Other admirable, even pleasant, inmates also inhabited the House. Nurra, a Daghestan Tartar, whose body had been virtually "hacked and scarred all over by bayonets and bullets" prior to his arrival, was always cheerful and pleasant. What kept him alive was his hope of one day returning to the Caucasus. The narrator was also drawn to Aley, another Daghestan Tartar, "for his good-naturedly straightforward face." His imprisonment resulted from having lived in keeping with tribal Islamic law, which required younger brothers to obey older ones without question. In so doing, he participated in a raid in which he helped rob and kill an Armenian merchant. Despite his killer potential, the narrator found his comportment in the prison dignified, reserved, strong, persevering, and gentle. "There are certain natures so inherently beautiful, so richly endowed by God that the very notion that they could ever alter for the worse seems an impossible one."

Sadomasochism: Floggings and Punishments

The convict is one who, consciously or unconsciously, lives beyond the moral codes set up by society. In him are contained a composite of opposites: the criminal and the penitent, the judge and the judged, the sadist and the masochist, the redeemer and the redeemed. Ambivalence marks his psyche. A man of action, for the most part, the criminal wants neither society's help nor pity. He rejects society; he wants solitude. Yet he longs to be part of the community, insisting, although frequently unaware of it, on being punished for his acts. A criminal act (considered a sin in moral terms) requires decisive judgment and audacity. Some criminals experience psychological ineffectiveness (considered guilt in moral terms) as an aftermath of their act. Such anxieties as guilt (moral terminology) or ineffectiveness (psychological terminology) can be assuaged or obliterated through sacrifice, the greatest being that of the self. With sacrifice, there occurs an unconscious transformation from one attitude toward another; that is, a liberation of the feeling of inefficacy and a new-found purity in a sinless life.

The idea of sacrifice and of expiation dates far back into humanity's history and can be seen in the ritual slaying of kings when a crop failure occurred. Such crop failure indicates, symbolically, impotence on the part of the ruler. The kings, then, were guilty of having acted ineffectively and so had to be sacrificed. In some societies the king was killed in order to improve his subjects' position. Christ was sacrificed for the same reason: the salvation of humanity (Jung, *Collected Works*, 11:269). The transformation process that occurs through sacrifice is similar to an initiation ritual that permits the initiate to pass from one stage of life to another.

Masochistic punishment makes it possible in certain cases for the person experiencing torture, either real or symbolic, to reach a new state of awareness or to be reborn psychologically. Sacrifice, then, is a stripping-away or a liberation of the old attitude. Death, the supreme form of sacrifice, serves to wash away the sin of the individual. The reborn person, like the newborn, is clean. When in turn this newborn attitude becomes unproductive, when bitterness sets in, a similar drama of life's eternal cycle is then reenacted: sin (act), guilt (feeling of ineffectiveness), sacrifice (liberation through destruction of old attitude), resurrection (birth of new attitude). As Jesus said: "Except a man be born again, he cannot see the kingdom of God. . . . Ye must be born again" (John 3:3, 7).

Expiation for a crime is an indispensable means of leading a convict to his destiny and eventual transformation and liberation. "I beseech you therefore, brethren, by the mercies of God, that ye present your bodies a living sacrifice, holy, acceptable unto God, which is your reasonable service" (Rom. 12:1).

Infractions in *The House of the Dead*, such as stealing, obscene behavior, drunkenness, murder, or rape, demanded and were awarded floggings. Sometimes more than a thousand lashes were effected, either by a cane or birch stick. For those who endured the excruciating pain of flogging, it "was truly a case of total victory over the flesh. It was evident that this man had boundless self-mastery, that he had nothing but contempt for any kind of torture and punishment, and that he was not afraid of anything under the sun."

Such a man, however, never lost his thirst for revenge, nor did he retreat from attaining, by any means, whatever the goal he had set for himself. Arrogant in his acceptance of punishment, he considered himself a hero of sorts, having, like the ascetic, transcended the flesh. Superior to others because of his ability to control physical pain, "he looked at everything with a kind of unexpected calm," accepting adulation and respect from the other convicts as if they were his due.

The narrator tried as best he could to penetrate the complexities of the criminal mind, to discover the "astonishing motives" that drove men to kill and then to seek expiation in floggings. How, he questioned, could a house servant, peasant, serf, artisan, soldier, who had lived his whole life in peace and quiet, be suddenly impelled to murder? Did something within his brain snap? Did his endurance run out, yielding to his urge to plunge a knife into his enemy? Although the killer might have thought he was destroying his oppressor the first time, how did he justify the repetition of such acts? Did they become an amusement? If so, this means that for some individuals nothing holds the killer-instinct in check. If no punishment acts as a deterrent for the criminal who considers murder an example of unlimited freedom, then he sees himself virtually deified, as beyond good and evil.

Such a brute killer, the narrator notes, is the very one who demands chastisement, and with a kind of "desperation." He yearns to be "*dealt with*, because in the end his . . . *desperation* has become too much for him to bear." Paradoxically, when some of these so-called strong men reach the scaffold, they seem to undergo a complete personality change, turning into "limp rags," whining and sniveling, "begging the onlookers for forgiveness." So different is such an individual from the man who arrived in prison that one wonders, the narrator remarks, how this "slobbering, snivelling, abject creature" could have murdered half a dozen people.

In the narrator's prison, strong and hard guards earned the respect of the inmates and were "treated with caution." One of these, a major, whose "fatal presence" inspired both dread and admiration in the convicts, "was severe to the point of insanity." Inmates understood that there was no way they could escape from his "Eight-Eyes" nor protect themselves from his "lynx-like stare," which was able to pierce their very depths. His "acts of vicious fury," although increasing the convicts' bitterness, never led to any attempt on his life. Another guard, Akim Akimych, exercised his "almost unlimited power over two hundred souls" at all times. If his "crimson and malevolent" face burst into the barracks at night to see if anyone was sleeping on his left side, when he had ordered them to sleep on their right side, the guilty party would be flogged the following morning.

Not surprisingly, the narrator mentions the infamously sadistic Marquis de Sade and Marquise de Brinvilliers when depicting the birchwood sticks used to strike a convict's naked body and describing the sensations this act aroused in the tormentors who directed the punishment, the soldiers who administered it, and the victims who received it. What is striking and revealing at the same time is the narrator's emphasis on both the details and the ritualistic and religious dimensions of these floggings. Each case takes on its own "sweet and painful" savor.

> There are people like tigers, who thirst for blood to lick. Whoever has once experienced this power, this unlimited mastery over the body, blood and spirit of another human being, his brother according to the law of Christ; whoever has experienced this control and this complete freedom to degrade, in the most humiliating fashion, another creature made in God's image, will quite unconsciously lose control of his own feelings. Tyranny is a habit; it is able to, and does develop finally into a disease. I submit that habit may coarsen and stupefy the very best of men to the level of brutes.

To observe crimes and punishments over and over again, as did the narrator, and to depict incidents involving men "whose backs were flayed raw," reveals a need on the narrator's part to understand evil in the human personality so as to be able to deal with it as a reality in a God-created world. Important, as well, is what such probings disclose within the narrator's psyche. Does his personality reveal "callous coarseness and depravity?" Do beatings after a while become "pleasurable to the mind and the senses"? If so, does such a commentary indicate sadomasochistic tendencies in the narrator?

There were convicts, he notes, who insisted "on being punished even when they were ill." So severely had some been beaten that they were brought to the hospital, and despite freezing conditions, soaking wet rags were applied to their lacerated and suppurating backs. Nor does the narrator omit the most minute details.

> Another form of aid was the deft extraction of wooden splinters from the blisters. These splinters were often left behind in a man's back by rods that had broken. Such an operation was usually very painful for the patient. But in general I was always surprised by the extraordinary capacity for enduring pain that was shown by those who had been beaten. I saw so many of them, sometimes beaten beyond endurance, and yet hardly one of them ever uttered a groan. Only their faces seemed to alter and grow pale; their eyes would burn; their gaze would be distraught, restless, their lips

would tremble so that the wretched fellows would bite them compulsively until they almost drew blood.

Floggings, as in the conducting of any theatrical, musical, or religious performance, follow their own rituals and scenarios. At times the actors, resorting to subterfuges and tricks, play with tremendous power on the convicts' or spectators' creative imaginations. Tormentor, convict, and spectator are, to some degree, mirror images of each other. The tormentor, as the aggressor, is the actor, but he also becomes a passive recipient by identifying himself with his victim. The same duality holds true for the convict, who, seeing himself in the role of the persecuted, martyred, or sacrificial agent being acted upon, also identifies with the tormentor, thus becoming a persecutor. The interaction between the two serves to provoke and accentuate a sexual as well as a psychological bond, metacommunication being established between the two. The observer, or *voyeur*, identifying with both tormentor and victim, becomes subject and object, actor and spectator, delighting in the sadistic orgy of beatings and the penitential bloodletting. During these interchanges, levels of perversion are reached that could be likened to a *mise-en-abîme:* the accomplishment of a happening with the purpose of destroying the perpetrator or the victim.

Dostoevsky's narrator, viewing the floggings, is caught up and confused by the ceremonial round enacted before him; he becomes, unconsciously, both victor and victim. Is what the narrator observes reality? Illusion? Both these questions may be answered in the affirmative: not only does the narrator create, but he re-creates, in his account, a world of deception that takes on reality for him and for the reader. By projecting himself onto the happenings, as the narrator has been doing with regard to the beater and the beaten, he, as voyeur, unconsciously adopts the identities of one and/or the other. In so doing, he has, but for only a short time, rejected his own. Such self-rejection is, in some cases, tantamount to an unconscious self-destruction or self-murder.

Tormentor and penitent, as depicted by the narrator, take on virtually mythical grandeur: as aggressor or victim, actor or passive recipient, sufferer or voyeur, they are endowed with feelings of authority. Because the same roles are performed over and over again at the prison, the performers achieve a sense of eternalness. They fulfill both an individual need and a collective function in a collective institution. Such role-playing also conceals an opposite unconscious attitude: that of a dependent and susceptible inner personality craving its own destruction. Rejected by society, the convict seeks punishment with an inner joy, seeing it as a test of his endurance, which is deserving of admiration. In this regard he is like Herostratos, who, in order to earn both fame and punishment, burned the

Temple of Artemis in Ephesus on the day Alexander the Great was born. The Herostratic act, proof of endurance and strength, dispels the unconscious sense of inadequacy and momentarily fills the individual with feelings of well-being and achievement.

Although many ritual floggings are depicted by the narrator, the proceedings always take on a sense of intense theatricality. Rules, codes, and gestures: all have been set in advance. The tormentor enters the punishment area smiling and joking; he asks the convict questions about his personal life, then sits down and lights his pipe, after which the birches to be used to beat the culprit are brought in. Once these preliminaries have been attended to, the scenario runs its course. The convict begs the tormentor for mercy, whereupon he is asked whether he knows how to pray. If so, he is told to begin: "The convict would know what to recite, and he would also know what would happen when he recited it, as this trick had been played thirty times previously on other convicts." As he begins reciting his lines, the soldier called upon to do the actual flogging begins doing just that. Thus are voice and gesture enacted simultaneously. Action and sound cease at a specific moment, whereupon the tormentor starts to "roar with laughter, fit to burst," while the soldiers, including the one who did the flogging, knowing what has and will happen, grin, as does the now-redeemed victim.

There are two kinds of tormentors, the narrator writes: the involuntary and the voluntary. Although the latter is the "more debased," the former is loathed "with an uncontrollable, almost mystical terror." Because the involuntary tormentor considers his work an art, he feels no emotion while carrying out his sentence. "His skill in applying the strokes, his knowledge of his craft, his desire to show off to his companions and to the public excited his self-esteem." Knowing that wherever he goes he is considered "a universal outcast" intensifies his "fury and bestial proclivities," thereby adding to his pride and his sense of achievement. The more contempt is heaped upon him, the greater are his feelings of personal satisfaction after a performance. The "spectacle and theatrical pomp of the surroundings in which [the participants] appear before the public on the scaffold" heightens the effect, giving him an even greater sense of excitement at the thought of being capable of inspiring terror in the hearts of victims and spectators. During such times, he becomes master of their fates.

The narrator also takes note of the variety of psychological reactions of the flogged. Some experience feelings of "involuntary and inexorable" terror prior to the event, yet face the actual punishment with fortitude and equanimity. Others approach their punishment with "joy" in their hearts, anticipating, after the completion of their ordeal, a cleansing of the soul. When three thousand strokes are ordered, the victim is usually hospitalized after the completion of the first fifteen hundred. In the hospital, his wounds are allowed to heal, after which he returns to the prison to endure the last half of his punishment. Some victims are sullen, stupefied, and annoyed by the length of time their backs take to heal, thus delaying the completion of their martyrdom. Some even die during the performance of the event.

Sadism and masochism play a significant role in *The House of the Dead*. The former, named after the Marquis de Sade (1740–1814), is defined as a perversion from which sexual pleasure is derived by the infliction of pain, cruelty, or humiliation upon another. Masochism, named after Leopold von Sacher-Masoch (1836–95), reduces the victim to the playing-out of a passive or subordinate role, completely subjected to the will of another.

Viewed by some psychiatrists as a defense against fears of castration (what could happen to a subject passively is enacted actively upon another), sadomasochistic rituals purge the aggressor's fears through action and also encourage the victim's identification with the aggressor, thus liberating the victim (he erroneously believes) from the occurrence he fears. When after the floggings the tormentor, like a punishing parent, expects, forces, or invites the victim to beg for forgiveness, the recipient interprets it unconsciously as a pardon, thus removing any onus of guilt or sexual malfunction he might experience.

The many flogging incidents depicted in *The House of the Dead* suggest a growing need on the narrator's part to suffer through pain and humiliation himself via projection. Indeed, there are times when he seems to long, unconsciously, to be beaten by an authority or father-figure, even if it means destroying himself in the process. Such an attitude is not unusual, given the many ascetic rituals practiced by Christian flagellants, martyrs, and saints, such as Saint-Jean Labre, Marie Alacoque, and Saint Sebastian; and those performed by Shiite Muslims during the holy day commemorating the murder of the sacred martyrs Hussein and Hasan, grandsons of Muhammad. Psychologically, such activities suggest a distorted expression of an aggressive drive. The discharging of invasive energy in sadistic or masochistic acts, whether for religious, political, or any other reasons, discloses a pleasure principle rooted in violence, its goal aimed at destroying oneself or that part of oneself projected onto others. Thus the death instinct is also implicit in sadomasochistic acts.

Does the narrator experience mental chastisement or sadistic enjoyment when questioning the convicts about their reactions to punishment? "Sometimes I had a desire to find out just how great this pain was, and to learn with what it might be compared. I really don't know why this was."

The numerous times the birch stick and cane are mentioned as the flogging instruments suggest phallic sadism: the penis being fantasized as a weapon of violence and destruction. The birch, the narrator informs us, not only stings far more acutely than the cane, but the pain is intensified, its effect becoming all the more irritating to the convict's nervous system, straining it to the point of killing him. When referring to the Marquis de Sade, he remarked that the sensations evoked during the beatings he inflicted made his heart stop, "something at once sweet and painful" taking over.

The narrator's pleasure/pain principle is not only evident in his descriptions of sadomasochistic happenings, but also when revealing his ambivalence about leaving the House he had called home for four years:

> "But who knows? Perhaps I shall be sorry when in many years' time I have to leave it." I added, not without a touch of that malicious joy which sometimes becomes a desire to rub salt in one's own wounds, as though one wished to admire one's own pain, as though from the consciousness of the enormity of one's misfortune there were some real pleasure to be derived.

Parricide

Parricide is considered "the principal and primal crime of humanity as well as of the individual" (Wellek, 103). Evident in many myths (Zeus/Cronos; Oedipus/Laertes; Orestes/Agamemnon), the murder of a father is considered to be one of the most important sources of guilt and expiation. A boy's relationship to his father is at best ambivalent: he hates him as a rival for his mother's affections and loves him as the protector of the family. Such an irresolute relationship activates a sense of identification with the father: the son wants to be like him because he admires him, but also wants him out of the way because he stands in the way between him and his mother. Freud notes: "You wanted to kill your father in order to be your father yourself" (parricide). "Now you *are* your father" (identification), "but a dead father. Now your father is killing *you*" (punishment). The punishment befitting such a crime is castration (Wellek, 105).

In suggesting Dostoevsky's own latent tendencies toward parricide, Freud remarks upon the author's astoundingly accurate rendering of Feodor Pavlovitch Karamazov's murder in *The Brothers Karamazov*. Dostoevsky's brief mention of parricide in several passages in *The House of the Dead* may also be noted, their brevity suggesting that he was fearful, unconsciously, of exploring the matter any further (Wellek, 105).

To understand the forces at stake in *The House of the Dead*, let us briefly examine certain facts relating to Dostoevsky's childhood and his relationship with his father. The author, his parents, and seven siblings lived in confined quarters in an apartment next to the Marinsky Hospital in Moscow, where the father, Mikhail, served as staff doctor. During Dostoevsky's childhood and adolescence, described as "painful and cheerless," his father ruled the family with an iron hand. Friends were never allowed to penetrate the family circle. Gloom, monotony, and a terrible sense of fear—his father had an uncontrollable temper—dominated the boy's world. The situation grew virtually intolerable when his father, unable to find a Latin tutor for his children, decided to teach them himself. He was devoid of patience and angered by the smallest of mistakes; the future writer, standing erect at all times during the lessons, bore the brunt of the man's volatile temperament.

At fifteen, after the death of Dostoevsky's mother, whom he loved, he, along with his older brother, Mikhail, was sent to a military engineering college in St. Petersburg. He never saw his father again, although they did write to each other on occasion. After his father's retirement to his small country estate, the old man took to drink and beat his serfs mercilessly. Dostoevsky was eighteen when he learned that his father had been murdered by his serfs as an "act of vengeance."

Dostoevsky may have unconsciously thought that the feelings of hatred he had harbored for his father—his death wish—had in some mystical or inexplicable way been instrumental in bringing about the old man's demise. If such were the case, it might account to some extent for the continuous feelings of excoriating guilt conveyed throughout *The House of the Dead* and, in fact, in all of his other works. Punishment, to pay for his sin, was the penance needed for redemption. As the Gospels said: "And if thy right hand offend thee, cut it off, and cast it from thee: for it is profitable for thee that one of thy members should perish, and not that thy whole body should be cast into hell" (Matt. 5:30). Suffering is required for expiation. Only then can the human/ego (center of consciousness) become aware of Self/God (the total psyche). Not meekness, but fortitude and aggressivity are needed for redemption. In Isaiah we read:

> He is despised and rejected of men; a man of sorrows, and acquainted with grief: and we hid as it were our faces from him; he was despised, and we esteemed him not.
>
> Surely he hath borne our griefs, and carried our sorrows: yet we did esteem him stricken, smitten of God, and afflicted.
>
> But he was wounded for our transgressions, he was bruised for our iniquities: the chastisement of our peace was upon him; and with his stripes we are healed. (53:3–5)

Dostoevsky's exile to Siberia was, in Freud's view, a fitting chastisement at "the hands of the Little Father, the Tsar, as a substitute for the punishment he deserved for his sin against his real father" (Wellek, 106). Under such conditions, political exile became acceptable to Dostoevsky as an example of the state's justifiable punishment for the author's wishful parricide. So, too, was chastisement warranted in the religious domain. According to some critics, Dostoevsky's wavering faith in the Church as an institution and even in God increased his sense of guilt vis-à-vis his Heavenly Father. Critics in general believe that Dostoevsky suffered very real anguish concerning the deity, as attested to in his later, unforgettable "Legend of the Grand Inquisitor." Crucial also in attempting to understand Dostoevsky's emotional laceration is the existence of evil on earth and the reality of universal suffering in a God-created world.

One of the narrator's implied goals in *The House of the Dead* was the discovery of a way of liberating himself from the guilt brought on by his sin of "arrogance" in questioning God's intent. He attempted to assuage his abrasive feelings through a firm belief in Christ; in so doing, he used suffering as a technique leading to an *imitatio Christi* with its consequent feelings of redemption. In *Writer's Diary* (1873), Dostoevsky stated: "The need for suffering in its most extreme form" is "the fundamental need of the Russian people," because they have "been infected with the desire for suffering since time immemorial" (Magarshack, 140).

Although Dostoevsky did not witness his father's murder or see the corpse, the written descriptions given him to read depict in detail his father's gruesome end and remained indelibly imprinted in his mind's eye. The serfs had grabbed his father by his genitals, which they then twisted, after which they poured liquor down his throat and then stuffed a rag into his mouth, accounting for his death by suffocation. The image of his father's death was so real and so unnerving to Dostoevsky that he remained prone to nightmares for the rest of his life. Nor is it surprising to learn that he considered all of his dreams revolving around his father as premonitory, announcing a future misfortune in his life (Magarshack, 10). To wish for someone's death, consciously or unconsciously, is a double-edged sword. Not only does it indicate a desire to do away with that person, thereby eliciting guilt feelings, but it also suggests an identification with the murdered party. As such, it is a yearning for suicide as well as an expression of fear of one's own imminent death.

Dostoevsky's narrator in the first third of *The House of the Dead* tells of a nobleman who, despite his imprisonment for parricide, possesses greater "decency and humanity" than many others living in freedom. Reintroducing this same figure at the end of the volume, the narrator does so in a protective and deeply feeling way. Court officials, and officers and guards in the prison as well, he writes, believe the man guilty of having murdered his father to pay for his gambling debts, although he never confessed to such a crime. Nor was there any real evidence to substantiate the indictment. On the basis of testimony attesting to the accused's dissolute nature, his flippant ways, and his continuously cheerful state of mind, he was judged devoid of feeling.

The narrator, understandably, as the author's spokesman, sides with the alleged criminal: "It goes without saying that I did not believe he had committed this crime." With restrained, but very real joy blended with bitterness, the narrator announces that after serving a ten-year prison sentence, the nobleman has been exonerated; the real murderer has been found and has confessed. That the narrator refrains from expatiating further on the tragedy of this case and the ruination of a life suggests a reticence on his part to probe his own very wounded feelings concerning the matter of parricide.

The Play Within the Play

The theatrical performance by the inmates of the Omsk prison fortress during the Christmas season played to a full house, made up of convicts, guards, guests, and townspeople. Excitement ran high for weeks prior to the event, especially because the fifteen participating in the production insisted on maintaining secrecy concerning all its details. The makeshift costumes and rudimentary sets they acquired demonstrated great ingenuity and imagination on their part, adding a sense of achievement to their pleasure. Indeed, the narrator wrote, the convicts were so exhilarated that they behaved like real children: their "imaginations were inflamed to such a pitch of high fever" that nothing else seemed to matter.

On the program were *Filatka and Miroshka* or *The Rivals*, a popular vaudeville by the St. Petersburg actor P. G. Gregoriev (1807–54), followed by *Kedril the Glutton* based on "A Fragment of the Comedy of Don Juan and Don Pedro" from the eighteenth century. The skill and creativity that went into the making of the luxurious theatrical curtain greatly impressed the narrator. Trees, arbors, ponds, and stars were painted on bits and patches of material contributed by strangers or given by the convicts themselves. "The effect was overwhelming." Its uniqueness gladdened even the most morose among the convicts. The few tallow candles used during the performance added just the proper lighting effects.

The curtain was raised and the orchestra struck up: violins, balalaikas, guitars, accordions, tambourines, some of which were actually made by the convicts. Although screeching and sawing sounds emanated from the string instruments, "the agility with which the musicians shifted their

fingers on the strings stood comparison with the deftest conjuring trick."
The uniqueness of the performance, the spirit, dash, and "reckless bravura
of the Russian melodies," and the harmony of the ensemble, were simply
remarkable.

The plays began. Filatka, performed by the convict Baklushin, was enacted "with astonishing lucidity." It was obvious that he had studied his
role, thought about his every word and gesture; his acting was always in
keeping with the character. Baklushin's "authentic gaiety . . . straightfor-
wardness and lack of artifice" marked him as a born actor. Some of his
antics were "killingly funny." For example, just before Filatka and Miroshka kissed, Filatka shouted to Miroshka, "Wipe your nose!" and instead
wiped his own. "Everyone fairly rocked with laughter." The narrator considered Baklushin's portrayal superior to that of actors he had seen in
Moscow and St. Petersburg theaters, because city-bred performers tried
too hard to act like peasants. Baklushin was a natural.

The costumes for *Filatka and Miroshka* were remarkable. Lord Bountiful appeared in an old adjutant's uniform with epaulettes, a cap, and a
cockade; he sported a cane. Lady Bountiful, bare-armed and bare-legged,
wore a tattered muslin dress which looked as though it had once served as
a floor cloth. The convict's farcical face, smeared with an excessive
amount of powder and rouge, was equally impressive. The calico nightcap
tied under the actor's chin, in addition to the parasol he held in one hand
and the painted paper fan in the other, added a parodic note to the
production, eliciting a "great howl of laughter." So caught up was the
actor in his performance that he finally could not hold back his own
laughter.

"The general mood of exhilaration reached its highest pitch towards the
end of the play," fascinating and later haunting the narrator. He contrasted the humor and lightness of touch on stage with the fate of the
convicts in the audience, weighted down with fetters and with the pain of
knowing they had so many "long, dismal years stretching ahead" of them
in this isolated, monotonous place of subzero temperatures. As long as the
narrator's attention was focused on the stage happenings, however, the
tyranny of his oppressive thoughts vanished.

The second play, *Kedril the Glutton*, a Russian version of the Don Juan
legend, takes place in an inn. A gentleman wearing an overcoat and a less-
than-elegant round hat is followed by his servant, Kedril. The latter is
wearing a sheepskin coat and a footman's cap and is "carrying a trunk and
a chicken wrapped in brown paper." Showing master and servant to their
rooms in an inn, the innkeeper informs them that the rooms are haunted
by devils. Kedril, a coward, begins to tremble. He would like to run away,
but he fears his master; he is also very hungry.

"This servant character," the narrator notes, "was a remarkable one, in which the features of Leporello might be glimpsed distantly and vaguely, and it was played in truly remarkable fashion." When, during the supper scene, the doors creaked and the devils appeared, Kedril "shivered and hastily, almost unconsciously, stuffed into his mouth an enormous gobbet of chicken which he was unable to swallow." Incomprehensible to the audience, however, was the "outlandish" entry of the devils, "shrouded in white, with a candle lantern instead of a head." Kedril was terrorized at the thought of being carried off by the fearful devils, but not sufficiently so as to put down his bottle and glass.

> His mouth wide open with horror, he sat still for a moment, his eyes goggling out of his head at the audience, with such a killingly funny expression of abject consternation on his face that he would have made a fitting subject for a painting. At last he was borne aloft and taken away, bottle and all, kicking his legs and bawling for all he was worth.

The spectators roared with laughter during both plays. The improvisations were unforgettable, as were the pantomime, ballet scenes, facial expressions, and gestures. Without formal training, the narrator commented, and perhaps unknowingly, the inmate-actors were continuing a tradition of folk theatre handed down from one generation to another.

The humor implicit in *Filatka and Miroshka* and in *Kedril the Glutton* is based to a great extent on caricature. This technique is not only accessible but appealing because it succeeds in inflating certain patterns of behavior so that the protagonists and the events depicted are taken out of the world of reality and placed into one of artifice, thereby underscoring the ridiculous nature of their antics and eliciting true belly laughs. According to Bergson, caricature is a device marked with "insensibility" and "ulterior motive." It enables an actor to express in veiled terms his paradoxical feelings of inferiority/superiority, love/hate. The caricaturist, Bergson contends, like the puppeteer, can force his creatures to express the most outlandish or excoriating emotions under the guise of folly. "The art of the caricaturist lies in his ability to seize that frequently imperceptible movement, and to make it visible for all to see by inflating it" (Bergson, 9, 5, 20).

That both convict vaudevilles aroused such continuous laughter is also due in part to the depth of the spectators' projections onto the happenings. Identifying with the characters, they perhaps felt they were sharing their anguishes and joys; in the movement of the dialogue and antics, they forgot their own miserable plight. The facial and gestural expressions, the outlandish costumes and absurdity of the situations, allowed them to expel those tormenting powers imprisoned within them in a kind of collective catharsis. Thus did the convicts feel purged, purified, born anew, free from the shackles of reality.

Humor and slapstick served to magnify the ridiculousness of certain character traits, as well as of some of life's situations. Lady Bountiful's attire, for example, was as ludicrous as was her identification with such a titled person. Allowed to be played out on stage, then, were certain repressed desires considered socially unacceptable, serving, at least momentarily, to liberate the observer. Humor through performance mirrors to a great extent certain notions about comedy set down by Cicero: "The province of the ridiculous lies within limits of ugliness and certain deformity; for the expressions are alone, or especially ridiculous which disclose and represent some ugliness in a not unseemly fashion" (Feibleman, 88).

Not only did the clowning sequences give the impression of professionalism, but, even more incredible, they were divested of prurient images and innuendoes. The leveling of blows and counterblows by a plethora of insensitive personalities performing their antics on stage with marionette-like alacrity and verve served to devaluate what was distasteful in the personal and collective world: the terror of psychological and physical imprisonment.

Significant is the ludic element of the vaudevilles. Never is there any playing down or up to an audience. Since neither *Filatka and Miroshka* or *Kedril the Glutton* are designed to teach morality but are rather intended to entertain, stage action is emphasized. The goal is to sweep the convicts into the stage events, through language, gesture, costumes, makeup, and the rhythm of the absurd antics. The use of shock technique in the enactment of certain scenes as well as in the incredible costumes is also valuable: it stirs emotions, inviting spectators through identification to become active participants. No longer are they passive observers; they have joined in with the collective, willing and able to bring something of themselves into the stage happenings, thereby making the creative event possible. No longer exiles or outcasts, they have entered into the spirit of things and are warmed with a sense of belonging.

The convict audience, at least temporarily, becomes oblivious to its surroundings. For this reason, *Filatka and Miroshka* and *Kedril the Glutton* may be considered therapeutic psychodrama, releasing emotions and filling both performers and observers with a sense of liberation. Feelings of deliverance are also experienced through the mechanism of laughter, which offers a freeing of pent-up inhibitions. As the narrator remarks: "All that was needed was for these poor men to be allowed to live in their own way for a bit, to enjoy themselves like human beings, to escape from their convict existence just for an hour or so—each individual underwent a moral transformation, even if it only lasted for a few moments."

The Hospital

Consumption, scurvy, eye and skin infections, fevers, and venereal disease were reason enough to send the convict to the military hospital. Some inmates feigned illness just to have a rest from their arduous penal labor or as a temporary escape from corporal punishment. The narrator, also hospitalized at certain intervals, was able to view conditions at close range. No detail is spared the reader: the filth of the lice-ridden undergarments the convicts were given to wear, the bed-linens with their bedbugs, the open urinals, the oppressive stench of the contaminated air: all are depicted with clinical clarity. One consumptive, for example, after sneezing into his handkerchief would open it

> and closely examine the abundant gobbets of snot in it, whereupon he would immediately smear it all over his brown prison dressing gown, so that all the snot stayed on the dressing gown and the handkerchief was left only slightly damp. He continued to do this all week.

Understandably, after having witnessed this act, when the narrator was given a dressing-gown to wear on his body, he was utterly revolted:

> by now it had grown warm from the heat of my body, and it was smelling increasingly strongly of medicines, sticking plaster and, it seemed to me, some kind of pus. . . . [Its] lining was saturated in all kinds of unpleasant secretions, lotions, suppurations from broken blisters. . . . What was more, these wards frequently admitted convicts who had just been beaten with rods until their backs were flayed raw; their wounds were treated with medicated lotions . . . and the whole mess stayed on it.

Nor were those dying of consumption deprived of their fetters, which generally weighed from eight to twelve pounds. This additional burden for such skeletal torsos, supported by withered legs, hastened their demise. Why, the narrator wondered, were the fetters not removed at this point, allowing the criminals to die in peace? The narrator, however, was well aware of the symbolic value of fetters: a "public dishonor, a disgrace, and a shameful physical and moral burden." But then, moved by his compassion for humanity, the narrator asked: "Was it right to punish men who were dying?"

Landscape

Climate and landscape also played a role in increasing or diminishing the narrator's sense of exile and aloneness. With the coming of spring and the song of the first skylark, the weight of imprisonment seemed to afflict him far more cruelly than in wintertime. The renewal of life in all of its luxuriant verdancy had a "disturbing effect on the organism," encouraging a "vague melancholy" in the narrator, and a yearning for freedom made all the more painful by the sun's bright rays.

To alleviate somewhat his sense of depression as well as to encourage his imagination, the narrator used to look through the cracks in the stockade at the world beyond. As his eyes feasted on the green grass surrounding the prison ramparts and the endless deep blue of the sky, he wrote: "My restlessness and anguish would grow with every day that passed, and the prison would come to seem more and more hateful to me."

Nature, an archetypal power, represents that which is both hostile and loving, voracious and giving, demonic and angelic, sick and healthy. The narrator responded powerfully to its alterations, which in turn alleviated and/or magnified his despair.

> There was something dreary and heart-searing about this wild, empty landscape. But it was perhaps even more painful when the sun shone on the endless white sheet of the snow; if only one could have flown away somewhere into those steppes, which began on the opposite bank and spread out to . . . the south in a single unbroken expanse for some fifteen hundred versts to the south.

The labyrinthian House standing within the immensities of the Siberian icy wastes, primeval forests, and endless steppes and plains exiled Dostoevsky from the world of the living, forced him to contemplate continuously his own underworld and, through projection, to view himself in multiple fragmented mirror images in other inmates. Although functioning as a framework for punishment, the fortress prison at Omsk led him, through his fictionalized narrator, to divest himself of the mask (*persona*) he had worn unconsciously prior to his incarceration. In *The House of the Dead*, he laid his heart bare. Exile permitted him to live out his every mood, feeling, and instinct through the written word and within the framework of multiple themes: the Convict/Minotaur personality, the parricidal act, the sadomasochistic ceremony, theater, the hospital experience, the landscape.

The depth of the narrator's feelings, though conveyed always in a restrained manner, responded all the more poignantly and compassionately to the emotions of the other inmates: their sobs, laughter, grievances, sicknesses, hates, or simply the torturing pain of being.

He also discovered, with some surprise, that in many cases criminals experienced "not the slightest trace of repentance, not one sign that their crime weighed heavily on their conscience." Rather, they felt justified in their act. But then he adds, with humility, "Who can say that he has fathomed the depths of these lost hearts and has read in them that which is hidden from the whole world?" And he adds:

> Of course the criminal, who has rebelled against society, hates it and nearly always considers himself to be in the right and it to be in the wrong. What is more, he has already suffered its punishment, and he nearly always considers that this has cleansed him and settled his account.

Nor was there any earthly force that could make the narrator, or any criminal in the Omsk fortress, forget that although he was an outcast, he was also a human being and had to be treated as one.

> *Human* treatment may even render human a man in whom the image of God has long ago grown tarnished. It is these "unfortunates" that must be treated in the most human fashion. . . . A few kind words—and the convicts experienced something approaching a moral resurrection. Like children they rejoiced, and like children they began to love.

Exiled, shunned by all, cut off from society, Dostoevsky spent four years in prison that were physically harrowing and psychologically mutilating. The experience echoed throughout his body and soul for the rest of his days. The psychological torture that he endured pierced him like the Crucifixion. Although he was not suspended between two thieves, one of whom went to heaven and the other to hell, Dostoevsky did undergo the torment of a trial amid a multitude of criminals. Like Christ on the cross, who united with his opposite, the Antichrist, as symbolized by the evil thief, Dostoevsky became aware, through his ordeal, of the polarities existing within him and in the world at large. As Jung wrote: "This great symbol [Crucifixion] tells us that the progressive development and differentiation of consciousness leads to an ever more menacing awareness of the conflict and involves nothing less than a crucifixion of the ego, its agonizing suspension between irreconcilable opposites (Edinger, *The Christian Archetype*, 99; Jung, *Collected Works*, 9, part 79).

And when the narrator/Dostoevsky had been sufficiently punished and his guilt redeemed, he felt jubilation in his liberation: "Yes, God go with you! Freedom, a new life, resurrection from the dead. . . . What a glorious moment!"

2 Conrad's *The Heart of Darkness:* The Shadow in Exile

Joseph Conrad's[1] *The Heart of Darkness* (1902), written after his journey to Central Africa (1890), may be viewed as a search for an exiled *shadow:* unconscious personality traits the individual considers inferior and does not accept as his own. If the quest is successful, the previously rejected characteristics are assimilated into the personality, bringing wholeness in the place of divisiveness. That Conrad should have noted, upon his return to England, "Before the Congo I was just a mere animal" suggests the psychological significance the trip had for him. Important as well in underlining the crucial nature of his journey is the speed and fervor with which he wrote his long short story, begun in December 1898, and completed at the beginning of February 1899.

In the era of successful European imperialism, "a mere animal" was a derogatory term Westerners usually reserved for "savages," "primitives," or the "uncivilized." The so-called "civilized" Europeans viewed themselves as inherently logical, rational, good, and light-bringing, whereas black Africans (such as those in Conrad's narrative) were considered savage, undomesticated, unrestrained, instinctual, and evil. Accordingly, the Westerners were endowed with acceptable and laudable traits; Africans, with unworthy ones. Antiblack prejudice is less blatant today, but it still

---

[1]Joseph Conrad (Teodor Josef Konrad Korzeniowski) (1857–1924) was born of Polish parents in the Ukraine but lived in Volagda, northern Russia, where his father was a political exile. After his parents' early death, he was cared for by his uncle, Thaddeus Bobrowski. In 1874 he went to Marseilles, embarked on a French vessel and began living out his dream of sailing the seas. He became a British subject (1886) and finally settled in England in 1894, where he wrote, married Jessie George (1895), and fathered two sons.

appears to be widespread, and on an unconscious level it may be just as virulent as it was in Conrad's day. In Conrad's story the traits of the shadow—those the *ego* (center of consciousness) considers inferior—are attributed to Africans, but such traits could be attributed to any race or group. The shadow's traits, whatever they may be, are frequently personi-fied in dreams and creative works; when these traits are projected onto blacks, they may be imagined by dreamers or artists as dark and frighten-ing figures. The question arises as to how individuals are to rid themselves of components that their self-esteem views as negative. An erroneous and dangerous means of discarding unwanted personality traits is to project them onto others (individuals, groups, or nations). Such a giant discharge of undesired qualities is illusory, giving the initiator of the projection the feeling of liberation and the conviction that these despised characteristics really belong to others. Such "scapegoat" psychology has led to mass reli-gious and racial persecutions throughout history. An alternative, more positive and enriching, manner of coming to terms with the shadow is by facing one's rejected components and clarifying them by bringing them to the light of consciousness.

Evidently tormented by what he considered his animal-like or shadow characteristics, Conrad opted for a quest leading to a better understanding of those "demons of the dark" raging within him. His journey, which he considered mandatory for the healing process, took him into the Belgian Congo, as it was called at the time, to Kinshasa and Stanley Falls on the Congo River. Only by exiling himself from "civilization" could he confront and come to grips with his exiled shadow.

That Conrad's protagonist, Marlow, remarks that "the mind of man is capable of everything—because everything is in it, all the past as well as the future," elsewhere refers to "the earliest beginnings of the world," and to "primeval mud"—suggests that *The Heart of Darkness* takes us back to one of the most archaic levels of the human psyche. Conrad's reference to a primitive stratum within an individual may be associated with the mysterious, timeless, and spaceless inner ocean which Jung termed the *collective unconscious*. This deepest of levels within the psyche is accessible to consciousness through *archetypal images*, manifested in dreams, myths, visitations, initiations, legends, and other cultural manifestations.

Conrad's *The Heart of Darkness* may be read as a sociohistorical work, highlighting European colonial exploitation of the African. Our discussion will be a psychological approach, attempting to understand why Marlow needed to confront his exiled shadow, and why he literally had to exile himself from Europe to accomplish his mission.

European Enlightenment

Before proceeding with our analysis of Marlow's journey back into that archaic sphere within his psyche, which he identified with the Belgian Congo, we shall probe the questions of why the Europeans looked upon themselves as the harbingers of enlightenment, and why they were always attempting to convert others to their way of thinking.

The overevaluation of the rational function and the concomitant denigration of the irrational sphere in Western Europe established an approach to life by which, it was believed, humanity's knowledge would be extended. One day, reason would control all things, including character traits. The ideal, then, would become real and infinitely continuing progress would be a certainty. Centuries earlier, Plato had laid the groundwork for such a notion by dividing the human being into two unequal parts: reason was identified with the divine element, and instinct with the animal side. The latter, as of necessity, had to be controlled, minimized, repudiated whenever possible (Barrett, 83). In the centuries to follow, value judgments were added: the rational mind being associated with good, the bodily realm with evil. The question as to how evil could exist in a God-created world plagued such believers as St. Augustine, who wrestled with the problem and thought that he had solved it once and for all. Only good exists in the Christian Godhead, he stated. God, therefore, is not the originator of evil. Not only did St. Augustine deny the existence of evil in a God-created world, he refused to give it substance. He looked upon it, rather, as a *privatio boni*. In his *Argument Against the Manicheans and Marcionites*, St. Augustine writes:

> EVIL THEREFORE IS NOTHING BUT THE PRIVATION OF GOOD. And thus it can have no existence anywhere except in some good thing. . . . So there can be things which are good without any evil in them, such as God himself, and the higher celestial beings; but there can be no evil things without good." Evil, then, is relegated to a "defect in good things" or to the figure of the Antichrist. (Jung, *Collected Works*, 9^{11}:50–51)

Rather than solve the problem, St. Augustine merely added fuel to the fire of controversy. He widened the gap between what was good and rational and what was bad and irrational, thus paving the way for the manifestation of increasingly dangerous feelings of alienation by people of the twentieth century. The growing emphasis on the rational principle (equated with good) transformed the individual into a thinking process.

The body (equated with evil) had little or no importance and became a mechanism that had to be controlled and repressed. Emotions had to be directed into proper channels by cognitive means (*logos*): ethical, scientific, and other forms of progress were a matter of reason and knowledge; virtue and morality were questions of will.

What are the psychological ramifications of such an ego-centered view? Pride in knowledge and in the cognitive process, leading to their perpetual aggrandizement at the expense of the rest of the personality. Such an abstract system, however, goes contrary to human nature in that it disregards the *instinctual*, or what the European considers the *shadow*, world, which is part of the whole personality. To suppress everything that cannot be directed by reason is to deny an individual's entire affective or instinctual side. As a result, the animal within rages, hungers, and loses control, destroying whatever balance exists within the personality. What the Europeans did not take into consideration was the fact that when instincts are properly tended to (understood) and accepted, they may act in harmony with the other aspects of the personality, becoming positive forces. When unattended and rejected, however, they crave what is rightfully theirs and may become virulent and destructive. Not to take into account the individual's earthly, instinctual, or affective half (*physis*), but to cultivate merely the godly, spiritual, and rational side, is to cut the person off from life, to create a top-heavy being who may end his or her days groveling in mire.

The overevaluation of the rational principle, considered the light side of being, and the devaluation of the dark side, the irrational factor, accentuates not only social problems but psychological ones as well. Marlow, the product of "European enlightenment," felt "animal-like" forces seething within him. He might have been unaware of his repression of these corrosive forces, as Freud's discoveries (*The Interpretation of Dreams*, 1900) had not yet been published and the science of psychology was still in its infancy. Conrad's attempt at self-healing through the creative process is therefore all the more astounding and impressive.

The Heart of Darkness opens as Marlow spins his yarn to four listeners, seated in a yawl on the Thames. Are the facts he is to relate based on reality or is it a dream he is recalling?

> It seems to me, I am trying to tell you a dream—making a vain attempt, because no relation of a dream can convey the dream sensation, that commingling of absurdity, surprise, and bewilderment in a tremor of struggling revolt, that notion of being captured by the incredible which is of the very essence of dreams.

The question is not only not resolved, but grows increasingly complex in view of the amount of archetypal imagery implicit in the narrative. The panoramic view of the Thames at the outset of the narrative, interpreted psychologically, discloses a need to unite what is disparate. This waterway leads, Marlow remarks, "to the uttermost ends of the earth." Fluidity becomes a key element in the archetypal image because it enables disparate components within a personality to merge. That "the sea and the sky were welded together without a joint" further corroborates Marlow's yearning for harmony, setting the tone for his exile and his search for his shadow.

Why such a quest is necessary is immediately evident in Conrad's description of Marlow. Sitting "cross-legged," having "sunken cheeks, a yellow complexion, a straight back, an ascetic aspect, and, with his arms dropped, the palms of hands outwards," he "resembled an idol." He had "the pose of Buddha preaching in European clothes and without a lotus-flower."

Outwardly, Marlow gives the impression of a restrained, straight, and honorable man in full control of himself. Words such as "ascetic" and "sunken cheeks" indicate the practice of austerity and self-denial as measures of personal and spiritual discipline. His Buddha-like posture and the serenity exuding from his being are, however, a pose, a mask; in psychological terms, a *persona*. That the inner man is at odds with his social face, that both facets of his personality are neither well connected nor integrated, is indicated in Conrad's use of the word "idol." For many Westerners, even today, idols are remnants of primitive or "savage" societies, and are thus disparaged. Having lost their once-sacred nature, idols symbolize a false god or treacherous phantom. Because Christians consider their religious views further advanced than those of other groups, such objects of worship are looked upon as traps, lures, impediments to the development of religious experience that must be destroyed (Acts 19:27; 1 Cor. 10:28). That Marlow should be compared with an idol suggests tension between his persona (rational, thinking) and his shadow (archaic, instinctual) (Eliade, *Patterns in Comparative Religion*, 25).

Marlow, "unruffled," "tranquil," and Buddha-like seated against a background of water and sky, gives his companions a historical exegesis. By evoking "the great spirit of the past upon the lower reaches of the Thames," he takes his readers back to Roman times, when London (Latin, *Londinium*) had "been one of the dark places of the earth." Once Romanized, "nineteen hundred years ago—the other day. . . . Light came out of this river. . . . But darkness was here yesterday." The interplay of light and darkness may be regarded as a reification of a reciprocal activity in Marlow's psyche.

What were Roman values that their presence should have transformed the dark side of human nature into light? What significance did such transvaluation of values suggest in terms of Marlow? Prior to the Roman conquest of Britain (first century C.E.), this land was made up of a variety of "barbaric" tribes: Celts, Picts, Scots, Angles, Saxons, Danes, and others. In time, their "primitive" characteristics amalgamated with the "higher" achievements of the Romans: architecture, law, engineering, painting, sculpture, literature, music, military prowess. One may well ask what happened to the visceral and earthy elements of the tribal fathers of Great Britain. Were the spectacular Celtic mysteries, such as Druidism with its ceremonial rituals and supernatural realms, driven underground?

Like the Romans, who came to Britain and were strong enough "to face the darkness" confronting them, Marlow would also have to come to grips with the "incomprehensible," and the "detestable" yet fascinating abominations he would encounter. "Land in a swamp, march through the woods, and in some inland post feel the savagery, the utter savagery, [that] had closed round him—all that mysterious life of the wilderness that stirs in the forest, in the jungles, in the hearts of wild men. There's no initiation either into such mysteries."

To identify with one's persona, which corresponds in some way to one's social face, conscious or unconscious attitude, religious feelings, and group environment, is far from new (Jung, *Collected Works*, 6:590). Celts donned masks when enacting their sacred mysteries, as did the tribesmen Marlow would visit in Africa. In both cases, masks were used to pave the way for the worshipper to enter into his animal nature (bull, stag, horse, boar, cat, etc.), enabling him to experience the latent powers within him. Contemporary men and women perform similar acts when putting on their "social faces," the difference being that they attempt to *hide* their animal natures rather than to connect with them (Sharkey, *Celtic Mysteries*, 8–12).

What factors are churning beneath Marlow's masklike stance? Why does he seek exile from the world of light into a disturbing, turbulent, and dangerous domain of darkness? Harassed, perhaps, by an inability to adapt to people and circumstances, or by gloomy forebodings or painful subliminal stirrings, he feels compelled to explore what he calls those "blank spaces on the earth" and "the farthest point of navigation." By sailing up the Congo River, which he likens to "an immense snake uncoiled, with its head in the sea, its body at rest curving afar over a vast country, and its tail lost in the depths of the land," he feels he will be able to fathom those elemental forces hidden deep within him.

Since jobs as skippers of steamboats navigating down the Congo River are at a premium, Marlow needs to take advantage of any available personal contacts to help him in this regard. Therefore, "I, Charlie Marlow, set the women to work—to get a job. Heavens!" He asks his aunt, who is ready "to do anything" for him and who knows influential people, to obtain the post for him. She succeeds. Marlow goes to his employers' offices in Brussels forty-eight hours later.

Brussels: "A Whited Sepulchre"

Why does Marlow call Brussels "a whited sepulchre"? The Westerner looks upon white as a paradigm of purity and spotlessness, as that unlived part of the life process, as absence, or as death. Because white is the sum of all colors, potential is enclosed within its substance. That Marlow should refer to Brussels as a "sepulchre" or burial place, indicates, psychologically, the existence of a cemetery within him. Such dead or repressed components of his psyche may refer to lost loves or other forms of vanished happiness or potential. The juxtaposition of "whited" with "sepulchre" intimates only an apparent end to things, thus the possibility of renewal.

Marlow reacts affectively and in sequences of paradoxical images when entering the trading company's offices. Outside, he is greeted by the "dead silence" of the "deserted" street, the "grass sprouting between the stones." Inside, by two fearsome figures, "one fat, the other slim," rising seemingly from nowhere, knitting black wool "feverishly." The latter rises, and walks toward him, never once putting down her knitting, giving Marlow the impression of being a "somnambulist." No sooner is he ushered into a waiting room than he sees a map on the wall and focuses on the Belgian Congo, the *yellow* area: "Dead in the centre."

Yellow, with its high concentration of energy, is a strident and violent color. Like the sun's rays, it may be blinding in intensity. Herein lies the paradox: light tones, representing consciousness, are used to delineate black Africa, the antithesis of consciousness: the shadow, the unconscious, the fearsome. That Marlow's journey leads to the "dead centre" of the African continent, and by extension to his own psyche, should enable him to penetrate his own axis, his own blackness and blankness. Or will the radiance of the illumination serve to blind him?

The "dead centre" of the African continent, which Marlow seeks to reach, may be viewed mystically as that privileged and sacred area where a religious experience may transform the nonmanifested into the manifested, the unlived into the active and potent. Some African tribes equate the umbilicus with the area of the body from which life spawns, viewing it metaphorically as the center of the earth, and thus according it greater importance than the phallus. To tap an individual's potential requires a descent into his *center*, or, psychologically, into subliminal realms.

The two women Marlow sees when entering and leaving the company's offices arouse "something ominous," "eerie," "fateful," within his psyche. It is as if they know all about him, and like the Moerae (the Fates), they are spinning the thread of his life, or like the Erinyes (the Furies), the daughters of Night, are avenging transgressions. These guardians of "the door of Darkness, knitting black wool as for a warm pall," may be regarded as archetypal figures, phantasms emanating from the deepest strata of Marlow's psyche. That they take on such negative functions indicates the urgency of Marlow's venture and the dangers involved. To regress to the most archaic and arcane levels of subliminal spheres may lead to an eclipse of the ego, to insanity.

Prior to his departure, Marlow pays a visit to his aunt, who had represented him to the company's chiefs as a most remarkable fellow: "an emissary of light, something like a lower sort of apostle," one of those "Workers" who would be instrumental in "weaning those ignorant millions from their horrid ways." The divergency between Marlow's realistic intent and his aunt's exalted view of him is evident in his judgmental statement about women:

> It's queer how out of touch with truth women are. They live in a world of their own, and there has never been anything like it, and never can be. It is too beautiful altogether, and if they were to set it up it would go to pieces before the first sunset. Some confounded fact we men have been living contentedly with ever since the day of creation would start up and knock the whole thing over.

While in former days Marlow used to be able to brush off opinions with which he disagreed, his aunt's flamboyant view of him going to Africa to reform and reeducate the savages make him feel like an "imposter." His reasons for journeying to Africa are neither altruistic nor condescending; his annoyance at his aunt's credulity are early examples of his attempt to clarify and come to terms with an untenable psychological condition.

Symptomatic of Marlow's inability to relate to women, having lived for so long in a patriarchal sphere, is his rationalization of the feminine principle. Women are viewed by him as "ominous" forces, as gatekeepers of Death, as emissaries of deadly whitened purity, or idealists who have never allowed themselves to be sullied by life's earthiness.

The Great Nekyia or Night-Sea Journey

The ship taking Marlow to Africa will be the first step in living out his "Night-Sea Journey" (or *Nekyia*, from Homer's *Odyssey*). Such a perilous voyage had been accomplished by Oriris in a boat; by Jonah in the belly of a whale; by Theseus in the labyrinth; by Moses in the desert; by Christ from an entombment. Each of these paradigms is viewed as a re-actualization of a death/rebirth ritual. The individual undergoing such psychic suffering exposes himself to his collective unconscious: to the limits of human endurance, to "the very threshold of the beyond," taking destiny, as it were, into his own hands.

The Great Nekyia, then, requires the novitiate to regress into the very heart of mystery—Origin—prior to *fiat lux*. Such a trajectory, if leading to a depersonalization of the ego, may result in an eclipse of consciousness or insanity, as previously mentioned. If, however, the individual experiencing such trauma survives the ordeal, enlightenment may ensue, and with it expanded consciousness and salvation (Jacobi, 156).

Such journeys, while pressing the ego to confront its own autonomous unconscious contents, generate psychic energy (*libido*). In so doing, formerly dormant components not only are churned up, but are pushed into new areas, and sometimes into the view of consciousness. Thus they are revived or reborn, becoming capable once again of nourishing new creative forces existing at the very base of life. The excitation engendered during the Great Nekyia is crucial to the effectiveness of the transformation process, and libido plays its part in an individual's destiny in altering ideations, values, and feeling tones (Jacobi, 183).

Once Marlow arrives at the company's Outer Station in Africa, masks are dropped. Stunned by the condition of deterioration all around him (as exemplified by decayed machines, a railway truck lying on its back), he wonders whether he is penetrating some outer or unreal dimension. Is he of this earth? Even the slave gang working at building a railway passes him by with "complete, deathlike indifference," as if he were some kind of invisible force. Is the "pain, abandonment, and despair" he reads on the faces of these "moribund shapes," these "black shadows of disease and starvation," a mirror image of his own inner geography? A prelude to disaster?

In sharp contrast with the sense of demoralization Marlow observes around him is the utter elegance of the company's chief accountant. A man sporting a snow-white starched collar, white cuffs, white trousers, a light alpaca jacket, and varnished boots in this no-man's-land is a man of "backbone," he believes. Two ways, then, are open to him: decadence and death or survival and renewal.

The wetness of the heat, the stabbing of the flies, and the innumerable other discomforts of jungle life are made easier to bear by the thought of the "remarkable" man Marlow is to meet: "Mr. Kurtz, a first-class agent stationed in the heart of ivory country and in charge of an important trading post that is in jeopardy because of his illness."

Ten days later, Marlow begins his arduous 200-mile trek with a sixty-man caravan through the jungle, traversing flatlands, matted vegetation, thickets, and ravines, walking hours on end in the blazing heat. His eyes are forever focused on the rapacious white men, who, "like a lot of faithless pilgrims," pander/pray to their God—"ivory"—a sacred power that brings bullion. The allusion to his fellow travelers as "pilgrims" reinforces Marlow's repugnance for their pseudophilanthropic pretensions, their intriguing, their slandering, and the murderous ways in which they preach Christianity in the name of loot.

While talking to the manager of the station, "a papier-mâché Mephistopheles," Marlow spies an oil sketch of a woman painted by Mr. Kurtz: "draped and blindfolded, carrying a lighted torch. The background was sombre—almost black. The movement of the woman was stately, and the effect of the torchlight on the face was sinister." What did such a proleptic image indicate? Was Mr. Kurtz really "an emissary of pity and science and progress . . . a prodigy," a man who would one day be general manager of the entire company?

Returning to the "Earliest Beginnings of the World"

During Marlow's two-month venture down the river to reach Kurtz's Inner Station, he feels he has become "captive" to some absurd, bewildering, terrifying, "incredible" power, living a "*dream*," a *dream-sensation*." Psychological regression has already taken hold in the hypnagogic state Marlow describes: that veiled period just preceding slumber. It is at this juncture that he becomes privy to the "earliest beginnings of the world," when "vegetation rioted on the earth and the big trees were kings."

That Marlow describes his journey as an "unrestful and noisy dream," as "moments when one's past comes back to one," is an analogical depiction of his reentry into the primitive heartlands of his own psyche. The metaphor of vegetation rioting discloses a condition of turbulence and confusion, as well as an opening-up onto a "strange world of plants," where kingly trees inhabit an "impenetrable" forest." Everything around him crackles with life and activity, reifying his own brooding. No longer living in his head as a top-heavy Westerner cut off from his roots, Marlow is beginning to feel some kind of connection with that steaming African earth, that primordial mud, unknown to him prior to his regression in time. It is via his descent into his own archaic psyche that he will reach out to that "inner truth" for which he so desperately yearns.

What does Marlow's regression or backward thrust into a space/time continuum entail? Such a psychological condition indicates a damming-up of libido in the unconscious with a suspension of conscious activity. The increase of energetic forces flowing into Marlow's subliminal sphere, accompanied by an escalation in its activity, results in a blockage of thought processes, such as the ability to differentiate, evaluate, and abstract. When bathing in such archaic or elemental waters, Marlow can no longer dissipate or channel the fiery subliminal impulses that are restrained under normal conditions by the thinking principle. Understandably, he will live through deeply disturbing periods during which certain subliminal contents may be constellated. On the other hand, these same clusters may also disclose new insights, associations, and mediating forces, inviting different conscious directions to become operational.

The continuously cradling effect of the steamboat as it makes its way up the river lulls Marlow still further into his regressive dream state, where mythical time prevails and space is eternal. While observing the stagnant, torpid, somnolent waters, his attention is increasingly drawn to the immense number and variety of trees that come into view as he proceeds more deeply into the African continent.

> Trees, trees, millions of trees, massive, immense, running up high; and at their foot, hugging the bank against the stream, crept the little begrimed steamboat, like a sluggish beetle crawling on the floor of a lofty portico. It made you feel very small, very lost, and yet it was not altogether depressing, that feeling.

That trees are archetypal powers for Marlow—dynamic nuclei, energy centers, sacred forces—is in keeping with ancient religious traditions. Let us recall that their numinousness was also significant for the ancients: the Celts (oak), Scandinavians (ash), Greeks (pine), Hebrews (Tree of the Knowledge of Good and Evil), Christians (the wood of the Cross) (Jacobi, 183). As an archetypal image, the tree is identified with transpersonal forces. Its appearance in dreams or in fantasy images suggests an opening-up of an individual's internal and personal drama to universal external forces. That the tree's growth, proliferation, and regenerative process symbolize life's eternality enables Marlow, when depicting trees, to review his entire existence onirically as a space/time continuum (Eliade, *Myths, Dreams, and Mysteries*, 19).

In the above quotation, Marlow identifies with the little steamboat, which he then compares to a "sluggish beetle," thereby deemphasizing the traditional narcissism of the white man who considers himself the focus of God's interest and superior to all other earthly entities. Associated so frequently with the human body, the boat represents, psychologically, the ego's struggle to remain afloat throughout the perils of the life process and the onslaughts of the collective unconscious. That the boat, a closed universe or microcosm, should be sluggish like a beetle (scarab) in no way diminishes its strength. On the contrary, according to the Egyptian myth, this minute entity is powerful enough to push the sun-globe along between its claws. In this regard, the beetle is also identified with renewal, as are trees and the waters within which the boat/body travels.

As Marlow penetrates ever more deeply "the heart of darkness," and his own center, nature's extreme quiescence enhances his already well developed sense of mystery. When, for example, he hears the faint drumbeats in the distance, their rhythms and tonalities seem to replicate his own heartbeat in some strange way. So, too, are his phantasms ever burgeoning, likening him and his group to "wanderers on a prehistoric earth, on an earth that wore the aspect of an unknown planet." A kinship with those ancient inhabitants and their descendents now living on the land takes hold; he responds as they break "into a burst of yells, a whirl of black limbs, a mass of hands clapping, of feet stamping, of bodies swaying, of eyes rolling, under the droop of heavy and motionless foliage."

In time, Marlow no longer sees the frenzied blacks as complete strangers, as *others*, but rather as living and breathing prehistoric counterparts of himself at another stage of evolution: vestiges of an archaic and arcane stratum within himself. He now begins to feel attuned to these once-incomprehensible howling, leaping, spinning beings and their horrific faces. What was once severed by Marlow's "sane" and "rational" upbringing is contained, he feels, somewhere within him. He will have to learn how to reconnect with these wild, elemental, but also thrilling shadow forces he has unconsciously rejected during the course of time. He also begins to question the fundaments of his own identity. Who is he? A "phantom"? An apparition? A man without substance? He seems to be visiting a "madhouse" while "travelling in the night of first ages, of those ages that are gone, leaving hardly a sign—and no memories." Marlow now understands that he does not understand: "The earth seemed unearthly."

Now that Marlow has observed his double in the black tribesmen, does he still pride himself on his "reason"? Now that his irrational domain has been tapped and he has been stirred empathetically by the wild and howling black men, by the mysterious drumbeats, by the primeval trees and primordial mud, he feels alienated from the "pilgrims" on board. Convinced of the notion of perfectibility, of their theological, biological, and scientific superiority, they have become real strangers to him now.

Confusion still prevails in Marlow's psyche, dominated as it is by strange, turbulent, and muddled impulses. Nevertheless, the tenuous connection already made between him and the natives is deepening; he no longer feels so fragmented as he did at the beginning of his journey. In keeping with the opening archetypal image of the flowing Thames River, a linking or consolidation of heretofore disparate components of his psyche is taking place. That he feels a "remote kinship" with the wild and passionate natives, with their ugliness and their instinctuality, is no longer surprising, in that he is no longer a creature only of reason. He has learned to *feel* into situations and moods, identifying more fully with qualities that motivate all people in all ages: "joy, fear, sorrow, devotion, valor, rage." Herein lies "truth stripped of its cloak of time." Sham and hypocritically induced "fine" or "civilized" sentiments no longer answer Marlow's emotional and spiritual needs.

After anchoring the steamboat about fifty miles below the Inner Station, Marlow walks to shore and comes upon a dismantled reed hut, once occupied by a white man. His curiosity is aroused by an unexpected item he finds inside: a book entitled *An Inquiry into Some Points of Seamanship* by a master in his Majesty's Navy. That he cannot decipher the "astounding" notes scrawled on some of its pages makes the volume that much more intriguing. To whom did it belong?

Sailing on, Marlow notices a change in the topography; it becomes more violent and increasingly impenetrable. He feels as if a barrier had been erected between himself and the natives. No longer does he feel that link, that fluid relationship with the outside world, that he had enjoyed just hours before. Something hard, cutting, and jarring now prevails. "The living trees, lashed together by the creepers and every living bush of the undergrowth, might have changed into stone, even to the slenderest twig, to the lightest leaf. It was not sleep—it seemed unnatural, like a state of trance."

What Marlow had formerly labeled *dream* is now termed *trance*, thus paralleling the increasingly dramatic and mysteriously opaque landscape. Unlike the dream, the trance suggests a far deeper foray into subliminal spheres, corresponding to a state of hypnosis or to a profound absorption in some archaic stratum within the unconscious. The *entranced* individual may be said to be living a completely separate existence, somewhere within a continuously descending underworld or collective unconscious. The pronouncements, or voices, heard within this profoundest of levels are usually expressed in the first person, giving the impression the individual is attempting a breakthrough.

The completion of the Great Nekyia requires confrontation with dangers. The multiple physical and evolutionary levels Marlow traverses during the course of his trajectory bring him closer to his undifferentiated center (or beginning, chaos, that mythical level within him), making his return to the differentiated world that much more arduous. Marlow's descent, however, is crucial to his future well-being. It alone will put him in touch with those fearsome demons and spirits that must be experienced in human or animal form. Only then may these rejected or exiled characteristics be assimilated by and later integrated into the whole personality (Eliade, *Rites and Symbols of Initiation*, 96). Is Marlow to know perhaps the most threatening power of them all: physical, spiritual, and psychological cannibalism?

Cannibalism

The fog, growing increasingly dense as Marlow approaches the Inner Station where Kurtz lies ill, halts the boat's journey temporarily. May not this be viewed, symbolically, as another barrier set in Marlow's path? Another test that he must pass prior to the completion of both the healing process and the Great Nekyia?

Fear again dominates as the "towering multitude of trees," the "immense matted jungle," and the "blazing little ball of the sun hanging over it" wait ready to devour the intruders. Marlow is stunned by the "complaining clamor, modulated in savage discords" which suddenly arises from everywhere, "as if the mist itself had screamed," followed by an "outbreak of almost intolerably excessive shrieking" culminating in an "appalling and excessive silence."

Although virtually in a trance state, Marlow realizes that were the natives to attack, no help would be forthcoming because "the rest of the world was nowhere." Would these cannibals butcher and eat them? Or was he passing through the "Gaping Jaws of Hell" as had so many heroes of past epochs?

Marlow's understandable fear of the cannibalistic African tribesmen, vestiges from "the beginnings of time" may also be explored as a psychological phenomenon. The terror of being swallowed, eaten, or consumed usually precedes the ego's entry into unknown or unexpected dimensions. Feelings of dread nearly always occur during the course of the Great Nekyia, as attested to by personifications appearing in many ancient epics, such as the "Mouth of Hell" or the "Jaws of Cerberus"; in the depiction of the Inferno by Dante, by Bosch, and by Brueghel; in Egyptian Pyramid Texts; in Creation myths; in religious rituals such as Christian communion; in contemporary food cults and diets; and in certain linguistic usages such as "eaten up with jealousy" or "consumed by work" (Neumann, *Origins and History of Consciousnes*, 27).

Marlow's fear of being eaten stems from both an outer and an inner reality. The tribesmen, now viewed as enemies, are described as "powerful" and ravenously hungry men. The psychological factor is the dread of something small (Marlow's ego) being swallowed by something large (his collective unconscious). Since hunger and food are such powerful catalysts in the empirical world, the digestive tract becomes virtually the focus of human existence. Generally speaking, the stronger eats the weaker, and the same may be true psychologically: when an ego is said to be weakly structured, as is Marlow's, the possibility of its ingestion, never again to surface into consciousness, is very real (Neumann, *Origins and History of Consciousness*, 27–28).

The idea of being swallowed or eaten is of such universal and eternal magnitude that it is said to be of archetypal dimension. Every form of eating, swallowing, and masticating symbolizes a pattern of behavior belonging to the psychic structure of humankind: a structure of instincts that are impossible to represent, their effects and meanings being communicable only in primordial or archetypal images via metaphors (Jacobi, 35). The amount of primitive symbolism implicit in *The Heart of Darkness*, from the outset of Marlow's narrative to its conclusion, gives evidence of his corrosive fear of the cannibal, since he is still disconnected and divided; his personality is not yet whole or operational as a unit.

Marlow is the one who must take sustenance, be it of a material or nonmaterial nature. Psychologically speaking, to eat is the equivalent of gaining understanding of, and thus power over, those factors within himself that might otherwise overwhelm him. The realization of the process of eating conveys the notion of assimilation by consciousness of an unconscious content. The question remains as to whether Marlow will eat or be eaten. Will his ego be strengthened? Or will it be devoured by forces beyond his control?

His dread, as we have noted, is not only the justifiable dread of real cannibals but also the materialization of a psychic content, the projecting of an inner condition onto an unknown quantity. Such projection makes intense feelings even stronger. Hence, when he first hears the clamor of natives in the fog he assumes that they are hostile, but once his terror dissipates somewhat he interprets the same sounds as an expression of extreme grief, "a great human passion let loose." Instead of being driven by his fear of attack to continue navigating through the fog, he decides to take the more prudent course and not to continue traveling until the fog dissipates.

Such thinking factors as are now operational in Marlow are due in part to the birth of new insights and of greater humility. To pursue a journey when one is not fully prepared is to run the risk of unnecessary danger. Like the natives who remain on land, rather than getting lost in the fog, Marlow will not allow himself to be consumed by terror. He will not budge until the fog lifts, that is, until he sees more clearly into his own murky underworld. That he no longer takes the tribesmen's strange voices to be aggressive forces but realizes they are expressions of inconsolable pain suggests greater understanding of their feelings and their needs. His empathy with his own shadow, which he still sees in projection through them, is increased.

Although Marlow's assessment of the situation is correct and no attack is forthcoming, when the fog lifts and the boat pursues its course it soon hits a snag: arrows and spears come its way from all directions. Again Marlow uses his head; fright no longer cannibalizes his ego. He closes the shutter to keep out the death-dealing weapons.

An Allegorical Helmsman

As the ship creeps slowly on, Marlow's eyes, riveted to the land, meet another fearsome sight: "naked breasts, arms, legs, glaring eyes—the bush was swarming with human limbs in movement, glistening, of bronze color." Although the "pilgrims" on board have preached calm incessantly, they now open fire into the bush, and the earth is filled with agonizing howling: the "tremulous and prolonged wail of mournful fear and utter despair."

Reacting to sensations of warmth and wetness on his legs, Marlow looks down to see blood covering his shoes. He recalls having seen, just moments before, his helmsman open the shutter he had so carefully closed, and wave an empty gun at the enemy. This incident leads Marlow to another discovery about himself: until he sees the helmsman lying dead before him, he does not realize how deeply he had felt about him. Although feelings of attachment to a "savage" might appear strange to some, Marlow notes, he considers him a type of "partner." After all, he had "steered" for him. During the course of their journey up the Congo River, a "subtle bond . . . like a claim of distant kinship affirmed in a supreme moment," had been born between the two men, revealed with such poignancy by the look the helmsman gave Marlow after the spear had pierced his body. Never will this image leave Marlow's memory.

Only after putting on a pair of dry slippers does Marlow jerk out the spear from the helmsman's side, doing so with eyes closed. The parallel images of the closed eyes and the closed shutter are attempts on his part to seal off the outside world, to occlude what could cause conflict. But his attempt to barricade himself from any jarring or wounding event, be it physical or psychological, proves to be in vain.

As Marlow drags the helmsman's body onto the deck, pressing his shoulders to the "savage's" breast, he "hug[s] him from behind desperately," then pulls this "heavy heavy" man to the railing and tips him overboard. How can Marlow claim that the very slim helmsman is "heavier than any man on earth"? Similarly the giant, St. Christopher, carrying the Christ child on his shoulders across a river, was told: "Thou hast borne all the world upon thee, a terrible burden and its sins likewise." The immensely heavy weight dragged by Marlow consists of the burden of his adolescent personality, of all those childlike traits which he loves in himself and loved in the helmsman through projection, and which reason tells him are not only unadaptable, but nonfunctional in the real world. That Marlow has taken this undeveloped part of his psyche so lightly all these years is now experienced as a crushing handicap obstructing his maturation. To sever himself from these youthful traits that he has grown to love is painful, and he hugs them "desperately" in a last farewell to his adolescent and vulnerable self. By casting the helmsman's body into the sea, Marlow is returning those nonserviceable aspects of his personality to the limitless waters of his collective unconscious.

When, shortly thereafter, the company's agent tells him that he supposes Mr. Kurtz as well as the helmsman to be dead, Marlow experiences crushing feelings of disappointment. Why should he react so intensely to the demise of a man he has never even met? So shocked is he, indeed, that he unthinkingly flings one of his bloodied shoes overboard. Shoes, for Europeans, in that they facilitate walking, come to represent a person in possession of his earthly life and of himself. That Marlow casts one of his shoes overboard because it is filled with the helmsman's blood, representing the depletion of his life principle, is understandable, as a bond had existed between them. When he identifies with Kurtz, however, whom he has never met, yet who is coming to occupy an increasingly powerful place in Marlow's psyche, his throwing his shoe into the ocean is unconscious, signifying a rejection of his earthbound condition in favor of a higher principle. Let us note that to remove one's shoes, in biblical texts, symbolizes an act of respect (God said to Moses: "Draw not nigh hither: put off thy shoes from off thy feet, for the place whereon thou standest is holy ground." [Exod. 3:5]) and also the discarding of unnecessary matter (Christ, sending his disciples out to "heal all manner of sickness and all manner of disease," admonishes them not to provide those they meet with "shoes" [Matt. 10:10]).

What pains Marlow most acutely is not the fact that he might never see Kurtz, but that he might never hear his voice. The inner dialogue with his fantasy figure, Kurtz, that has sustained Marlow throughout his harrowing ordeals, viewed psychologically, identifies Marlow with ego and Kurtz with Self (the total psyche). Because of Kurtz's demise Marlow has "been robbed of a belief" and "deprived of his destiny in life," which is tantamount to Marlow's having been divested of an invisible Mana or Godhead.

A voice. He was very little more than a voice. And I heard—him—
it—this voice—other voices—all of them were so little more than
voices—and the memory of that line itself lingers around me, impalpable, like a dying vibration of one immense jabber, silly, atrocious, sordid, savage, or simply mean, without any kind of sense.
Voices, voices.

The voice Marlow hears, psychologically, is a manifestation of an autonomous complex. Despite the fact that it is projected onto Kurtz and
seems not to belong to Marlow, it is in fact a content emanating from his
own unconscious. What Marlow is experiencing is another bout of psychological cannibalism: affect holds sway as ego is "swallowed up" by a more
formidable force. Of what this autonomous complex consists, only a confrontation with Kurtz himself could bring to light and break its hold
(Jacobi, 13).

Affects are crucial to the healing phase of an initiation process. In such
texts as the *Ramayana*, the *Mahabharata*, the *Odyssey*, *Gilgamesh*, and
Parzifal, the moments of shock following the *catastrophe* or *grace* stimu-
late powerful reactions, which in turn fragment or dissolve the autonomous complex holding sway. In Marlow's case, the crucial element is
Kurtz's voice. The trauma he experiences upon learning of Kurtz's possible
death transforms his psyche so radically as to allow new components and
fresh groupings to coalesce and solidify, opening up to a different view of
the world.

Kurtz's "inner voice" has served until now to awaken dormant unconscious contents in Marlow, which have shed some light as to his future
course. The possibility of Marlow's having to seek elsewhere for a new
ruling system in life fills him with a sense of panic. Until now Marlow's
truth, his authenticity, have come to him through the voice, a transpersonal source. Like the totem for the primitive, Kurtz's voice has been
experienced as Marlow's guardian spirit, leading directly to inner revelation. Such a power, however, can take an individual only so far; the rest of
the work must be done alone, in exile.

An Allegorical Harlequin

When the steamboat finally anchors at the Inner Station, Marlow is
greeted by a cheerful, beardless, boyish white man. After conversing with
him and feeling buoyed up at first, Marlow examines him more closely
and fails to understand the young man's continuously altering moods,
moving from light and bantering humor to moments of gloom and doom.

The patched and brightly colored clothes the boyish man wears so intrigue Marlow that he calls him Harlequin. The archetypal harlequin, or clown-figure, is frequently viewed as an inversion of supreme royal powers and attitudes. Drollery, irreverence, insurgence, and earthiness are at odds with majesty, sovereignty, and divinity. Harlequin is Kurtz's antithesis: the king and his jester. Like the archetypal harlequin, the young man Marlow meets conveys in the most innocuous of terms the most serious of matters, and, in serious tones, the most humorous. Beneath his comic appearance there exists a lacerated, victimized being, desperately searching for acceptance and love from his master, his deity, Kurtz. A *puer*, Harlequin flits here and there, with only one purpose: to please and serve his king/Kurtz. He is unable to carve out his own way or assume his own destiny, and his heteroclite vestments are symptomatic of his fragmented psyche. What does the reader know of this "bewildering," enthusiastic, miming and gesturing person? At twenty-five, he can boast of being the son of a Russian archpriest, of running away to sea and wandering about the earth until he met Kurtz, after which he functioned as his jester.

Harlequin proves to be a helping force for Marlow. From him he learns that Kurtz is still alive, though desperately ill; that the natives, though they had attacked the white men, meant no harm, but did so because they did not want Kurtz, their deity/king, to be taken from them. Nor does Harlequin, who says devotedly, "I tell you, this man has enlarged my mind. . . . "He made me see things—things." As for the tribesmen, they "adored" him.

Nevertheless, things have not been easy for Harlequin. Instead of thanks for his loyalty and love for Kurtz, when he nursed him through two illnesses, he received threats on his life. Harlequin, forever worrying about his deity/king's well-being, wandered days and months at a time in the jungle, he tells Marlow, searching for lost villages and raiding others for ivory. Kurtz has "filled his life, filled his thoughts, swayed his emotions."

Marlow learns that Kurtz, who commands such love and admiration from so many, is given to violence and will shoot anyone interfering with his ivory trade. As the complexity of the man's attitudes indicates, all Europe, including the best-intentioned members of the so-called International Society for the Suppression of Savage Customs, "has contributed to the making of Kurtz," who is of English and French extraction. When the members of this group asked him to report on the conditions in Africa, he did so in seventeen closely written pages, forwarding the opinion that the whites, as "supernatural beings" able to "exert a power for good practically unbounded," were more highly evolved than the blacks.

Reading Kurtz's pages, Marlow feels virtually hypnotized by the "magic current" of the words. At the end of the document, however, after a "moving appeal to every altruistic sentiment," Kurtz added a postscript of

a different nature, written, Marlow rationalizes, in an "unsteady hand";
that is, after his nerves had gone wrong and he had been accused of
presiding at certain midnight dances and their "unspeakable rites." The
words in question, according to Marlow, "blazed at you, luminous and
terrifying, like a flash of lightning in a serene sky: 'Exterminate all the
brutes!' "

The Epiphany

Marlow knows that if he wants to approach Kurtz he must proceed with
caution, because Kurtz, as king and deity, is guarded by a whole army of
invisible men from the lake tribe. "The woods were unmoved, like a
mask—heavy, like the closed door of a prison—they looked with their air
of hidden knowledge, of patient expectation, of unapproachable silence."

Something awesome leaps into view in the field glasses that Marlow is
focusing on the dilapidated hut in which Kurtz lies: encircling the structure are posts upon which heads have been impaled. All but one looks
toward the house: "black, dried, sunken, with closed eyelids—a head that
seemed to sleep at the top of that pole, and, with the shrunken dry lips
showing a narrow white line of the teeth, was smiling, too, smiling continuously at some endless and jocose dream of that eternal slumber."
Stunned, Marlow attempts to rationalize: Kurtz "lacked restraint in the
gratification of his various lusts," one of them being his "appetite for
ivory." Or was it the wilderness taking "on him a terrible vengeance for the
fantastic invasion."

> He felt he had . . . been transported into some lightless region of
> subtle horrors, where pure, uncomplicated savagery was a positive
> belief, being something that had the right to exist—obviously—in
> the sunshine.

Marlow turns around in time to see his idol, Kurtz, a skeletal form, an
apparition, an "atrocious phantom," being carried out of his hut on an
improvised stretcher. And a

> cry arose whose shrillness pierced the still air like a sharp arrow
> flying straight to the very heart of the land; and, as if by enchant-
> ment, streams of human beings—of naked human beings—with
> spears in their hands, with bows, with shields, with wild glances
> and savage movements, were poured into the clearing by the dark-
> faced and pensive forest.

Transfixed, Marlow knows that one word or a single gesture from Kurtz will result in the extermination of the whites.

> I saw him open his mouth wide—it gave him a weirdly voracious aspect, as though he had wanted to swallow all the air, all the earth, all the men before him. A deep voice reached me faintly. He must have been shouting. He fell back suddenly.

The tribesmen retreated into the forest.

Has the vision of Kurtz been an epiphany? It was certainly a manifestation of divinity for the tribesmen. Has Kurtz's long-awaited image catalyzed some unknown component within Marlow's psyche that endows his world with new meaning?

Kurtz is still a power principle for Marlow, representing both adoration and terror. These polarities become overt when Kurtz is finally brought on shipboard and Marlow visits him in his cabin and describes him in cannibalistic terms: "This shadow looked *satiated* and calm, as though for the moment it had its *fill* of all the emotions." Kurtz is a psychological cannibal who wants to take the world into himself before being *swallowed* by it. Aggressive, lustful, possessive, voracious, he wants to live life fully and on his terms.

Marlow, having made his connection with Kurtz, will have to take matters into his own hands. The allegorical Harlequin and what he represents—a helping, mediating, youthful, adventurous, loyal, loving figure—is no longer needed and will return to the darkness of the forest, as had the helmsman to the sea. Marlow knows that he alone has to grapple with his shadow figure, Kurtz; that he alone must try to fathom those ravenous, omnivorous, and predacious contents living and pulsating within his unconscious.

Confrontation with the Tutelary Spirit

Like Jacob wrestling with the angel, Marlow has to struggle with Kurtz, his tutelary spirit. Only after coming to grips with those aspects Kurtz represents in Marlow's psyche can Marlow face and internalize them. Confrontation precedes revelation. A higher and broader understanding of what seemed at first to be only a personal problem is at stake.

Marlow now proceeds to the crucial stage of his Great Nekyia. With no allegorical figures to allay his suffering, no palliatives to diminish his sorrow, he must stand naked before his truth, and be ready for any eventuality, even cannibalization. Just as Jacob engaged in his hand-to-hand combat with the dark angel at the ford, so Marlow has to be prepared to stand his ground and accept the challenge, reacting straightforwardly and fully to those "unspeakable secrets" existing within him. To be the aggressor against Kurtz, his inner divinity, while also remaining the vessel in which his potential is to be realized, requires heroism (Jung and Franz, 211; Jung, *Collected Works*, 10:461).

The grim confrontation takes place at midnight. Marlow is looking over the ship's rail, straight into the thick forest where Kurtz's "adorers were keeping their uneasy vigil." The continuous beating of the drums, replicating the primordial rhythms of his own heart, in addition to the chantings and the incantations, have "a strange narcotic effect" on Marlow's semiawake senses. He dozes off momentarily, only to be awakened by the sound of yells from the forest. Shock. Terror. He runs to Kurtz's shipboard cabin only to discover he is no longer there. Monstrous feelings well up within Marlow. Again he is terrorized by the fact that he will be robbed of his destiny for lack of the essential confrontation. Although fearing a massacre, Marlow does not call for help. He knows that he alone must experience the crisis in a hand-to-hand contest. He makes his way to shore, robotlike, guided only by that inner transpersonal voice he had so feared would vanish from his hearing:

> it was ordered I should never betray him—it was written I should be loyal to the nightmare of my choice. I was anxious to deal with this shadow by myself alone—and to this day I don't know why I was so jealous of sharing with any one the peculiar blackness of that experience.

Raging, with clenched fists, Marlow follows Kurtz's trail. To do so is relatively simple, as Kurtz, too weak to walk, must have crawled to his destination. Marlow reaches Kurtz, who "rose, unsteady, long, pale, indistinct, like a vapor exhaled by the earth, and swayed slightly, misty and silent before me." The invisible figures in the forest, which is crackling with fires and sounding with muffled voices murmuring among the blackened trees, are prepared to destroy, in a matter of seconds, anyone interfering with their totem figure, their deity/king. Kurtz does not call out to his worshipers. Protective of Marlow, Kurtz, like so many divine figures, warns him of his dangerous course and counsels him in deep and awesome tones, "Go away—hide yourself."

Marlow does not budge. He stands his ground. He has only one thought in mind: "to beat that Shadow—this wandering and tormented thing." Kurtz must come with him, he warns him, back to the ship. Otherwise,

"You will be lost . . . utterly lost." Kurtz refuses: he has "immense plans"; he is on "the threshold of great things." Marlow threatens. Kurtz pleads to remain. No longer can Marlow allow him to gratify his "brutal instincts" and "monstrous passions." No longer can he be permitted to yield to the "mute spell of the wilderness." If Kurtz shouts for help, Marlow will smash his head.

The dreadful battle begins. Marlow against Kurtz, soul against soul: "If anybody ever struggled with a soul, I am the man." A soul gone mad. "Being alone in the wilderness, it had looked within itself . . . it had gone mad. I had for my sins, I suppose—to go through the ordeal of looking into it myself." Soul for soul, Marlow and Kurtz were interchangeable, each hearing the other, each seeing the other, peering into "the inconceivable mystery of a soul that knew no restraint, no faith, and no fear, yet [was] struggling blindly with itself." Marlow/Kurtz wrestle mysteriously and secretly with unconscious forces: greed, lusts, appetites, brutal and monstrous passions, and obsessions—for power through ivory.

Mute horror. Despair. Marlow understands Kurtz's power over him as well as the depth of his own instinctual rapacity and violent cruelty, that of the white man living in the heart of the African jungle, that of a shadow in exile. Kurtz has to be carried on board to save their lives. Marlow is winning the first round. They walk slowly toward the ship. Kurtz's "bony arm [is] clasped around Marlow's neck." As in the case of the helmsman's corpse—and just as strangely, because Kurtz weighs no more than a child—Marlow remarks that it feels as if he is carrying a ton on his back.

The Postpartum Ordeal

The ship slowly slipping forth, like a leviathan, is the focus of two thousand eyes, "each pair, following the evolutions of the splashing, thumping, fierce river-demon beating the water with its terrible tail and breathing black smoke into the air." Minutes before it begins its withdrawal from the Inner Station, a woman with "helmeted head" appears. Marlow, who had seen her before, when Kurtz had first been brought on board, describes her as "a wild and gorgeous apparition of a woman" who walks

> with measured steps, draped in striped and fringed cloths, treading the earth proudly, with a slight jingle and flash of barbarous ornaments. She carried her head high; her hair was done in the shape of a helmet; she had brass leggings to the knee, brass wire gauntlets to the elbow, a crimson spot on her tawny cheek, innumerable necklaces of glass beads on her neck; bizarre things, charms, gifts of

witch-men, that hung about her, glittered and trembled at every step. She must have had the value of several elephant tusks upon her. She was savage and superb, wild-eyed and magnificent; there was something ominous and stately in her deliberate progress.

Who is this woman in whose face Marlow detects such a tragic and fierce note of sorrow and pain? Who is this black phantom who once visited Kurtz in his hovel when he was ill? When Kurtz was transported to the boat, she had suddenly

> opened her bared arms and threw them up rigid above her head, as though in an uncontrollable desire to touch the sky, and at the same time the swift shadows darted out on the earth, swept around on the river, gathering the steamer into a shadowy embrace.

Why had this regal figure gestured so frantically, as she sought to communicate her feelings of sorrow to one man, to her king/son? How is it that Kurtz, from within his shipboard cabin, had cried out from the depths of his unconscious: "Save me! . . . I will return"? She alone, this "barbarous and superb woman, who merely stretched tragically her bare arms after us over the sombre glittering river," alone stands firm as the departing boat's whistle rings out and the natives look on in "abject terror."

This Great Earth Mother, paradigm of a black, rich, and fertile domain, mourns with the other tribespeople, as her king/son is forcibly taken from her. From this archetypal figure emerges all vegetation and all living things. Proud of her wild and triumphant motherhood, gratified that the seed gestates and grows within her darkness, she is loving as she yields the fruit of her womb to the light of earth. But this "superb woman," though she shelters, contains, and nourishes, is also a complex of opposites.

As a paradigm of wholeness, she stands for an undifferentiated, primordial, matriarchal world. She is *uroboros:* the state of psychic beginning, the original condition prior to ego-consciousness. And this "Great Container," as the archetypal figure has been called throughout history, seeks to hold fast to her progeny and to her votaries, subjecting them to her power and making them dependent upon her for their well-being. When unconscious forces allow her to cannibalize consciousness, putting it permanently under her sway, ego is annihilated. It is no wonder then, that this formidable power's great enemy is consciousness (Neumann, *Great Mothers*, 18, 48, 255).

As the boat withdraws from the reach of the Great Earth Mother, she knows her battle has been lost. Her postpartum pain, visible on her face, indicates her acceptance that Marlow has broken free from her shadowy power, as he had from Kurtz's when leading him back to the ship after their struggle. No longer does he suffer from a hypertrophied consciousness, nor does he allow his destiny to be cannibalized by those formerly voracious, insatiable unconscious shadow forces once pulsating within him.

Until now, Marlow's relationship with the archetypal feminine has been polarized. The two women knitting their black wool in the company's offices in Brussels were negative principles, "guarding the door of Darkness." His aunt was their opposite: bathing in light, idealistic, thus "out of touch with truth."

Kurtz, too, experienced the feminine principle in extremes. One extreme took the form of the African Great Earth Mother: visceral, energetic, sexual; but also a castrating power, possessive and domineering. The other extreme was Kurtz's "Intended," whom he described to Marlow on shipboard as perfection incarnate. Although Kurtz believed that European women were "out of it" (meaning they were detached from reality), he also felt that men "must help them to stay in that beautiful world of their own, lest ours gets worse." For him, women were dolls, objects, playthings, pure in spirit, not real beings. In fact, just before Kurtz died, he said, "My ivory . . . My Intended, my ivory, my station, my river." Woman was like ivory: to be hoarded and possessed, worshiped voraciously, continuously, brutally. Ivory's worth is great; its attribute is hardness: when shaped as teeth, it ingests and cannibalizes; as ornament, it is beauty; as object of worship, it takes on the power of a fetish.

Kurtz had not accounted for the fact that in the jungle ivory was considered the progeny of the Great Earth Mother, and therefore beyond his reach. Unaware of his drive, he allowed his appetite for object possession to run wild, thus acting against the Great Earth Mother. The irrational prevailed: ivory brought him money and power. His increasingly aggressive and greedy unconscious was sated only after it devoured his own ego, driving him mad. Unprotected and vulnerable, this unthinking man was returned to the uroboros, his origin, to the womb of the Great Earth Mother. Ruled by his alimentary canal, Kurtz had allowed the "swamp" or pregenital stage to dominate where even sex is not yet operative; food alone remaining the driving force (Neumann, *Origins and History of Consciousness*, 27).

Nevertheless, Kurtz's voice rang "deep to the very last," as did the psychological legacy of this man who lived in "impenetrable darkness." Just before he died, he gave Marlow a packet of papers and a photograph. Marlow describes what happened next as he looked on during Kurtz's last gasp:

> It was as though a veil had been rent. I saw on that ivory face the
> expression of sombre pride, of ruthless power, of craven terror—of
> an intense and hopeless despair. . . . He cried in a whisper at some
> image, at some vision—he cried out twice, a cry that was no more
> than a breath: "The horror! The horror!"

Having "peeped over the edge myself," Marlow understands the meaning
of Kurtz's deathbed stare: it "was wide enough to embrace the whole
universe, piercing enough to penetrate all the hearts that beat in the
darkness. He had summed up—he had judged. 'The horror!' He was a
remarkable man."

Awareness spells victory for Marlow. Never has he felt more in touch
with his innermost nature. Having lived the Great Nekyia authentically,
Marlow is now able to objectify his feelings, to put them to work, to carve
out a new way for himself.

Upon his return to "the sepulchral city," he delivers Kurtz's letters and
portrait to his "Intended," thus surrendering all that remains of Kurtz.
Kurtz's Intended is beautiful because she is truth without guile. As she
comes "forward, all in black, with a pale head, floating towards me in the
dusk," she takes Marlow's hand. She is not "girlish," he realizes, but
endowed with a capacity for suffering and feeling deeply. When observing
her look "of awful desolation" at the thought of living her life without
Kurtz, he understands also that she is not one of those "playthings of
Time." As an archetypal figure, she represents the *mater dolorosa*, the
counterpart of the Great Earth Mother. The destiny of this white, supernal,
mourning figure is to grieve. Her face "remains illumined by the unextin-
guishable light of belief and love." Reacting to this deeply moving figure
and seeking to spare her greater sorrow, Marlow says: "The last word he
[Kurtz] pronounced was—your name." An "exultant and terrible cry"
emanated from her, ushering in feelings of "triumph and of unspeakable
pain." Hiding her face in her hands, she weeps.

The lie Marlow has spoken reveals the burgeoning of latent contents in
his psyche: the ability to evaluate women and the feeling world of women
and the strength to adapt to their needs in conjunction with his own.
Marlow no longer lives only in primordial darkness, but in light as well.
No longer is he the victim of his exiled shadow; he works in partnership
with it, integrating what had once been his unbridled need for power and
possession into a harmonious and fluid wholeness.

3 Huysmans's *Against the Grain:* The Willed Exile of the Introverted Decadent

Willed exile and the deepest condition of introversion was the way chosen by Duke Jean des Esseintes in Joris-Karl Huysmans's[1] extraordinary novel *Against the Grain* (1884). Inability to face reality, uncontrollable ennui, and hatred for a society he saw as superficial, banal, vulgar, and materialistic: all motivated des Esseintes's withdrawal from the world and seclusion in a country home not far from Paris. Alienated from his fellow beings, Huysmans's antihero hoped that by cutting himself from the intellectual, spiritual, and philosophical morass of contemporary society he would be left untainted and free to indulge his every wish. To this end, he regulated his life in such a way as to keep his mind and senses forever active in the creation of his own world of fantasy and artifice. His dehumanized existence revolved around the acquisition of rare and exotic objects: furnishings, paintings, books, flowers, foods, liqueurs.

The duke's exile, then, was based on neither a need for increased consciousness or understanding nor a desire to attain higher spiritual values.

---

[1] J.-K. Huysmans, *A Rebours.* 116. Shortly after Huysman's birth in 1848 in Paris, his father became ill and his mother spent long years caring for him. When his father died in 1856, Huysmans was deeply depressed. He considered his mother's remarriage (to a Protestant) an act of betrayal to his father's memory. The birth of his half-sisters increased his sense of neglect and the rancor he felt against his mother. After passing his *baccalauréat*, he held a job at the Ministry of the Interior, did a stint in the army, and then began writing. His mentor was Zola, to whom he dedicated his novel *The Vatard Sisters* (1879) and *Down Stream* (1882); morose and misogynistic works followed. Only the world of art offered him some semblance of contentment and feelings of relatedness. *Against the Grain* was followed by *Down There* (1891), *En Route* (1895), *The Cathedral* (1898), and *The Oblate* (1903), his last works dealing with his search for holiness and need for penitence. He became deeply religious and spent some days among the Trappist monks.

It was designed to cultivate sensual highs, states he would then analyze with the finesse and perspicuity of a scientist. His home, transformed into a virtual hothouse, resembled a laboratory for experimentation, offering him the visceral pleasures of the synesthetic experience. The resulting reveries and dreams, revolving for the most part around sexual encounters, including voyeurism, sadomasochism, homosexuality, and extreme misogyny, indicated a condition of severe psychological disequilibrium, unalleviated and in fact accentuated by exile and escapism.

Arthur Symons called *Against the Grain* "the breviary of Decadence." Indeed, it was just that. The word *decadent* (from the Latin, *cadere*, to fall, to decline), is an exact description of Huysmans's hyperaesthetic, misanthropic, morbid antihero. It has been claimed that des Esseintes's comportment and inclinations were modeled on those of the effete Baron de Montesquiou-Fezensac and on Ludwig II of Bavaria, as well as on the author himself. Mention must also be made in this regard of Edmond de Goncourt's protagonist in *Faustin* (1882), a work that had much impressed Huysmans. Above all, Baudelaire and Poe were Huysmans's mentors. Like them, des Esseintes was morose by temperament, and a dandy who longed to bathe in an ideal world of eternal beauty and artifice. Unlike these writers, however, he was not a creative type; his yearnings were focused solely on the most efficacious gratification of his senses.

Neurologists and psychiatrists have ascribed des Esseintes's pathologically passive and morbid nature to *erethism*, a malady causing abnormal irritability of the nerves and hyperresponsiveness to stimulation. Inordinate acuteness of the sense of hearing (*hyperacusis*), of touch (*hyperesthesia*), and of smell (*hyperosmia*) encouraged him purposefully and systematically to excite his senses, allowing these to impact as powerfully as possible on his psyche and body.

Exile/Escapism

The Duke des Esseintes, the last descendent of an illustrious, noble, and inbred French family that had received its education from the Jesuits, lost his parents when he was seventeen. Never having received their love, he had always lived a lonely and detached existence. Thin and handsome, with steely blue eyes and overrefined aristocratic manners, he was deeply disdainful and resentful of his restrictive upbringing. That he opted for a life of debauchery and indulged in all types of excessive and unhealthy sexual experiences undermined his health and accounted for a turning-inward. Having sold the Château de Lourps, his ancestral manor, he moved to a villa in the outskirts of Paris, at Fontenay-aux-Roses, where he took up residence with only two human presences: the elderly couple who had cared for his mother.

The world of artifice into which des Esseintes exiled himself could, in some ways, be likened to that of a religious ascetic. Like the Trappists, for example, when des Esseintes gave up enslavement to society he opted for another rule: obedience to a dogma. His daily routine, like that of a monk, followed certain disciplines: he slept by day and remained awake at night; his meals followed certain culinary specifications; and silence was maintained at all times in his home. However, unlike the religious ascetic, who lives on a spiritual level, des Esseintes deluded himself that he sought solitude because of his hatred for the vulgar, his contempt for the mediocre, his hostility toward bourgeois entrepreneurs, and ignorant masses.

The evils this post-Romantic young man attributed to the outer world were, psychologically, a projection or a mirror image of his own empty and arid inner world. Unable to create or to give of himself and incapable of sounding out those factors which troubled him, he spent his time cultivating the exotic, preternatural, and involuted world of his fantasies.

Unbeknown to des Esseintes, exile was really a strategy: the elimination of the world of people and its replacement by a world of things. This strategy was instrumental in further dehumanizing an already severely alienated young man. His extreme cerebralness was focused on finding ways to take him out of himself by transcending empirical reality. Just as monks were constantly occupied with prayers or litanies, des Esseintes was obsessively concerned with the most effective way to ascend to supernatural spheres through ritualistic uses of objects.

The duke's approach to the world of things also had sexual implications; it was a means of sublimating his erotic impulses. Like fetishes, objects upon which certain values are projected, des Esseintes endowed paintings, rugs, plants, or even a bejeweled turtle with dynamic energy; this energy in turn activated his subliminal world. The redirection of his libido (psychic energy) from his unconscious to the outer world impregnated objects with certain virtues and powers. In des Esseintes's case, such excitation titillated his senses, thus arousing him sexually. The *abaissement du niveau mental* and the concomitant rise in emotional level put an end, at least momentarily, to his underlying fears of castration and impotence. So effective a healing technique did des Esseintes consider the world of things, that he looked upon objects as having medicinal value. The aged couple who were his only companions, in keeping with the hospital environment he had created for himself, were dispensers of drugs.

Des Esseintes's belief that seclusion would help him find release from his paralyzing and fearsome ennui was, of course, an illusion. Seclusion was an escape mechanism his superficial and undeveloped psyche consid-

ered a panacea. Such a view, however, is not unusual. Indeed, it is characteristic of some unformed and immature *puer aeternus* types who have
never evolved or strengthened their ego (center of consciousness). Like the
puer aeternus, des Esseintes wandered about from one experience to another, yielding to bouts of despair, despondency, and helplessness. Incapable of dealing with the problems at hand, of facing and struggling through
the difficulties marring his life, he sought answers in the world of objects
and the erotic fantasies, dreams, and hallucinations triggered by them.

House/Womb/Tomb/Unconscious

What does the house signify that des Esseintes chose not only to withdraw
into it but to furnish it in keeping with his aesthetic sense? A mother
symbol, it represents a containing, protective womb, and it is also
tomblike. Like the mother, it is empowered with both positive and negative attributes: if the house is creative, nourishing, and fertilizing, it encourages growth; if it imprisons mind and psyche, it has the power to
destroy life, to encourage rot and decay.

Psychologically, the house may also be looked upon as a symbol for the
unconscious. Closed, hidden, filled with shadowy and mysterious elements,
it is the setting within which des Esseintes performs his insalubrious rituals.
Governed by subjective factors, he relies on what the outer object, the *thing*,
constellates in his subliminal sphere. His already weakened ego is further
devitalized, precipitating a condition of morbid subjectification.

Books

Books, particularly those of Classical Latin writers, hold des Esseintes in
thrall. His choice of authors and works reveals a correspondence between
his inner climate and the one depicted in the particular work he is reading.
As a mirror image or reflection of his unconscious, specific volumes may
be viewed as mediators between invisible and visible worlds, encouraging
cogitation. Let us note that the Latin word for mirror is *speculum*, the
implication being that this object encourages speculation, contemplation,
understanding.

The emphasis the duke places on books, and his boundless knowledge of
literature in general and Latin texts in particular, indicates his highly
developed thinking faculty. Everything in the outer world is related to or
associated with the intellect through the *logos* principle, which connects,
structures, abstracts, and conceptualizes all facts. Des Esseintes, therefore,
feels comfortable theorizing on everything from mathematical problems
to colors to perfumes, and he does so with the exactingness of a scientist.
His meditations, focusing on harmonious gradations and degradations of
tones, colorations, and ideas, act as catalysts, ushering him into a dream-

world. Thus is he able to continue to escape ever more deeply into his world of delusion and phantasmagoria.

As suggestive powers, books encourage him to displace himself via reverie or dream without ever leaving his chair. As a thinking/sensation type, he can experience with ease distant lands, mountains, ports, continually varying sounds, textures, odors, and sights. The libido he concentrates on the book (or any object) is so intense that it leads to its overvaluation. Moreover, his apperception of a volume encourages an introjection of his own inner state: a transfer of an unconscious content onto the object. The aesthetic enjoyment he derives from a book, and the rationalization that he believes is an objectification of his sense of pleasure, is in fact, an indication of his poor adaptation to life in general and to the volume—object/stimulus—in particular (Jung, *Collected Works*, 6:309, 360).

Because he is an introverted thinking/sensation type, his senses are conditioned to his thoughts. This determines the type of book he will enjoy, and indeed the works des Esseintes likes most are those that release the strongest sensations within him. Understandably, then, certain books have a strong erotic hold and act as a kind of instinctual or vital function.

The Latin writers he identifies as "decadent," whose works line one wall of his orange and blue study, are des Esseintes's favorites. For him, the "decadent" period is positive, in sharp contrast to the negative characteristics the Sorbonne professors attach to it. Vergil's *Aeneid*, written in the so-called great period, he finds derivative: a mass of borrowings from Homer and others. Nor do Theocritus, Ennius, and Lucretius hold any interest for him. Cicero and Caesar are "dry" and "constipated." Seneca, Suetonius, Tacitus, Juvenal, Quintilian, Pliny, Plautus, and Titus Livius incite no emotional reaction in him whatsoever.

The duke's favorite work is the *Satyricon* of Petronius. This author's vivid, sardonic, and intensely accurate vision of the vices and luxuries of imperial Rome is written objectively and without concern for humanity, like "decadent" novels, which contain no criticism of sociopolitical regimes and no attempt to reform noxious conditions. No better example of this genre can be found than *Satyricon*, which analyzes in the most delicate and perspicacious ways the mores of a period.

Petronius spares the reader no details, des Esseintes maintains, in his stagings of sodomy and lubricity, analyzing these with the finesse of a jeweler, while also omitting all moral commentaries. The duke's visceral reactions to *Satyricon*, as well as to other works of the period, such as the *Metamorphoses*, of Apuleius, are overt. He openly enjoys the erotic stimulation aroused by his readings and visualizations of happenings revolving around sadomasochistic pantomimes, voyeurism, enactments of lustful and perverse relationships, and debaucheries of all types. He visualizes the details like film clips, pondering one image after another: naked women on the prowl, men and women peeking at lovemaking in bedrooms through doors slightly ajar. Such mental voyeurism allows him to be the passive recipient in his own fantasy world. *Satyricon* opens him up to the bejeweled domain of exciting erotic and masturbational sensations.

Jewels and Stones

As a thinking/sensation type, des Esseintes is aroused by the continuously changing colorations of stones, depending upon their cut, shape, and the intensity or dullness of the light rays shining upon them. For him, they are living and active entities, just like books. Stones, like the duke's steely eyes and unfeeling heart, are hard and compassionless. The thirty-year-old nervous, hollow-cheeked bachelor experiences the luster, texture, and shape of stones in his house of dreams as yet another way of escaping. He bypasses the banal empirical world, penetrating an earthly paradise of his own manufacture.

The search for rare and exotic objects to furnish his solitude is uppermost in the duke's mind. Artifice, as opposed to objects emanating from the natural world, is what he most prizes. The many pages Huysmans devotes to descriptions of heteroclite jewels—their shapes, textures, and tints ranging from electric to cobalt blues, multiple nuances of indigos, blacks, greys, turquoises, salmons, roses, cinnabars, viscous reds, violets in all of their shadowy intensities—are not only marvels in themselves, but also disclose the author's empathy for his antihero's intensely sensual nature.

That stone is durable and less subject to the laws of birth and decay is a truism. As used by des Esseintes, however, the stone does not represent continuity, any more than does a mood or thought. Like fleeting luminosities or scintillae that shine when the lighting is right, the powers of stones are ephemeral, tenuous, and fragmented, concrete manifestations of des Esseintes's split psyche, when fantasies emerge, either beauteously prismatic or in horrific and deformed images. The thinking/sensation type cannot assimilate such ephemera into his psyche (Franz and Hillman).

The gem merchant, the only visitor allowed in des Esseintes's home, brings with him a most singular object: a living turtle with a shell that is painted brilliant gold and encrusted with rare stones. Des Esseintes has ordered it for a very special purpose. It is to be placed on his Oriental rug of yellow and purple tonalities, where the sparkling brilliance of its bejeweled carapace will create a sharp contrast, thereby lending the rug just the antique look he wants.

The turtle, from the Greek word *Tartaros*, a part of Hades sectioned off for punishment of the wicked, is complex in its symbology. The Egyptians looked upon the turtle as a chthonian entity, a fearsome power because it emerged clandestinely from beneath the waters or earth. To ward off any harm the turtle might inflict, such phrases as "May Ra live and may the turtle die" were formulated by this ancient people. As representative of the dark or shadowy aspects of the underworld, the turtle represented a negative factor in many cultures. Its domelike carapace, identified at times with a cosmos, house, or cranium, was frequently an unwelcome sight. However, because its four paws were firmly planted upon the earth, the turtle has also been associated with solidity, stability, longevity, and a material rather than a spiritual approach to life. An engraving in a fifteenth-century allegory, *The Hypnerotomachia Poliphili*, depicts a woman holding a pair of outspread wings in one hand and a turtle in the other, contrasting spiritual and material domains (Fisher, 195).

Other attributes of the turtle explain the duke's choice of this animal. Because of its carapace, the turtle has a containing quality about it, and accordingly, is identified with woman and lubricity. In that its head and feet have the ability to protrude or withdraw, a phallocentric image is suggested. Interestingly enough, this androgynous animal, depicted in *The Chimeras* by Gustave Moreau, one of the duke's favorite painters, is featured with a woman's head; in his *Orpheus*, it stands for everything that is disquieting and negative. With respect to des Esseintes's psychology, the turtle signals dark, shadowy, regressive, and inverted powers within him. Its slowness represents stagnation; its involuted and obscure nature suggest confusion; its grounded condition enslaves it to matter alone.

Des Esseintes had chosen a cluster of flowers in Japanese arrangement for the turtle's lapidary decoration. The petals, leaves, stems, and border were to be set in brilliant and tastefully colored gems. Any jewels that might appeal to the upper bourgeoisie or to the masses, such as diamonds, emeralds, rubies, and the like, were anathema to the duke. His eyes were fixed on exotic stones: beryls, peridots, olivines, micas, cat's-eyes, cymophanes, and others. He would have these blended according to their tones, thus highlighting their inner flame and enhancing their effects upon each other. The uniqueness of the art object, which combined the natural with the artificial, made des Esseintes "perfectly happy."

In addition to the immense pleasure brought him by the bejeweled turtle, he indulged his senses in yet another manner: by taking advantage of his *hyperechema:* the exaggeration of auditory sensations. With this in mind, he had built what he called a *mouth organ:* a closet filled with the rarest liqueurs, each bottle lying horizontally and each having its own silver spigot. By pressing a button hidden behind the closet's paneling, he controlled the spigot he wanted as well as the combinations and amounts of liqueurs to be decanted into his glass. Even more fascinating was the fact that each liqueur corresponded for him to the sound of an instrument: kummel was an oboe; mint and anisette were both flutes; kirsch was a trumpet. Certain virtually scientifically blended mélanges triggered his taste buds to such an extent that they would in turn heighten his auditory nerves, thus enabling him to hear entire symphonies, concertos, quartets, quintets, trios, chorales, pastorals, romances, whatever he programmed for himself.

Des Esseintes's synesthetic experience was so complete that he could hear complicated melodies in major and minor keys, as well as intricate rhythmic patterns, in terms of what he called mint solos, rum duets, and the like. Once his taste buds had been activated, his hearing became intensely acute, as did his olfactory sense; his thought patterns followed suit, triggering all types of melodies and revivifying memories from a distant past.

The synesthetic experience, as practiced by T. E. Hoffmann, Baudelaire, and other creative persons, is defined as a fusion of the senses, allowing the visual to be heard, smelled, touched, and tasted; the heard to be seen, touched, tasted, and smelled; and so on with all the senses. Synesthesia has been described as a great awakening, a psychic happening within the unconscious. In des Esseintes's case it affected his whole nervous system, with sometimes soothing but mostly shattering results.

The simultaneity of sense impressions during the synesthetic experience took des Esseintes into the timeless dimensions of reverie and of hallucination. During periods of heightened awareness, he succeeded in escaping his prosaic present and savoring the beauty and refinement of the fleeting sensation. On certain occasions, he was ushered into an incredible world of fantasy, ranging from the most exquisite to the most gruesome of privileged moments. One such reverie, brought on after the bejeweled turtle's arrival and following a synesthetic experience resulting from his use of the "mouth organ," re-created an excruciatingly painful experience that had taken place three years previously: a toothache that had caused des Esseintes to awaken in the middle of the night. The pain was so acute that after waiting until seven in the morning, he ran out in search of a dentist. Stopping at the first dentist's premises he saw, he ran up a flight of filthy stairs. Although nauseated by the dirt and bloody spittle he saw around him, his torment was so great that he let the dentist push his index finger into his mouth, then take an instrument, and, with nothing to alleviate the pain, extract the decayed tooth. Strangely enough, after it was all over, des Esseintes felt "happy, younger by ten years."

That the reverie focused on the extraction of a tooth is symptomatic to a great extent of the duke's psychological condition. In that teeth cut and dismember food, thereby paving the way for its ingestion into the stomach to enrich and strengthen the body, these entities are associated with the aggressiveness needed both to persevere in and preserve life. Because des Esseintes's tooth had split, rotted, and caused him lacerating pain that only extraction could remedy, one may view his reverie as a premonitory happening: his extreme introversion and reclusion was leading to a disintegration of his own ability to nourish himself, and was an important factor in depleting his vital energy. No longer was he able to defend himself from inner decay; no longer could he assimilate or cope with anything from the outside world. The extraction of the tooth indicated the necessity of ending the self-imposed exile that encouraged his introverted way of life.

Following des Esseintes's reverie, he happened to look down at the rug where the turtle had been placed to notice that it was no longer moving. After palpating it, he realized it was dead. Accustomed to a simple life of obscurity, the turtle did not have the stamina to bear the dazzling array of jewels embedded in its coat. It was so out of tune with itself that it could no longer function.

The synesthetic experience, the reverie focusing on the extraction of the tooth, and the death of the turtle indicate a disequilibrium within des Esseintes's psyche. Slowly and methodically, he was poisoning himself. Extreme seclusion and introversion were suffocating his very life. He had become a man imprisoned in his own mind. The ending of all communication with the outer world had cut off all flow of new air into his world. Thus did his ideas and the sensations to which they gave rise atrophy. Depleted and solipsistic, des Esseintes's world had become fungal and parasitic, feeding exclusively on itself. The psyche had offered him a premonitory *sign:* "extraction" from his hermetic life-style was the only alternative to death.

The Art Object

Des Esseintes was not yet ready to give up an existence that seemingly gratified all of his wishes. In the world of art, as in other domains, he veered away from any painting that might appeal to the masses or to the bourgeoisie. What haunted and mesmerized him were "subtle, exquisite" canvases "bathing in an ancient dream" and in utter corruption. Scenes of this type worked on his nerves and, by intensifying their perceptiveness, were instrumental in plunging him into unknown dimensions and bringing on the nightmares that were henceforth to plague his existence.

Des Esseintes was enraptured by one artist above all others: Gustave Moreau. He responded erotically to the depraved and seductive details and colorations in Moreau's painting *Salomé.* Its palace/cathedral with its crystalized mosaics and brilliant semiprecious stones, its architecture combining Muslim and Byzantine styles, mesmerized him. Most exciting to him, however, was Salomé's "solemn, almost august" stance as she began her lecherous dance. Her sensuality was strikingly enhanced for the duke by the "odor of the perverse perfumes" that emanated from her body through the shapes, rhythms, and textures embedded in the canvas itself.

Because des Esseintes viewed Salomé as an eternal and universal figure capable of transcending centuries—"superhuman" as "indestructible Lewdness" and "cursed Beauty"—she takes on archetypal stature. She is the Terrible Earth Mother, that feminine principle who demands the head of the Christian martyr as punishment for thwarting her desires. Destroying everything that lies in her path to sexual fulfillment, she becomes the agent of the enormous energy buried within the archetype. For the ascetic Christian, in this case John the Baptist, she is an abomination. For the materialistic Herod, whose weakly structured ego is under the complete dominion of his wife, Herodias, she is the incarnation of sensuality.

The more powerful the denunciation of Salomé in the Gospels, the more formidable does this erotic archetypal force become, and the more she seeks to transform John the Baptist into an object to manipulate, dominate, and conquer. As depicted dancing in Moreau's canvas, her feet touch the Great Earth Mother, drawing from it sustenance and power. Having completed her lustful dance, she is served John's head on a silver shield. Seizing it, she kisses it, trembles, delighting as she looks deeply upon its eyes, tongue, hair; her fervor remains unappeased even as she kisses the martyr's mouth. Unguided by any moral credo, Salomé lives out the most primitive level of her instinctual world while salivating for her prey. Huysmans writes:

> In the works of Gustave Moreau . . . des Esseintes realized at last the weird and superhuman Salomé he had dreamed of. No longer was she merely the dancing girl who extorts a cry of lust and concupiscence from an old man by the lascivious contortions of her body . . . she was now revealed in a sense as the symbolic incarnation of indestructible Lust, the goddess of immortal Hysteria, of cursed Beauty supreme above all other beauties . . . the monstrous Beast [of the Apocalypse], indifferent, irresponsible, insensible, poisoning, like Helen of Troy . . . everything that approaches her, everything that sees her, everything she touches. (Muehsam, 409)

So enraptured is des Esseintes by Salomé's sadistic play and so dependent is he upon her ability to arouse his whole erotic world that this archetypal figure has come to represent for him a grave psychological dancer. Men, exploited by her, become her votaries, passive recipients of her needs and desires, never aggressive or energetic in their own rights.

Salomé has intrigued men of the cloth as well as creative spirits ever since Christian times, as attested to by the Gospels and many Patristic texts. Writers such as Flaubert and Wilde, artists such as Beardsley and Moreau, composers such as Richard Strauss: all were inspired by this awesome archetypal figure.

Psychologically, Salomé represents the castrating female who entices and then destroys the male while initiating him into her arcane and libidinous world. Like the prostitute, she is a woman degraded, who unconsciously chastises herself every time she performs a service for the man. By the same token, when the man buys her services, he is experiencing similar feelings of shame and debasement. It is not he who is of import to her, but what he can offer in material gifts. Without gold or lucre of some sort, he is valueless; hence each is an object and not a subject for the other. Both, therefore, experience schizoid attitudes; neither is able to relate to the other or to him/herself.

Des Esseintes—like Moreau, who drew Salomé over a hundred times in settings of sumptuous palaces, mosques, cathedrals, and Hindu temples— was haunted by her image. The intensity of his sensual reactions to Moreau's paintings of Salomé discloses his penchant for the harlot in general, and her in particular, as she swirls and swoops, rotates and pivots.

Other paintings by Moreau also electrified, vivified, and disquieted des Esseintes: for example, *The Apparition*, featuring Herod's palace, which now resembled the Alhambra, and an almost nude Salomé after the decapitation. Des Esseintes, the voyeur, seemed especially stimulated sexually by the gory details he ferreted out in this canvas: John the Baptist's flaming, gleaming, shining head, the tints radiating from its coagulated blood ranging from deep purple to lighter tonalities depending upon their placement near the beard and hair. The duke's identification with the old king, who "remained crushed, destroyed, overcome with vertigo," as this "dangerous idol" danced in all of her eroticism, had a hypnotic effect upon him.

Some of Moreau's paintings preyed on des Esseintes's mind in the same way as did some of Baudelaire's poems. Both in their own way were "symbols of perversity," of "superhuman loves," of divine depravity. Moreau's canvases, unlike those of other painters whose works had been influenced by past masters, "derived from no one," des Esseintes believed. Moreau had neither ancestors nor would he have any descendents.

Other works of art also hung on the duke's walls: the fantastic, lugubrious, and terrifying *Religious Persecutions* by the engraver Jan Luyken; Rodolphe Bresdin's landscapes bristling with their terrifying trees (*The Comedy of Death*, *The Good Samaritan*); El Greco's sketch of a Christ with its exaggerated lines and "ferocious colors"; Odilon Redon's horrific heads, his fearful humanized spiders, his stagnant livid heavens, monstrous flora and fauna, fearsome faces with their immense crazed eyes. The duke's taste in paintings was drawn to all that was freakish, abnormal, and distorted.

The archetypal images delineated in such paintings not only twisted and triturated the duke's optical and auditory nerves, but activated all of his senses, forcing them into the deepest of subliminal realms. Battling in his psyche were the Divine Christ (all Light, all Purity, all Good), versus Salomé (the Beast of the Apocalypse, the Terrible Earth Mother, the Evil and Sordid Harlot). In that both figures, psychologically speaking, are archetypal in nature, the power they exerted in des Esseintes's collective unconscious (that suprapersonal and nonindividual layer within the psyche) was inordinate.

The duke's erethism, accounting for his abnormal responsiveness to stimulation, was becoming acute, creating havoc with his psyche as well as with his digestive system. Rather than inspiring serenity and wholeness, his protracted contemplations of paintings, engravings, and drawings, particularly those revolving around the Salomé archetype, had a psychologically dismembering effect. Certain sexual proclivities, such as voyeurism, sadomasochism, and homosexuality, which des Esseintes had lived out during his years of excesses in Paris, had again taken hold in his world of reverie and dream, indicating the destructive nature and effect of these visualizations.

Homosexuality

That des Esseintes is fascinated by the Salomé archetype, which is identified, psychologically, with the *vagina dentata*, indicates the power this devouring female has over him. In myths and legends, this kind of woman not only devours her lover emotionally, but tears his psyche to pieces by pulling and tugging at it with her demands. Unless the young male succeeds in breaking or at least loosening the stranglehold this Negative Earth Mother has on his psyche, he cannot hope to free himself from her, not will he ever experience ego consciousness or evolve psychologically. Throughout the centuries, the men associated with dragons and snakes, such as Saint Patrick, Saint George, and Saint Michael, to mention but a few, have succeeded in destroying the *vagina dentata* women in their mythical battles, thus disentangling themselves from the tentacles of the man-eating feminine principle.

Des Esseintes's extreme passivity and solipsistic nature have never entered into conflict with the *vagina dentata* power. Instead, he has allowed his psyche to be aroused and dominated by Salomé's energy and force.

Because of des Esseintes's inability to relate to either men or women, and therefore to himself, his *eros* cannot connect or empathize with or even understand others, and is so repressed as to be virtually nonexistent. He frequently regresses in his reveries and dreams to childhood images and incidents revolving around homosexual and bisexual episodes. One icy evening, for example, seated in front of a warm hearth-fire, he recalls an experience he had a few years earlier, when he met a street urchin, probably about sixteen years old, so pale and thin as to be almost girllike. "Sucking on a cigarette" that would not draw, he approached des Esseintes for a light. After giving him one of his finest aromatic cigarettes, des Esseintes began chatting with the boy and then invited him for a drink, followed by a visit to an elegant brothel. Because it was the young man's first time, des Esseintes took pleasure in the lad's naiveté, gaucheries, and the mocking he received at the hands of the prostitutes. Significant as well was des Esseintes's goal of turning the young man into a thief. He reasoned that by indoctrinating him into a world of sexual pleasures, he would become accustomed to these joys, and that the moment des Esseintes stopped giving him the funds necessary to support his habit, the lad would steal to maintain it.

Although the duke's confusion as to gender identification, frequently evident in the *puer aeternus* type, is apparent in the above episode, what is particularly arresting is the fact that the lad is a mirror image of des Esseintes as he used to be at that age. He projects upon him (and the exquisite pleasure he derives from using the lad as a sex object in the brothel is increased by alluding to his feminine and virginal nature) a symbolic way of violating, of deflowering him. Whatever sadism is involved, it calls into activity the other half of the dynamic: masochism. Des Esseintes wants to experience the rejection and humiliation of the sophisticated ladies and the chastisement of society by becoming a criminal. Let us note that sadomasochism has frequently been identified with a death wish.

Flowers and Plants

Des Esseintes's attention now focuses on the acquisition of rare and exotic species of flowers and plants. His personification of these brings a completely new dimension into his search for sensual gratification.

Flowers played an important role in antiquity. Certain gods, such as the handsome Tammuz, Attis, Adonis, Hyacinth, and Narcissus, were identified with their ephemeral natures: they died young, never developing into full manhood. Psychologically, they were prevented from doing so by the mother figure (symbolized frequently by the dragon or snake): the *vagina dentata*, a castrating force.

The aforementioned gods, also associated with the *puer aeternus*, lived through the woman (or the male partner) and were unable to grow firm roots into the soil (the world). They existed in a state of perpetual psychological incest with the mother or with what she symbolized for them. It is she whom they loved, feared, or sought to destroy. As appendages of the mother and, like an evanescent force or dream, they lived ephemerally, as does the flower (Neumann, *Origins and History of Consciousness*, 44).

In that flowers and plants are associated with the *vagina dentata* type, it is understandable that des Esseintes should be drawn to them. They are usually chosen for the home because of their beauty and sweetness of aroma, but the duke's tropical varieties are chosen for just the opposite reasons. The more bizarre, grotesque, terrifying, and destructive they are, the more he is attracted to them.

Used by him for ritualistic purposes, these Negative Earth Mother archetypes are animate in every sense of the word. Their branches, like venomous and constrictive snakes, are ready to coil and strangle any male approaching them. Their petals or "skin" are scarred, hairy, encrusted with scabs and blotched like ulcerated canker sores, rot, and gangrene. The leaves are engraved with furrows ("false veins") and are covered with syphilitic and leprous pustules.

Moreover, many of the "vegetal ghouls" inhabiting the duke's home are carnivorous: there are Insect Eaters from the Antilles, Droserae of the peat-bogs "garnished with their glandular hairs," and Cephalothi "capable of digesting, absorbing real meats." Some flowers and plants with their tumorlike/tuberlike excrescences remind des Esseintes of the severely ill; others, endowed with long metallic leaves curling way down, he associates with umbilical cords. The very language used to describe these hideously scaled and deformed varieties suggests the visceral quality of his emphatic relationship with them.

The more macabre, grotesque, and spine-chilling these symbols of destructive feminine forces are, the more they arouse the duke's lust and passion. That des Esseintes's thinking also comes into play with regard to flowers and plants is evident in the scientific accuracy with which he enumerates and describes them. Nor can such verbal imagery be outdone even by such artists as Bresdin, with his hideous trees and plantings (*The Comedy of Death* and *The Holy Family*), or Redon, and his gruesomely fearsome faces (*The Cactus Man*, or *Marsh Flower, Eyes in the Forest*), which des Esseintes admires.

The second step in des Esseintes's ritualistic use of flowers and plants occurs in the olfactory domain. His exaggerated sense of smell (*hyperosmia*) has the power of bringing on hallucinations and dreams. Perfumes and other aromas are able to lead him into ever-profounder levels of introversion. Like primitive man and his magical ceremonies and sacrifices using incense of all types, des Esseintes sets his mind to work thinking up new ways of using things to enliven his autoerotic world.

As the air in the room inhabited by the flowers and plants becomes increasingly rarefied, their aromatic qualities exert an anesthetic effect. Like a narcotic (from the Greek, *narke*, numbness), they dull des Esseintes's rationality, while also encouraging his eyes to wander onto "the horrible tiger markings" of the Caladium, which he identifies with syphilis. Indeed, looking at them all, he remarks, "Everything is syphilis." His reverie then takes root as he sees all of humanity attacked by this ancient and eternal virus. Exhumed in fossils, having been passed on from father to son, it is still active today "in all of its splendor, on the colored leaves of the plants!" Premonitory signs of some future cosmic cataclysm, they are to be viewed as rumblings of the giant battle to be waged between perversity and purity.

The intensity of des Esseintes's archetypal vision, the stifling heat of the room, and the mélange of aromas emanating from the flora has a soporific effect upon him. Lying down on his bed, he falls asleep moments later—not a restful slumber, for des Esseintes becomes a prey to a nightmare. Among its many terrifying incidents, one finds him riding on horseback at dusk in an alley when, suddenly, a human form appears before him. His blood congeals. He feels nailed to the ground.

> This ambiguous sexless face was green; and opened onto violet eyelids; terribly cold, clear, blue eyes; and pimples surrounding the mouth; extraordinarily thin arms, skeletal arms, nude up to the elbows, trembling with fever, emerging from tattered sleeves; and emaciated thighs shivering in overly large cauldronlike boots.

The dread vision in question is that of Syphilis. As she (it) presses hard against him, des Esseintes breaks away, runs as swiftly as possible, only to see this "lamentable and grotesque" creature forever before him no matter what direction he takes. At one point she begins to cry; she tells des Esseintes she has lost her teeth, then taking some clay pipes from her apron, breaks them and plunges the shards into the holes in her gums. No sooner is this done than he warns her they will fall out and they do. His new attempt to flee leads to exhaustion. He shuts his eyes, again attempting to block out this diseased presence, whereupon he realizes that no matter what he does he can never evade or avoid "the horrific stare of Syphilis." Neither walls, nor barriers, nor flight can shut the Flower-Virus out of his world. She is always there in multiple forms and with outstretched arms ready to encircle and strangle him. Indeed, she is now doing just that, as she mutates into a ferocious Nidularium with bladelike leaves that cut him severely. As blood flows and des Esseintes, now insane with fear, makes a superhuman effort to disengage himself, he awakens to realize that it is "only" a dream.

That des Esseintes associates destructive, though alluring, flowers and plants with the feminine principle and with Syphilis is a commentary on his fear and hatred of women. As castrators, these Flower-Women are *vagina dentata* types waiting to work their wiles on the unsuspecting male. In des Esseintes's dream, the narcotic effect of the Nidularium's aroma forces his defense to drop, making him all the more vulnerable. As he attempts to extricate himself from the grasp of this Flower-Woman, the blood oozing from the cut symbolizes castration, a loss of energy, and a wounding of the psyche. Unconsciously, women, for des Esseintes, are viewed as practitioners of sacred feminine rituals who wreak havoc upon young, innocent males. As they unleash their pent-up emotions, until then lying buried beneath a mask of voluptuous and enticing sensuality, they wound the young men for life.

That des Esseintes should identity women with flowers, plants, and disease also suggests a regressive approach to life. Vegetative imagery also abounds in Poe's "The Fall of the House of Usher" (1839), a work Huysmans admired immensely. Fungi and rotting or moldy plants delineate a comatose condition or severe mental illness. Since vegetation feeds directly on inorganic matter, it is looked upon as being connected with the chemical somatic process. To express this condition, Huysmans, like Poe, introduces plant life into his narrative, and in its most rudimentary and negative form, thereby underscoring the retrograde and miasmic elements involved.

The Sex Change

Recurring nightmares work on des Esseintes's already taut nerves. As his olfactory, visual, tactile, and auditory senses became increasingly acute, so, too, does his sense of taste, as previously noted. When he sucks on *sarcanthus*, violet candy, its strange properties, described as "a drop of feminine essence," evoke an even more revealing reverie from his distant bawdy past.

The image of Miss Urania appears full-blown in his mind's eye. He re-sees her as she was in the past: an American circus acrobat of renown, with muscles like steel and arms like cast iron, who succeeded in arousing him sexually because as he peered at her she seemed to be undergoing a sex change. Her serpentine wiles, airs, affectations, and all those "sickening womanly sentimental ways" suddenly vanished, to be replaced by a highly developed, strong, agile, and powerful male. Concomitant with

Miss Urania's sex change, des Esseintes felt himself becoming more feminine and overpowered by a desire to possess this woman/male. Needless to say, disappointment followed the consummation of the sex act. Instead of relaxing in the powerful and brutal arms of a Hercules, he was faced with woman in all of her "stupidity" and "puritanical" reserve. Worse, his reactions to her "glacial fondlings" made him increasingly impotent.

Such *intersexuality*, a shifting from one sex to another, indicates confusion and a lack of sexual identity, resulting often from a fear of castration. The derivation of Miss Urania's name in itself suggests the nature of the emotional distress: *Uranus*, the primordial Greek God of heaven, unwilling to allow his children to be born to the light of day for fear they would overthrow him, concealed them in the depths of the earth. His wife, the Great Earth Mother, encouraged them to rebel against him. The youngest, Cronus, waiting until Uranus was asleep, grasped his father's genitals with his left hand and castrated him with the flint sickle his mother had given him.

Symbolically, castration by the Great Earth Mother suggests the destruction of all creativity, aggressivity, and direction in life. In that *puer aeternus* types, such as des Esseintes, are her slaves and votaries, they are owned by her and involuntarily sacrificed to her. Psychologically, we may say that the duke's adolescent ego (sense of identity), has been drowned by the unconscious, which is tantamount to the ego's dismemberment. The phenomenon of castration, although implicit in previous images, is most overt in the Flower-Woman-Syphilis and Miss Urania sequences.

Since the fear of matriarchal castration has so deflated and degraded des Esseintes's ego, he loses all sense of reality with regard to his own body and sexuality. His regressing libido reactivates parental images, reestablishing an infantile relationship with them (Jung, *Collected Works*, 5:204). In des Esseintes's case, the devouring Great Mother is held accountable for the amputation of his ego, to be equated with the loss of his penis (Neumann, *Origins and History of Consciousness*, 117). Is it any wonder that his exile from society increases his already powerful feelings of alienation and cuts him off from any connection with life?

Although other visions of beguiling and powerful *vagina dentata* types point to des Esseintes's castration complex, an encounter of another kind, reveals his homosexual bent. One day, years earlier, near the Invalides, he had met a young schoolboy whose slim torso and thighs attracted him. What he looked upon with the greatest of pleasure, however, were the youngster's cherry lips. A liaison followed, and he confesses that he had never known such "perils of the flesh" nor felt more "painfully satisfied."

Des Esseintes's hallucinatory reveries and dreams and his synesthetic experiences are draining his strength, leaving him devastated and distressed to the extreme. Suffering from double vision, dizziness, and continuous nausea, he finds himself unable to digest any food. His intensely nervous state is followed by high fevers and chills. A doctor is called. After examining des Esseintes he tells him that he has to leave "this solitude," for it is a question "of life or death." The reader is not told exactly what happens to him, but it is assumed that he reenters the venal city of Paris, for he does not seem cut out to lead any other kind of life, certainly not that of a Trappist.

Exile and introversion might have been a salutary way for des Esseintes had he analyzed his acts objectively and assimilated his fantasies consciously. Because they were used exclusively to cultivate his eroticosexual pulsations, to encourage hallucinatory reveries, and to fill the void which was his life, exile and willed introversion endangered his already weakened ego to the point of virtual dismemberment.

Throughout his months of exile, des Esseintes lived out the fate of the *puer aeternus*. As a personification of the infantile or inferior side of his character, he was fated to remain the undeveloped and callow youth about whom he fantasized in his sadomasochistic, transsexual, and homosexual encounters. That he experienced (temporary) satisfaction only with Miss Urania and in the consummation of the homosexual act suggests that it was only through the male that he could come into contact with the feminine aspect of himself, which he lived out through projection.

The scenes of voyeurism depicted in his reveries revolving around certain paintings and episodes in *Satyricon* allowed him to experience lascivious acts vicariously. His constant yearning for what he lacked, sexual consummation and the concomitant feelings of fulfillment and serenity, did not indicate a need for love or for the sexual act (as such yearning is commonly thought to indicate) but rather showed an inability to love. Had des Esseintes experienced real love from his parents during his early years, he might have related to others and to himself, understood and responded to the feelings called into play. Deprivation, however, had denied him the possibility of bestowing love upon others by giving of himself in a relationship.

4 Malraux's *The Royal Way:* Heroes in Exile

The three heroes in André Malraux's[1] novel *The Royal Way* (1930), exiles from Western Europe, struggled through life-threatening situations in their attempt to carve out their destinies in the forests of Cambodia. Each had undergone periods of crises, personal suffering, and loss. Each in his own way had a driving desire to find fulfillment, to *renew* a life considered

---

[1]André Malraux (1901–76) was born and brought up in Paris by his mother, who had separated from his father four years after André's birth and divorced fifteen years later. After leaving the lycée Condorcet, in which he had been enrolled in 1919, without taking his *baccalauréat*, he worked for booksellers, editors, and publishers (René Louis Doyon, Simon Kra, Daniel Kahnweiler); published his first articles in *Action* and *La Connaissance*, his semisurrealist fantasy *Lunes en papier* (*Paper Moons*) appeared in 1921, and *Le Royaume farfelu* (*The Mad Realm*), in 1922. In 1921 he married Clara Goldschmidt. They later divorced.

Malraux's interest in art in general, and in that of the Far East in particular, made him an inveterate visitor of museums and art galleries; he also viewed a performance of the ballet of the Court of Phnom Penh at the Paris Opera.

Setting out with his wife from Marseilles for Indochina on 13 October 1923, he hoped to locate ancient Khmer temples near the Royal Way, once a Buddhist and Brahman pilgrimage route through the jungles of Cambodia and Laos. The thirty-mile trek through the jungle, described in *La Voie royale*, was arduous. Malraux's goal was to reach the temple of Bantai-Sre, mentioned by Parmentier. Having achieved his goal, he and others in his party, among them his friend Louis Chevasson, dislodged seven stones decorated with bas-reliefs and brought them back to their ship. The ship sailed. After it docked where the Mekong joins the Tonle-Sap, Malraux was arrested for having taken archeological works protected by a Khmer royal edict.

Malraux's three-year prison sentence was reduced on appeal in Saigon in 1924, and finally annulled in Paris; the stay of execution brought Malraux home in November 1924. The details involved in Malraux's Indochina episode have been brilliantly researched and narrated in Walter Langlois's *André Malraux: L'Aventure indochinoise*.

Siam, referring to Thailand, was the name used throughout *La voie royale*, and will also be used in this chapter.

a failure. The quest for a different mode of existence, for that of Malraux's heroes, entails the killing or integrating of old frames of reference, thus inviting the enactment of the age-old mystery of death and resurrection.

Heroes, be they semidivine, mythical, legendary, or simply young people seeking to prove themselves in life, must have performed an outstanding *act* to merit such a designation. Symbolically, the heroic feat may be viewed as the reactualization of a primordial deed or an imitation in human terms of a celestial archetypal exploit. The courage, sacrifice, and endurance required of the hero to accomplish his outstanding or superhuman undertaking serve also to alter values, ideals, personalities, and modes of existence. Common denominators, once existing between the hero and the collective, understandably vanish in the process. Cut off or alienated from family, group, and society, and suffering from the aloneness of exile, some heroes feel compelled to look within to assuage their solitude and anguish. Meditating upon their situation, they not only learn to accept the separation involved, but they evolve as they integrate their newfound independence into their personalities. Thus do they become equipped to build a solid foundation upon which to structure their lives. Exile, leading to independence, becomes positive.

Claude Vannec, the youngest of the three would-be heroes in Malraux's novel, is a twenty-six-year-old French archeologist. He seeks to explore the ancient Khmer Royal Way, a road that had once linked Angkor and the temples of the Middle Mekong and the Menam River basin. His motivation for such a venture, taking him through the treacherous Dangrek Mountains, which are inhabited by fierce nomadic tribes, is not solely intellectual. Financially destitute, alienated from European civilization, obsessed with the continuous thought of death, Claude believes that the money gained by selling whatever ancient sculptures and bas-reliefs he can find in abandoned temples will enable him to change his life-style.

The middle-aged Perken, whose first name is unknown (as are details concerning his life—characteristic of many heroes), is of German-Danish nationality. An international adventurer and expatriate, having lived in the Far East for fifteen years prior to the events related in *The Royal Way*, Perken has taken on for Claude the dimensions of a legendary figure. Stories concerning his real and imagined exploits abound: he became the "white chief" of a tribe of natives whom he then led into combat against their enemies. His desire to acquire money was prompted by his wish to stem the tide of colonialism and Western "civilization" in the Far East.

Grabot, an army deserter and also an adventurer, a trafficker in gold and arms, and a subduer of hostile native tribes, is both Perken's hero-figure and rival. Grabot, who had left the West years earlier, making his way alone into dangerous areas inhabited by such fierce tribes as the Moi and Stiengs, had, so it was said, established a kingdom of his own in that area. Perhaps because of such competition, Grabot's fortitude and bravery are catalysts for Perken, accounting in part for the goal he has set himself in *The Royal Way*: of finding this man of mystery, who was perhaps living as a king somewhere in the forests of Cambodia.

It may not be coincidental that *The Royal Way* should have been divided into four parts, as were many of the ancient initiation rituals leading to herohood. As attested to in *The Odyssey, Beowulf, The Song of Roland*, and *The Tain*, each would-be hero must be prepared to live out (1) an aggressive phase, involving his exile from family and country; (2) a collective stage, requiring his successful passage of harrowing ordeals; (3) a more personal period, including ventures and adventures revolving around psychological and metaphysical questions, such as identity and the meaning of life and death; and (4) a "noble" period, that of maturation, with the integration of past deeds and personality traits, that serve to transform the course of the hero's life (Eliade, *The Myth of the Eternal Return*, 35–36, 85–86). Just as symbols, signs, and visions or visitations played a significant role in initiation rituals leading to the herohood of such figures as Hector, Achilles, Charlemagne, and King Arthur, so, too, do they reveal profound spiritual and psychological lessons in Malraux's *The Royal Way*.

Exile—The Ship

During his journey on shipboard, the young and naive Claude attempts to convince the defiant and blasé Perken to become his companion in arms in his Cambodian adventure. Because ships and sea voyages, symbolically viewed, involve a passage through space and time, they suggest an unconscious need on the part of the travelers to recast their life experience. Examples may be found in many navigation myths: the Judeo-Christian Noah's Ark; Buddha's role as "the Great Navigator," so called because he sees to humanity's safe passage from one bank of existence to the other; Osiris's "Night-Sea Crossing," taking him from the land of the living into the Realm of the Dead; Gilgamesh's voyage to the ocean of death; and the many sea journeys in *Tristan and Isolde*.

While the ship functions in *The Royal Way* as a conveyor into exile, its enclosed womblike shape serves to create and nourish bonds of friendship between the two protagonists and to trigger all types of fantasies as well. Moreover, the cradling motion of the ship as it sails through rough or peaceful waters lulls inhibitions and breaks down defenses, thus encouraging a state of receptivity and stimulating both conversation and confession.

That *The Royal Way* should open on shipboard with the image of Claude looking directly into Perken's face is revealing. If the two men are viewed as mirror images of each other (Claude being the antithesis of Perken, or both men being two sides of the same personality), the sea voyage becomes the first stage of an initiation ritual intended to bring these two polarities together. Claude is Perken *in potentia:* that undeveloped half that seeks one day to become a seasoned hero.

As the catalyst, the ship sets the initiation ritual into orbit, becoming the vehicle through which the desired end may or may not be attained. It plays a crucial role in helping Claude and Perken find their spiritual center, and the stability and understanding needed to heal their excoriating sense of despair. Exiling themselves from the comforts of so-called civilization, from a way of life they both detest, the two set out for different reasons to confront the perils associated with the unknown.

Claude, as the initiator of the shipboard dialogue with Perken in his desperate attempt to convince him to join forces with him, may be considered the aggressor in the relationship. His admiration for Perken, a virtually legendary figure and a father-image as well, is boundless. However, specific and verifiable knowledge of his hero's deeds, including his reputed military accomplishments in his semiofficial position as civil servant for the Siamese government, is lacking. Hero-figures thrive on generalities and vague exploits. Specific details might cut these giant figures down to size. Claude, a hero-worshiper, is not troubled by the need for documentation, and he would like to make Perken's qualities his own.

The question remains, however, as to why Perken should be so intent upon finding Grabot, a man the French government labels a deserter and a person whom he had once considered sympathetic but in whom he now has no confidence. Does he want to ferret out the truth about someone whose personality has eluded his understanding (just as *his* personality is not completely known to Claude)? Details of Grabot's life are vague and contradictory, but I have just remarked that hero-worship thrives on mystery.

Perhaps Perken had idealized certain of Grabot's acts, interpreting them as paradigms of freedom, as examples of man as master of his destiny: his exile, his desertion from France's African Batallion, his readiness to use his revolver against anyone who threatened his freedom. Perhaps Perken admired Grabot's choice of vengeance against an army doctor who had wrongly diagnosed his gonorrhea. What did Grabot do to vent his ire? He rubbed his purulent discharge into his own eye until he was blinded. Thus did he humiliate the doctor who prided himself on his medical knowledge, and who was forthwith punished by the authorities. Did Perken consider Grabot's self-inflicted blinding an act of courage? Did the act suggest his inordinate admiration for one who had learned to sacrifice something as precious as sight for a principle? Was this another lesson in the exercising of freedom and a further sampling of Grabot's disdain for bondage and for dependence?

That the eye, symbolizing visual and intellectual perception, should be the organ chosen by Grabot for destruction, rather than another part of the body, suggests his intent to seal the aperture that enabled him to look *out* onto the world. His way, henceforth, would be inward. Like Oedipus, who gouged out his eyes as an act of self-punishment, and Tiresias, who was blinded because he had revealed certain secrets to mankind, Grabot intended his act of revenge as a chastisement. He wanted to penalize himself by destroying or cutting out of himself what he considered a weakness or infection (dependence); he wanted to transcend it. That the act smacked of sadism (aimed at punishing the doctor) and masochism (aimed at hurting himself) is also evident. In that he had lost but one eye, his exile from the world of appearances was only partial. Neither complete herohood or independence had as yet been achieved.

Claude also seeks to extract himself from what he considers to be the detestable earthbound and pedestrian views prevailing in Western nations. Most powerful, however, is his longing for the excitement of adventure, which he believes will take him out of himself, relieving him of his corrosive anxiety. That he finds a similarity between his own grandfather, also an adventurer who sailed the seas and was hostile to the establishment, and Perken is not surprising. Such an identification not only increases his admiration for the middle-aged Perken, but triggers Claude into activity. More pragmatic reasons of money, as previously mentioned, also motivate Claude's need to alter his course. Virtually destitute after the deaths of members of his family, he now seeks a financial return from the years spent studying archeology. Solipsistic, never for a moment does he consider putting his efforts as an archeologist into restoration work, such as the rebuilding of ancient Khmer temples or the repairing of the Royal Way, which had been cannibalized by the forests.

Claude's and Perken's need to exile themselves from what they despise, or perhaps fear, is also a manifestation of a psychological condition. To reject one's origins, be it family, city, country, or hemisphere, mirrors an inner attempt to expel those very aspects of oneself that one cannot accept and therefore, projects onto others. The intensity of the feelings of rejection, hatred, and rage harbored by both Claude and Perken reveals a grievously oppressive inner climate: a shadow-dominated outlook in both men.

The shadow is defined as a subliminal part of the personality that contains characteristics considered by the ego (center of consciousness) to be inferior and weak. The ego does not recognize this part as belonging to it. Rather than bringing these factors to the light of consciousness, analyzing them, accepting them, and redeeming them, Claude and Perken project them onto other people, nations, or other external stimuli. The struggle in which Claude and Perken are involved requires a clarification of the confused and abysmal pulsations that dominate their evaluation of the hero-figure. Sometimes by performing an act of valor, by experiencing and understanding its psychological, physical, and spiritual consequences, one can heal a bruised or injured ego, and thus establish new connections within the psyche and with the world outside (Edinger, *Ego and Archetype*, 37). Not to perform their heroic feats might repress further those fearsome phantoms lurking in Claude's and Perken's shadowy kingdom, increasing their already powerful sense of alienation and estrangement from the world and from themselves. To succeed in routing an enemy might dissipate the noxious powers imprisoned within them by bringing these to the light of consciousness.

That eroticism should be one of the first themes broached by Claude and Perken during their conversations aboard ship, is natural, but also psychologically revealing. In that sexual union is most frequently the culmination of the erotic interlude, it may be considered a repetition on a mortal level of the primordial hierogamy: the fusion between Heaven and Earth. Such coalescence, which led to the birth of humanity, symbolizes a conjunction of opposites. Erotic symbolism, for example, in Shaktism and Tantrism, practiced by Buddhists, Brahmins, and Taoists throughout Asia, has metaphysical impact and is considered a paradigm of cosmic harmony. Although the religious element is certainly not present in Perken's penchant for the erotic, the collective aspect of such acts is an important factor. When, for example, Perken tells Claude that "not to know one's partner" is crucial in eroticism, the implication is that the individual is for naught and gratification alone is of import. Perken's ostensible need for emotional detachment hides the opposite condition within his psyche, where he experiences unconscious feelings of alienation from the world and from himself. His need for eroticism discloses a fear of the feeling domain in general; love, affection, relatedness are all considered weaknesses, entrapments, and imprisonments. Since these are associated with the feminine principle, one understands why the worldly Perken and the intellectual Claude choose to reject relatedness with a woman and live he-man adventures on an exclusively patriarchal level. Because neither has ever known the meaning of real love, they have been estranged from it and are incapable of giving of themselves. They fear what they consider to be emotional bondage. Alienated from everything that is feminine, experiencing it only as a negative power, they may perhaps redeem their initial scarring through the heroic adventure.

What Perken really seeks, when fantasizing about the erotic, though he is unaware of it, is *eros* (the Greek root of "erotic"). Born of Chaos and the comrade of Aphrodite, Eros was viewed by Hesiod not only as the god of sensual love, but also as a power that forms the world by means of an inner union between disparate elements. Eros, then, represents those forces within the psyche that spell relatedness and love. The deprivation of love, be it a mother's love (Claude's case) or a sweetheart's (Perken's), is abrasive. Malraux's heroes, who seek autonomy over themselves, rationalize their situation and believe that what they cannot dominate must be rejected. Everything relating to feeling, emotion, and love, which are identified with the feminine sphere, is viewed as restrictive and imprisoning, and thus banished from their world.

Claude avoids thinking seriously about the repercussions of his scheme to steal a nation's art treasures. Like other archetypal heroes (Heracles, Tristan, Arthur, Lancelot), he is so centered upon himself and his struggle for affirmation that the gravity of disregarding the laws of the land is overlooked. Only one determinant is focused upon: his search for sculptures and bas-reliefs on the now cannibalized Royal Way of the Khmers. Like Jason leading the Argonauts, Claude reconnoiters the familiar markings he has made on his map of Cambodia, which "he knew better than his face." His chartings have been meticulously thought out, in keeping with Western logic and intellectual discipline. Cambodia is shown to be bordered by Laos on the north, by Annam (South Vietnam) on the east, by the Gulf of Siam (Thailand) on the south, and by Siam on the west. Neatly blocked out is the capital, Phnom Penh, as well as the dead cities and the thick forest areas covering three-quarters of the country.

As long as Claude is armed with map and compass, his sense of security, based on the Westerner's arrogant confidence in the rule of rationality, remains intractable. The map, with its surface delineations and mathematical correspondences to locations, allows Claude to measure and visualize his trajectory. The circular compass orients him in the real world. For the Easterner, and this may also be a factor involved in Claude's growing understanding of other ways, the compass is a cosmological symbol, relating Earth to Heaven, spirit to matter, East to West, the mortal to the immortal, the whole to the particular. Thus, Claude's venture becomes virtually all-inclusive, encompassing the rational and the irrational spheres.

Although intellectually prepared for what he has anticipated as a grueling journey through the virtually impassable Dang Rek Mountains into Siam, Claude little understands the traps awaiting the inexperienced explorer. Neither the intense humid heat, nor the tropical vegetation, poisonous insects, or dangerous reptiles, however, will be allowed to interfere with his project. Nor will the warning of government officials—after disclosure of the murder by tribesmen of two white leaders of an exploring party—dampen his enthusiasm. Like Siegfried, Claude seems impervious to danger, so driven is he to succeed.

That Claude has chosen archeology as a profession indicates a fascination on his part for the past, as well as a haunting need to go back into time to the *cradle* of civilization, to an *ab origine*, where non-time prevailed and gods and heroes roamed the earth. Viewed psychologically, Claude may be seeking escape from an untenable present reality into a world of infinite riches endlessly fed by the imagination. The search into the collective past that a return to archaic humanity offers him reveals Claude's unconscious need to discover his own raison d'être, his own sense of the meaning of life and death.

The ship docks at Singapore. Perken goes to Bangkok before joining Claude at Phnom Penh, where they will start to live out their adventure together.

The Ordeal—The Forest

The second stage in the hero's evolution corresponds to a period of growth: the more ego-conscious he becomes, the more aware he is of *Self* (total psyche); that is, his own person in terms of the world as a whole. His newfound understanding leads to the development of greater powers of differentiation and discernment with regard to his actions and their repercussions in his life and that of others. Thus far, Claude and Perken have little comprehension of themselves. To clarify the reasons for their exile, their obsession with death, and their hunger for adventure is crucial to the growth process.

Perhaps Claude's encounter, shortly after arriving in Phnom Penh, with a blind bard intoning the verses of the *Ramayana* (500 B.C.E.) may be viewed in part as a premonitory indication of the difficulties in store for him. Like the blind Homer, who wandered through the streets of Athens intoning heroic exploits in his *Odyssey* and *Iliad*, the aged Hindu chants the religious text ascribed to the poet Valmiki, recounting the exploits of the young hero, Rama (an avatar of the god Vishnu): his exile in the forest with his bride Sita, her capture by the demon-king, his struggle to free her, and their final reintegration into society. Is Claude being forewarned of the dangers awaiting him on his journey to the north of Angkor? Is there any connection between his trial and the years of anguish that Rama and Sita had suffered?

What shocks and dismays Claude as he listens to the chanting of the *Ramayana* is the audience made up of slaves and beggars. In ancient days, the inspirational verses of the Hindu epic served to nourish the body and soul of all classes. Then Cambodia was growing, building, expending its energies in creativity. Under the rule of S'rutavarman, the Khmer Empire (fifth century) rose to prominence; its march toward greatness began under Jayavarman III (ninth century), with such constructions as the royal city of Angkor Thom (tenth century) and the temple of Angkor Wat (twelfth century). Cambodia's decline (fourteenth century) made it fertile field for conquest and exploitation by neighboring Siam and Cochin China. Its final death rattle came with the establishment of the French protectorate in 1863. The creative energy once used to build a nation had foundered, as had interest in spiritual and aesthetic matters. Claude's vision of the old blind bard surrounded by slaves and beggars evidently spells spiritual decline in a country already politically and economically decadent. Does it not mirror as well that inner state of decomposition which Perken fears so desperately and of which Claude, until now, has been unaware?

The trek Claude and Perken are planning through the Cambodian forest may be viewed paradigmatically as a test that heroes, such as those in the *Ramayana*, must pass in order to acquire wisdom. The forest, as a symbol for the unconscious, is awesome and fear-inspiring. A journey into its depths parallels a plunge into the unknown, into disorienting chaos. A treacherous yet infinitely fertile area, the forest may be regarded as the container of repressed or unsuspected fears, but of marvelous treasures as well. Behind each tree, bush, stone, leaf, blade of grass, poisonous flora or fauna, may lurk an animal, reptile, insect, or savage tribesman. Still, what is considered poison for one may become a healing and revitalizing agent for another. To succeed in the journey through one's abysmal depths may lead to greater awareness in dealing with life's continuous hazards as well as to expanded consciousness of the individual's own performance. It must also be noted that deeply forested areas in general are, symbolically speaking, the domain of the Great Mother, the Hindus' Kali ("Dark One"), the "world nurse," and are the source of new living forms. A composite of opposites, she is both nourisher, in that she suckles her offspring, and devourer, consuming them in human and animal sacrifices. Her behavior varies, depending upon whether she rules over nature left in its natural state or nature that is cultivated, in an ordered and restrictive manner, as in gardens or fields.

The remote and chaotic realm of forest is analogous to a womblike sphere. Identified with the most primitive level of the psyche, the collective unconscious, this protective/destructive maternal shelter will, for a certain period of time, hold Claude and Perken in a kind of psychologically incestuous thrall. Particularly intriguing in the forest sequence is the manner in which Claude and Perken cope with what they fear most: the Terrible

Mother, or the destructive aspect of the female principle. Just as Perseus, Siegfried, St. George, St. Michael, and St. Patrick each struggled and slew a dragon, a symbolic representation of the Terrible Mother, so it is incumbent upon Malraux's he-men to do likewise. The slaying of this beast is tantamount to the annihilation of the would-be hero's primordial enemy: that powerful and domineering force buried deep within the unconscious. To free the hero of this virtually autonomous power is to liberate his feeble and tottering ego (center of consciousness). Once emancipated, the ego is no longer obliged to dissipate its energy warring with an increasingly demanding negative principle within the psyche. It has strength enough to develop in its own right, to take stock of itself, and to consolidate its position with regard to the collective unconscious. Alert to the ever-present danger of becoming vulnerable to the power of the Terrible Mother, the ego will never again allow itself to be off-guard. Fear and obsessions have been replaced by the nourishing powers of Mother Earth, who loves and cares but does not dominate.

After only four days in the forest with their native guides, the meaning of "decomposition of the mind in this aquariumlike light" takes on meaning for Claude and Perken. The monuments they come upon have been so completely cannibalized by the Terrible Mother as to be worthless to them. Proceeding on their journey, they search carefully for ancient stones, coming upon some that have been crushed and others, intertwined with roots of plants and trees, that sport superhuman, even grotesque shapes, as if they had been sculpted by beings long since vanished from the earth. They see firsthand the remains of the once-celebrated Royal Way. The Terrible Mother, having devoured its own creation, leaves in its wake detritus, skeletons, fermentation, and decay, as well as a whole world of "scintillating atoms" in the form of insects, spiders, termites, fungi, vermin, and reptiles. "Everything was ramifying, softening, trying to blend into this ignoble and enticing world."

Walking becomes difficult and dangerous, particularly when they attempt to scale a severely crumbling wall. In ancient times, walls were erected to protect inner sanctuaries—cities, temples, or palaces—from vandalism. Thus did the people assure the safety of what is alluded to in so many myths and legends as the "treasure hard to attain," either material or spiritual.

In Claude's case, "the treasure hard to attain" took the form of valuable sculptures and bas-reliefs. To obtain them required him to find some way of circumventing the barriers preventing entry into the religious sanctuary. Ingenuity, courage, and fortitude had to be applied to avoid accidents; to break a limb or to suffer an abrasion of any kind in a tropical climate could easily lead to gangrene, the "mistress of the forest."

Claude moved slowly and carefully, at times on his belly, through gluey underbrush and viscous, moss-ridden plantings permeated with the stench of putrefaction. Doggedly and painstakingly he went on, stopping every now and then to wipe away the intrusive black and red ants, wasps, worms, spiders, chiggers, and multiple other moving things, who liked nothing better than to slip between his fingers, to roam about his hair and neck, or to find their way under his clothes. Finally, he found a way of passing directly into the sanctuary. So well acquainted was Claude with Cambodian architecture that before allowing his hopes to rise, he realized that this particular religious edifice had never been completed and thus it would contain no monuments.

Although disappointed, Claude and Perken forged ahead, inspired by the memory of Angkor Wat, the renowned Sivaitic sanctuary they had glimpsed at Siem Reap, the "prologue" to the forest. They were also encouraged by the knowledge that the gigantic religious complex surrounded by a moat had included cloisters, courts, turrets, towers, galleries, step-pyramids, and intricately sculpted reliefs celebrating heroic epics, such as the *Ramayana*. It had been overrun by the forest and forgotten until its ruins had been discovered by the French in 1861. Might not they too come upon such a wonder?

As they continued their trek through the forest, they heard talk from their native guides of a great edifice, the Ta Mean, situated high on the Dangrek Mountains between Cambodia and an unexplored part of Siam. Although the many meters of bas-reliefs were said to be in relatively good condition, access to this region dominated by the Stieng and the Moi people was perilous.

Despite the dangers and the flight of their guides fearing for their lives, Claude and Perken continued on. In time, they reached another wall, much of which had been buried in greenery. Suddenly, the moment Claude penetrated the sanctuary he experienced elation. Something behind an "apron" of leaves captured his attention: a stone sculpted in the form of a bird in flight, its beak like that of a parrot. As he walked toward it, he saw more priceless sculptures.

What value, aside from the monetary, did these religious bas-reliefs have for Claude? Whether in the form of a bird, animal, or human figure, these sculptures were saturated with sacrality: each was a *hierophany*. Endowed with Mana, these awesome and once-sanctified cult objects were still impregnated, even for Claude, an agnostic, with some kind of atemporal force (Eliade, *Myth of the Eternal Return*, 4, 5, 18).

The powerful feelings these hallowed objects triggered in Claude as he approached them revealed a far deeper and more spiritual motivation than financial. Their very presence took him back to the beginning of time, to an *illo tempore*, when gods and heroes roamed the earth. By returning to the dawn, the very foundations, of humanity, Claude reverted to a collective past, losing track of himself and his present reality. His integration into eternal time abolished all sense of linear moments, inviting him to relive and re-create his life as he now saw fit.

The works of art found by Claude, stemming from the deepest archetypal levels of the psyche, were molded from contents within the collective unconscious. Although subject to decomposition and transformation, as is all else on the planet, they were nevertheless the product of an artist's or artists' *original experience*. Thus did they live both outside of and within historical time, containing past, present, and future within their structures. The sculptures that most impressed Claude featured women dancers of incredible beauty from the classical Khmer period.

The treasure hard to attain had been located. The hero's next battle revolved around its extraction from the tentacles of the Terrible Mother. Ingenuity, and tools (saws, hammers, scissors, machetes), as well as will, furor, and brute strength, were mustered to perform this next Herculean task. Try as Claude might to wrench the treasure from the Terrible Mother, she clung firm to her artfully concealed possessions.

Why was Claude so intrigued with the sculptures of the two dancing women (*apsaras* for the Hindu)? As mentioned in the *Ramayana* and the *Puranas* (traditional religious stories), these nymphs or fairylike beings, born from the churning of the ocean, are frequently called "the wives of the gods" and "daughters of pleasure." That Claude was so moved by their beauty and voluptuousness—he affirmed that they were "among the purest" specimens of their kind he had ever seen—suggests a development in his psyche, the emergence of a new relationship with the feminine side of his personality (*anima*).

Prior to his discovery of the treasure hard to attain, Claude had lived in a strictly patriarchal world. He had functioned through his head, that is, rationally, via his thinking principle, in keeping with his capacity to structure, synthesize, and conceptualize data. Relationships with the feminine world had been repressed, rejected, or experienced as negative—until now, when the Great Mother's extreme fertility, manifested by the virtually uncontrollable eruption of subliminal contents into consciousness, resulted in near-paralysis of Claude's ego, arresting all development. The viewing of the *apsaras*, a projection of Claude's *anima*, or soul image, was so intensely moving an experience that it affected his entire feeling world. The loosening and dislodging of the dancing figures from the monument, which had buried and imprisoned them during the course of centuries, was paralleled in the mythical sphere by the killing of a dragon, and in the psychological sphere by a release from bondage of those negative feminine forces incarcerated within Claude since childhood. Now the would-be hero could glimpse the positive side of the feminine principle, inviting ego-consciousness to evolve along a new royal way.

That the sculptures Claude had discovered were part of a temple complex suggests a fusion of what had formerly been severed: celestial/earthly, spiritual/sexual. Let us also note that dance, for the Hindu, represents the union of space and time within the process of evolution. As such, it is a creative force, and a paradigm of eternal energy, as attested to when Lors Shiva performed the *tandava*, his Cosmic Dance, bringing forth the universe.

Unlike Claude, Perken had not yet killed his symbolic dragon nor had he found the treasure hard to attain. Still at the mercy of the Gorgon-type, the destructive and monstrous infernal feminine image, he continued to resort to eroticism rather than to eros.

Because it had been decided that Claude and Perken would continue on through even more dangerous territory in their search for Grabot, the older and more experienced of the two men could still prove his mettle. The precious sculptures were placed in carts and drawn along, while Claude and Perken pursued their course through the mountainous terrain on horseback.

Sacred Terror: Human/Inhuman

The natural world of the Terrible Mother and the fascinating events involving the treasure hard to attain now recede into the background as the human/inhuman sphere predominates. Topography, atmosphere, and surroundings change during the course of Claude and Perken's journey into increasingly dangerous areas. No longer are they steeped in "the voluptuous nonchalance of Laos or Lower-Cambodia." They have been flung into a world of savagery, raw energy, and viscerality. They must now be doubly careful. Unlike the natives, ever-awake to visual or auditory warnings of danger, Europeans cannot rely on instinctive reactions.

Prior to his Cambodian venture, Claude had never experienced intimate contact with the earth; he had always relied on rationality and book-knowledge to protect him from the hazards of the unknown. Perken, on the other hand, having lived in Asia for so many years, had grown accustomed to dangers. It was he who stopped Claude just as he was about to step on a poisoned spearhead. Virtually invisible, it was one of those traps set by natives who knew the art of avoiding them, in order to kill colonizers.

Poison, used by people from time immemorial, be it for death-dealing or for healing purposes, plays an important role in myths and fairy tales (for example, *Parzifal, Tristan and Isolde, Snow White*). In *The Royal Way*, the natives implant their poisoned spearheads and darts in the ground, covering them over with leaves and greenery of all sorts. The unwary person who steps on them is pierced in the foot and leg, those organs which enable one to move, travel, and maintain balance. Impairment of these capacities indicates, psychologically, a disturbed relationship with the earth force, or *real* life.

Claude and Perken, unrelated to each other and to European and Asiatic social structures as well, are vulnerable in their approach and attitude toward people and society. Thus, they are easy targets for destruction. To be aware of their Achilles' heel, however, may serve as a protective device. When, in such myths as those of Siegfried and Arthur, spears, swords, lances, knives, or any cutting or piercing instrument divides or bruises what is whole, the ensuing separation or fragmentation allows light to penetrate where once only darkness prevailed. Viewed psychologically, segmentation permits more minute and profound examination of smaller sections of an important problem. Thus can various angles be scrutinized in greater depth, evaluated with increased precision, and judged more profoundly (Jung and Franz, 170–71).

Thus far, Perken has been the one to protect Claude from any tearing of the flesh. As they continue on their journey across rivers and glades, the atmosphere becomes increasingly oppressive, particularly for Perken. Haunted ever more persistently and brutally by his phantoms—thoughts of death, of the "irrefutable proof of the absurdity of life," of his sexual impotence and his ensuing feelings of mortification (which he had attempted to stave off through eroticism and voyeurism)—he now realizes they are symptomatic of his own decline. *Déchéance* (decadence) is no longer an abstraction; it is a reification. The more degraded he feels, the more powerful is his admiration for Grabot: a man he believes to be truly free, having accepted solitude and having risen above all human anxiety.

As they come upon the Stieng village where they believe Grabot to be living, Claude looks at its wooden ramparts as if he were confronting a complex of dangerous powers: he sees a tomb decorated with plumed fetishes and an enormous gaur's head. Once they enter the village, they learn they have finally tracked down their prey and are told which hut the "slave" occupies.

The oblique rays penetrating an opening on the roof of a windowless hut allow a shadowy, dank world to come into view. Stunned, their eyes growing accustomed to the darkness, they make out a form working a treadmill. Grabot is the one treading around the room on the periphery of a wide wheel with a horizontal axis. A type of punishment in olden days, it symbolizes a wearisome, monotonous, endless, and meaningless routine to the Westerner, paralleling the chastisement meted out to Ixion, bound as he was to a fiery wheel that perpetually rolled through the sky. For the Easterner, Grabot's circular trajectory around his hut (his earthly sphere) suggests an acceptance of and detachment from earthly considerations. Temporal concerns are no longer of interest to him who has been placed in atemporal spheres; he fits Perken's original image of a man who has transcended all he considered hopeless. Or is such an exile from life a paradigm of Grabot's own *déchéance?* Hadn't he said that freedom was what he most prized and that he would commit suicide were it ever endangered? The question is moot.

The figuration of the treadmill is particularly significant for Hindus and Buddhists. The wheel, as *mandala*, is a solar representation of a condition of liberation from material attachments, inviting an individual to reach his center and achieve balance and harmony within the personality. As a paradigmatic replication of Buddha, the wheel stands for Universal Man, Sovereign Man who has fulfilled the laws and the steps leading to the incessant mutations and the succession of multiple states of development. Could Grabot's circular and perpetual rotations of the wheel signify, not meaninglessness or punishment, as Westerners see it, but renewal?

Because Perken is unaware of Grabot's spiritual and psychological evolution or devolution, his initial reaction is one of horror at the sight of the man who had been for him a paragon of strength and freedom, and whom he now sees as a slave. Observing Grabot more closely, he sees that he is blind in both eyes. Later he learns that the Moi warrior to whom he had been awarded as booty had gouged out the second eye.

Grabot's blindness, the animal sounds he keeps making in answer to Perken's questions, and his ring-shaped permutations through time and space arouse what mystics have called that "sacred terror," or *mysterium tremendum:* feelings that overwhelm an individual in the presence of "inhuman" powers (Otto, 118). Stunned and dizzied by the endless discoid activity, Perken seems shocked into a new state of awareness, as if barriers had suddenly been abolished and fresh understanding born. Ambiguity, nevertheless, is implicit in his reaction. Does he see his idol as a slave, having regressed to a virtually animal state? Or does he believe this man to have passed from the profane to the sacred, from the outside world of appearances into an inner reality in which timelessness is experienced as an external present? (Eliade, *Myth of the Eternal Return*, 18).

Has the sacrifice of his vision allowed Grabot to see beyond *maya*, the obvious world with its snares and deceits, into an inner domain, thus becoming privy to the secrets of the privileged? Unmoved after Perken cuts him loose, Grabot walks slowly toward the open door of his hut, appearing "even more terrible in the light of day" than he had in his darkened habitat.

As Perken looks at Grabot, he begins to understand the meaning of the language of the flesh, body language: words that need not be articulated, but, as in the performing and pictorial arts of the Far East, are sensed semiotically and viscerally. Grabot exists beyond the world of contingencies. Like a visitation, a sign sent by some higher power, Grabot's image, bathing in a composite of light and darkness, catalyzes the until-now dormant emotions within Perken's psyche, paving the way for a momentous spiritual experience: the realization that something autonomous and beyond the "I" is alive within him (Jung, *Visions Seminars*, 2:260).

Energized by the power of the visitation and the resulting unconscious forces that have been released within him, Perken, along with Claude and Grabot, walks out of the hut into an open field. The moment to *act* is at hand. Fearlessly and alone, Perken walks toward the enemy at the other end of the terrain, despite drawn lances, crossbows, and arrows pointed his way. As coruscating tension quivers in an atmosphere already taut with hostility and dread, Perken's body is suddenly flooded with inhuman strength, as if some power beyond his control were alive within him and dictating the way. Slowly and methodically he keeps advancing across the field, staring fixedly and unrelentlessly at the enemy. As the rays of the setting sun cast their diagonal colorations on Perken, the Moi seem transfixed by the hypnotic gaze of this man proceeding into their camp. One thought alone prevails in Perken's mind: to defy the enemy by challenging and spurning the possibility of torture. Because his eyes never once leave the enemy, Perken, failing to see a poisoned spearhead in front of him, trips, falls, rises, and, although acute pain shoots through his leg, pursues his relentless course. Blood spurting from his wound, frenzy drives him on, and he walks erect into the "decomposing" light.

Astounded by Perken's bravery, the immobile tribesmen remain rooted to the ground. Instead of shooting their arrows, they speak, agreeing finally to exchange Grabot for whiskey jars they prize. "This man is worth a hundred jars!" Perken exclaims, thereby reducing a human life to that of a thing, but also pointing out the relativity of values.

To make certain that he and Claude are released from the Moi village, Perken resorts to magic: or is it miracle? He fires his revolver at an animal skull, from which blood suddenly starts flowing. The natives are benumbed. After the chief tastes the blood—not an uncommon practice among primitive peoples, who regard it as a potion of immortality (like the dragon's blood for Siegfried)—he declares it to be human (Jung, *Collected Works*, 5:350). Adding to the sacredness of the event are the sun's rays, which shine upon the now-sparkling drops of red blood in the process of coagulating. As understood by the natives, the coagulation of the blood, in addition to the extrahuman event, is the act of a redemptive power. What the tribesmen do not know is that the blood they saw issuing from the animal's skull was Perkin's own. He had poured the blood spurting from his wounded knee into an empty bullet shell which he then placed inside the skull.

No longer is Perken obsessed exclusively with his own life. The emotions that Grabot's "inhuman" presence have triggered within him have taught him to think beyond personal considerations. His willingness to sacrifice himself for the cause of others, as attested to by his march toward the enemy, indicates a broader, less solipsistic approach to existence, thus marking the successful passage of his initiation.

On the way back to "civilization," Perken's wounded knee, as is to be expected, becomes infected. The doctor called upon to examine him informs him that amputation alone can save his life. No medical man in the vicinity, however, is qualified to perform such an operation. The spreading infection grows increasingly painful and gangrenous.

Exile in Death

The fourth and most noble phase in a hero's maturation process takes place after the completion of his exploits. At this point, he is able to integrate into his personality the disparate forces, feelings, and passions that emerged during his period of travail.

Change occurred within the outlooks and psyches of the three heroes after having lived out their rite of passage. Grabot's fate is the strangest of them all. Or is it, considering the politics involved? Once considered a deserter, after his rescue by the Siamese military he will be viewed as a martyr, an excuse to invade regions heretofore uninhabited by whites. Thus will the mission of spreading "civilization"—the power principle— be fulfilled!

Perken's discovery of Grabot's whereabouts led to his rescue and enabled Perken to acquire the treasure hard to attain, which in his case is nonmaterial. The aftermath of his feat brought on the *mysterium tremendum:* the eruption of latent emotions into consciousness in the presence of inhuman or suprahuman powers. Strengthened by this surge of libido, Perken is ready to submit to the agony of death with the dignity and sagacity of a man who, having lived life fully, is prepared for the next phase of being. *Déchéance,* or disintegration, impotence, and rot—forces and conditions he had so desperately feared—have now receded in importance for him, taking their rightful place as part of cosmic cyclicity.

As Perken reviews his life and mulls over his former acts, taken so seriously at the time, they all seem hollow. His only reality at present is death. All else is illusion, sham, deception: *maya.* For the first time, and despite his pain, "he felt himself furiously alive." No longer intent upon discussing the life/death dynamic as an intellectual or philosophical concept, as an abstraction to be bandied about in conversation, he experiences it as a silent, indomitable, inexorable force that encroaches on his and everybody's world, relentlessly and ritualistically. As the hero prepares himself for that greatest moment of them all, his exile from the world of the living, he closes his eyes, aware that he has already distanced himself from the others. "It is impossible to make oneself understood by the living."

As Perken's face "ceases imperceptibly to be human," and he slips into death, Claude realizes that he, too, has changed. For the first time he understands the real meaning of eros as relatedness. The positive *anima*, or soul image, which had come to the fore after he discovered and extracted the bas-reliefs of the beautiful dancing women had released a whole new side of him: his capacity to feel for and with others, to experience the meaning of brotherhood and camaraderie. "To express with hands and eyes, if not by word, that desperate fraternity which cast him outside of himself! He hugged him [Perken] around the shoulders."

5 Agnon's "Edo and Enam": The Exile of the Feminine Principle—The Shekhinah

S. Y. Agnon's[1] "Edo and Enam" (1950) narrates the spiritual and psychological drama confronting a young bride, Gemulah, after leaving the land of her ancestors to follow her husband to Jerusalem. A descendent of the ancient tribe of Gad, one of the ten lost tribes of Israel, Gemulah lived with her people in a remote mountain region, perhaps some place in Southeast Asia. A practitioner of ancient devotional rituals and hymns spoken in a Hebrew long since vanished from the earth, her new environment arouses in her feelings of displacement and alienation. She feels cut off from the world of her origins and the security it had afforded her. More tragically, she mourns the loss of the spiritual and inspirational role she had once played for her people. An irremediable sense of bereavement fills her days. A soul in exile, Gemulah is incapable of adjusting to her new situation and surroundings.

On a mystical level, Agnon's tale implies another kind of crisis: a playing-out, terrestrially, a condition of uneasiness and disorientation experienced by God himself. In Kabbalistic (Hebrew mystical tradition) terms, trauma within the Godhead is said to occur when the Shekhinah is in exile. One of the Ten Manifestations of God, the Shekhinah, an extremely com-

---

[1]Samuel Joseph Agnon (1888–1970) was the first Hebrew writer to receive the Nobel Prize for literature (1966). Born in Buczacz, Galicia, he was brought up in a deeply religious family. After emigrating to Palestine (1907), the family changed their name to Agnon. After spending a year in Europe, Agnon returned in 1913 to Jerusalem which he made his permanent home. His tales and novels, such as *Bridal Canopy* and *And the Crooked Shall Become Straight* are known for their simple yet profound meanings, their insights into character, their ironies and subtle humor as well as their pathos. Agnon's writings may be read on many levels.

plex and ambiguous notion, first alluded to in the *Book of Bahir* (twelfth century), then in the *Zohar* (thirteenth century), for some symbolizes the feminine element within God himself. In the human domain, it is identified with the feminine principle, the soul, and the Community of Israel. Depending upon times and circumstances, the Shekhinah makes manifest either the beautiful (merciful, loving, and compassionate) side of her personality, or her terrible (stern, judgmental) aspect. When the Shekhinah is said to be in exile, her suffering is deeply intense since she is cut off from God and thus from the Whole. When she is united with God, joy and harmony prevail (Scholem, *On the Kabbalah and Its Symbolism*, 107).

Communion between God and his Creation is so close that divine torment, occurring when he is separated from his Shekhinah, or part of himself, is mirrored in the trials and torments of earthly persecution and wanderings. When such a cleaving takes place on earthly or celestial planes, the Shekhinah weeps in anguish: she "tastes the other, bitter side, and then her face is dark." The abandonment she feels as a result of her exile from God or, on a human level, during periods of individual and collective banishments, may leave the Shekhinah to wither and die from neglect and lack of nourishment. Severed from the Tree of Life or God, she becomes the "Tree of Death." Her role is also positive and protective: she guided the exiled Jacob and his people to their rightful destination (*Zohar*, 2:156, 171b). "When Israel were journeying in the wilderness, the Shekhinah went in front of them" (*Zohar*, 176b). The Shekhinah's enforced separation may also be used as a means of rekindling and rechanneling her power, helping to reroot and enrich those enjoying their earthly existence.

That "a part of God is exiled from God" may be interpreted psychologically as a projection of a harrowing drama occurring within a human personality. The banishment of the Shekhinah (as feminine principle, soul force, or Community of Israel) implies a one-sided emotional condition existing in an individual or in a nation. The alienation of the feminine principle and of that relational (eros) factor with which she is frequently identified creates such a vacuum in a personality as to lead to dissociation within the psyche. Rather than encouraging awareness and fomenting the healing process, the inner void may tear mind and heart asunder. Redemption, on the other hand, is brought about when God is reunited with his Shekhinah: then masculine and feminine powers flow unimpeded throughout the Godhead as well as within humanity. With the restoration of original unity and harmony, chaos has been transformed into cosmos.

Although applicable to all victims of persecution and banishment, the state of exile, as depicted in Agnon's tale, refers perhaps most specifically to the Jews of Eastern Europe, victims of centuries of persecution in their native lands. Those who could escape with their lives emigrated to nations the world over; or, if they were unable to find asylum, they wandered, anchorless, from one part of the globe to another in search of a home.

Ever since the Babylonian captivity (586–537 B.C.E.), when the Jews were forcibly exiled from Palestine, they dreamed of returning to the land their ancestors had inhabited after their flight from Egypt. Some Jews believe that those who do not make their home in Palestine/Israel are said to be living in the Diaspora (from the Greek, *diaspora*, a scattering), dispersed throughout the world—or in exile.

The two male protagonists in "Edo and Enam," Gamzu and Dr. Ginath, are wanderers roaming the earth in search of ancient, "scattered," manuscripts and writings pertaining to their people. The former, a dealer in rare books and texts, and a traditionalist in matters of religion, in one of his journeys, happened upon a remote mountainous area, where he met and fell in love with a beautiful young girl, Gemulah. A member of the ancient tribe of Gad, she lived the same way as her ancestors who had wandered there centuries before to escape persecution. Gamzu identifies Gemulah with the moon and stars, that is, with mystical climes. Dr. Ginath, a well-known, open-minded, and scientifically oriented philologist who also travels continuously seeking lost or "scattered" documents relating to his, but also other cultures, also fortuitously reaches the area of Gemulah's tribe. Cerebrally inclined, he sets about transcribing the strange grammar and language spoken in this remote region, most importantly, the Enamite Hymns that Gemulah sings in the lost Edo language.

Jerusalem: Archetype of the Self

That "Edo and Enam" should be set in the Holy City of Jerusalem suggests a fusion of mystical and empirical worlds. For the pious, Jerusalem is considered the center of God's Creation. It is a sacred zone, a sanctuary of absolute reality, that place where celestial and tellurian forces commune, and where light and darkness cohabit. All varieties of life, inanimate and animate, exist inchoate within this microcosm of the macrocosm (Eliade, *Myth of the Eternal Return*, 18). The belief in a heavenly Jerusalem was alluded to by most of the Hebrew prophets (Tobias 13:16; Isaiah 59:1Lff., Ezekiel 60, etc.) as well as by the Kabbalists. The latter believed that the Holy City was located in the region of the sun, moon, planets, and stars.

Because of their containing, protective, womblike, but also limiting qualities, cities in general—and Jerusalem is no exception—have come to symbolize the feminine principle. As a Holy City, however, Jerusalem is identified with Divinity, the masculine principle, and may be considered a composite of opposites. Given the right proportions, Jerusalem as a meeting-ground of polarities experiences periods of equilibrium; conveyed in psychological terms, of *centeredness* within the personality.

Many Jews living in Jerusalem, then, are said to have rooted themselves within its protective spiritual and empirical boundaries, or hope or intend to do so. Others, living elsewhere and finding themselves alienated from the cultures and ideologies of the lands in which they live, yearn to return to Jerusalem, fully aware of the dangers involved. Still others, living in the Diaspora do not consider earthly Jerusalem as home and are content to live in their adopted country.

As a paradigm for wholeness and centeredness, Jerusalem, for some of the protagonists in "Edo and Enam," may be looked upon psychologically, as the central archetype of the Self (total psyche), which encompasses and regulates all the others in the personality. In this capacity, representing an ideal state of wholeness or completion, it makes *holy* or is able to *heal* disparate or exiled contents within the unconscious and conscious realms that might otherwise be torn asunder. As an active ordering center, the archetype of the Self is a suprapersonal authority operating in every individual. It is just this sense of wholeness, completion, and harmony that rootless or wandering Jews ideally yearn for, particularly from the time of their real or symbolic "scattering," or fragmentation, in the Diaspora.

Agnon's modern/ancient city of Jerusalem, however, with all of its redemptive and messianic associations, does not represent security and wholeness for all the protagonists in Agnon's tale. Certainly it does for many of the survivors of the Holocaust, as well as for those who have experienced persecution in other lands. Some, however, find themselves psychologically unprepared to find integration within its confines. Not everyone fits the mold, Agnon suggests.

The House: Containment/Imprisonment

The locus of "Edo and Enam" is centered not only in the Holy City of Jerusalem, but also in a house. Like the city, the house functions as a centering device and world axis. Set in the valley, separated from the surrounding metropolis, it seems to contain not only a whole world within its walls, but is "rimmed with a crown of trees through which beneficent vapors flow, keeping it free from the taint of malign airs" (Agnon, 157).

The low-lying valley, with its feminine contours may be considered a zone or space receptive to celestial influences. As a cavern like the heart, it not only becomes a receptacle for rhythmical vibrations, but is fertile field for spiritual and psychological events. The valley's circular configuration, "rimmed with a crown of trees," represents the eternal value of spiritual enlightenment. The "crown" ("Kether" for the Kabbalist) symbolizes Divinity in his most remote and absolute form.

Like the ancient walled city of Jerusalem, the encircling and protected valley with its house in the center may be looked upon as an aspect of the feminine principle: the repository of occult wisdom and tradition. The house, then, is not only the meeting-place of the protagonists, but the matrix, the womb, the locus within which the events are dramatized.

The narrator of the tale, like an impersonal consciousness, visits the owners of the house, Gerhardt and Gerda Greifenbach, who are about to leave for Europe to visit relatives "in the Diaspora." During the course of their conversation, they tell the narrator they are looking for someone to keep an eye on their home. They also tell him that they have rented a room to the world-renowned philologist and ethnologist, Dr. Ginath. Impressed by this scholar's work, the narrator questions them about his "Ninety-nine Words of the Edo Language," his "Grammar of Edo," and his transcription and translation of what is considered his great discovery, the Enamite Hymns. When the narrator first set eyes on the latter work, he told the Greifenbachs that something deep within him had stirred: "It was the reverberation of a primeval song passed on from the first hour of history through endless generations."

Why was the narrator so impressed by Dr. Ginath's works as a whole and by the Enamite Hymns in particular? First, because Dr. Ginath's research had established "a newfound link in a chain that binds the beginnings of recorded history to the ages before." Second, his discovery of the Enamite Hymns, with their feminine rhymes and rhythms, disproves previous affirmations that the gods and priests of Enam were male.

The first point discloses the narrator's need to establish a sense of continuity with his ancestors. Such a link is crucial to psychological well-being, particularly for those who have been cut off from their lands and their cultural heritage. Jung notes:

> Just as the developing embryo recapitulates, in a sense, our phylogenetic history, so the child-psyche relives "the lesson of earlier humanity." The child lives in a pre-rational and above all in a pre-scientific world, the world of men who existed before us. Our roots lie in that world and every child grows from those roots. Maturity bears him away from his roots and immaturity binds him to them. Knowledge of the universal origins builds the bridge between the lost and abandoned world of the past and the still largely inconceivable world of the future. How should we lay hold of the future, how should we assimilate it, unless we are in

possession of the human experience which the past has bequeathed to us? Dispossessed of this, we are without root and without perspective, defenseless dupes of whatever novelties the future may bring. (Franz, *Creation Myths*, 203. Quoted from Jung, *The Gifted Child*)

Historical continuity, as Jung suggests, connects an individual to the archetypal foundations of his or her psyche. Rooting in this manner acts as a safeguard: it prevents a person from being carried away by illusions and delusions, or from a disintegration of the personality. To be divested of emotional support is to invite an atomization or dissociation of the psyche, as in schizophrenia. Under such circumstances, increasing fragmentation may lead to an eclipse of the ego, overwhelmed as it could be by the power of autonomous unconscious complexes.

So important is the motif of continuity to the stability of the psyche that in most religious texts (from Hesiod's *Theogony*, to the *Mahabharata*, to the Maya Quiché's *Popul Vuh*, to the Bible), genealogies of gods, kings, and ancestors establish a link with the beginnings of nations and their godheads. Such connections with a past make concrete what has seemingly vanished into oblivion, thus giving order, orientation, and a sense of unity where otherwise chaos would prevail.

That the names of Agnon's protagonists all begin with the letter *G*, the first letter of the Hebrew word *galut* (exile, Diaspora) emphasizes the harrowing need of these wandering beings to root themselves, to find some kind of bond with a mythical past, *in illo tempore*, thus endowing them with feelings of security and belonging. Not one of the participants in Agnon's tale is settled, not one is whole, not one lives in harmony with himself or herself.[2]

Wandering Scholars

What kind of man is the internationally famous scholar Dr. Ginath? Secretive, in that he deals with ancient, esoteric, frequently undeciphered, documents. A wanderer, in his continuous search for written texts or oral material that might reveal information concerning ancient tongues and primordial civilizations. A thinking type, because of the objective and scientific manner in which he goes about acquiring and recording information. Perception and judgment are most important to him in his continu-

---

[2]Agnon's pseudonym was derived from the Hebrew word *aginut* (bereavement). The title of his first story was "Agunot" (1908), suggesting solitude and a universal failure to find fulfillment.

ous quest to define objects and things with regard to name and concept. Rational, he proceeds in the most detached and determined of ways in reaching his goal. Never, however, does he allow himself to become emotionally involved. Never remaining for more than a night or two in one place, he leads a virtually nomadic existence that precludes any kind of bonding. Is it an excuse to escape commitment?

A restless man, Dr. Ginath is forever driven by his intellect. His world, revolving solely around the mind, has divested itself of the feeling function. So repressed or unused is the feeling side of his personality, that it has virtually atrophied. Dr. Ginath not only has cut himself off from any and all human relationships, but is even unaware of the existence of others. Eros is missing from his world.

Dr. Ginath, a delver into esoteric matters, is himself a man of mystery. When, for example, the inquisitive narrator learns that the Greifenbachs had heard a woman's voice, singing and speaking in a strange tongue and emanating from Dr. Ginath's room, he is intrigued. Because entertaining others was specifically forbidden in the lease, and the woman communicated in an incomprehensible language, he wondered whether Dr. Ginath had created her? Such things are said to have occurred, as in the case of the Golem.

Greifenbach then told the narrator that Dr. Ginath had given him and his wife a gift of extraordinary value: two parched brown leaves with strange lines and markings on them, which he kept in an iron box. Were they written in some secret code, he wonders? Although they look like nothing more than tobacco leaves, Dr. Ginath had specifically told them at the time that they were talismans from a distant land and had said no more about them.

After the Greifenbachs depart for Europe, the narrator keeps his promise and decides to spend a night or two in their house. One evening, he is awakened from his sleep by a strange scratching at the door. He opens it and recognizes his old friend, Gabriel Gamzu. A scholar like Dr. Ginath, Gamzu also spends his time traveling to distant, inaccessible lands in search of ancient texts. Strange things had happened to him. After his marriage to Gemulah, Gamzu's life had changed drastically. He has given up traveling, devoting his every living hour to nursing his bedridden wife. Rather than being grateful to her husband for his kindness, she, perhaps compelled by some inner rage, tears his clothes and scratches his face.

How and why did Gamzu come to the Greifenbachs' house when he did not even know them? Nor had he had any idea that the narrator was spending the night there; it had been a spur-of-the-moment decision. After returning from the synagogue, Gamzu tells his friend, he discovered that his paralyzed wife was no longer at home. How is such a phenomenon possible? the narrator asks. "Every night when the moon is full, my wife gets up from bed and walks to wherever the moon leads her." Even though Gamzu locks the doors and windows, Gemulah finds a way of escaping.

Somnambulism, a complex operation of the psyche, has haunted the imaginations of scientists and writers since early times. Shakespeare's Lady Macbeth reenacted fragments of her crime while sleepwalking at night; Kleist gave his readers a literary description of somnambulism in his play *Das Käthchen von Heilbronn* (1810). In the eighteenth century, the Marquis de Puységur, Mesmer's student, concluded after experimentation, that a universal fluid (electricity) could permeate a human body and endow it with extraordinary powers, even clairvoyance. Scientists have classified some types of somnambulism among hysterical illnesses.

Gemulah may have been a hysteric, simulating unconsciously an organic disease leading to her paralysis, sleepwalking, and aphasia. A victim of overdominant subliminal contents, she has allowed her consciousness to be virtually deprived of its ability to function. Dissociation of mental or bodily functions such as Gemulah experiences, invite fragmented energy packets to operate autonomously in the psyche. The weakened ego-complex, no longer in a position to channel disruptive elements, is unable to integrate explosive or disruptive facets of the psyche, permitting the hyperactivity of dissociative phenomena, such as split-offs and hysteria to dominate.

The somnambulist, suffering, as we shall see, from a dissociative disorder, is possessed of a double personality. Somnambulistic fugues or wanderings may be precipitated, scientists claim, by the freeing of blocked or repressed emotions, forbidden wishes, impulses, or prohibitions, and the memory of those traumatic events that the psyche is unable to face. Gemulah's psychogenic reaction to what she experiences as an intolerable situation compels her to seek gratification in some mysterious manner.

The question now remains as to how and why Gamzu went to the Greifenbachs' house. His response is: "Going to the south, turning to the north, turning goes the wind, and again to its circuits the wind returns." Was he, too, showing symptoms of hysteria? Was he perhaps enslaved by an idée fixe? by an obsessive or autochthonous idea? a thinking disorder interfering with his psychological functioning?

So traumatized had Gamzu felt upon finding his wife's bed empty, that he was suddenly deprived of any sense of recall. Living as he did on such an archaic level of the psyche, he had incorporated the object of his thought (his wife) into his ego (center of consciousness), which he then projected onto the outside world. Because his normal consciousness had been suppressed, no voluntary ego awareness or even memory of his action occurs.

A deeply religious man, Gamzu told the narrator that he had been led to the Greifenbachs' home by some extraterrestrial force. The word "wind," as he had used it, evokes biblical imagery: wind (*Ruach*) is synonymous with the Spirit of God (*breath*), as it had once moved over the primordial waters prior to the Creation" (Gen. 1:2); as "It breathed a living soul into Adam" (Gen. 2:7). Wind is also said to have lifted up Elijah, bringing him to the heavenly realm (2 Kings 2:11) (Kaplan, 42, 49). Psychologically, when wind is strong or agitated, it reveals an unconscious condition of turmoil and instability, as well as a yearning to supplant inner chaos with the comfort of cosmos.

Gamzu, along with his wife, was, indeed, psychologically troubled. His name reveals the personality he would like to have possessed. An ancient Aramaic word meaning "to graft" in fig culture, *gamzu*, describes an individual who intends to bring together (or graft) disparate factors of spirit and psyche with the understanding of integrating these into the whole. The unresolved dichotomies (feminine and masculine, rational and irrational, past and present, Orthodox and Reformed) within Gamzu's psyche were pulling him apart (Hochman, 66).

So involved had Gamzu become in his continuous travels and searchings for ancient volumes and first editions that the inner schism created by his divided and uncentered pulsations had not yet surfaced. Libido had been and still was repressed, exploding only in times of duress, and then manifesting itself solely in affective charges. Limited to a patriarchal environment with intellect or *logos* prevailing, he, like Dr. Ginath, had no time for eros. As a result, his experience with women was virtually nil; nor did he feel the need of developing such relationships. Vulnerable to the extreme, Gamzu had been unable to handle the emotions that had erupted upon first seeing Gemulah in her mountain environment. No confrontation with the volatile passions she had aroused in him occurred; no integration of these into the personality as a whole took place. Overwhelmed by her presence, he became her servant and votary.

The funneling of Gamzu's libido from one extreme (rejection of eros) to its opposite (obsession with eros) had eliminated the energetic tension inherent in a healthy personality. Thus did he became the victim of *enantiodromia:* "when one pair of opposites becomes excessively predominant in the personality, it is likely to turn into its opposite (Edinger, "Outline of Analytical Psychology," 2). Unlike Dr. Ginath, a cerebral, steady, logical, and detached fellow, Gamzu was fundamentally emotional. His behavior was affective, erratic, and, as suggested earlier, even showed symptoms of hysteria.

Gemulah: Shekhinah, Moon, Virgo, Angel

Gamzu first saw Gemulah after following complicated sea routes, then walking forty days in a desert wilderness where he was caught in a sandstorm that blinded him in one eye, whereupon he was finally picked up by a caravan that brought him to a remote area high in the mountains: to the ancient tribal community of Gad ("good fortune" in Hebrew).

That Gamzu spent *forty* days in the wilderness, as Moses had upon the summit of Mt. Sinai, is a number used countless times in both the Old and the New Testaments. The forty days has been prolonged to forty years in biblical texts, reminiscent of the desert wanderings of the Israelites prior to their arrival in the Holy Land (Numbers 32:13). The ordeals experienced are to be understood mythically, as part of an initiation process leading an erstwhile hero to spiritual and psychological development. Would Gamzu's trials expand his consciousness? Would he learn to relate to Gemulah rather than merely idolize her?

When Gevariah, Gemulah's father, realized how ill Gamzu was upon his arrival, he prepared charms that would heal him. Although he recovered, his eye had been destroyed during the desert sandstorm. He would remain blind, thus depriving him, from a symbolistic point of view, of his intuitive and perceptive faculties. His ability, therefore, to confront overwhelming emotional factors would diminish, as would his ability to evaluate, differentiate, or objectify situations and people.

When he first met Gevariah and Gemulah, the impress the two made upon his psyche captivated his every thought. His fascination was most potent during the twilight hours, when listening to them converse in both ancient Hebrew and in a secret language of their own creation. In the evening, when the sun's power (compared so frequently with the rational sphere) declined, the earth becomes enclosed in dimmer lunar luminosities (associated with subliminal spheres). It was then that Gamzu's fantasies roamed with increasing vigor. The sight of Gemulah seated with a white kid lying in her lap and of her father standing nearby, an eagle hovering over his head, transported Gamzu into a state of virtual ecstasy.

Because the goat is associated with lunar spheres (Numbers 28:22), and the eagle, with God (Exod. 19:4), the two were identified in Gamzu's mind, not with individuals per se, but with collective powers. It was as if father and daughter belonged to a mythical past: they were capable of connecting him with his ancestors, thus instilling in him the feelings of well-being that he so desperately needed.

Although mesmerized by Gemulah's outer beauty and gracious bearing, it was her voice, with all of its ancient rhythms, cadences, and feeling tones, that affected him most deeply. The music emanating from her

mouth was like a sounding board for conflating celestial and terrestrial
fluidic forces, for exciting electric currents, with all their affective charges,
to act on his nerves and psyche. "And when she sang, her voice stirred the
heart like that of the bird Grofith, whose song is sweeter than that of any
creature on earth."

Gemulah's strange song was also semantically alluring to Gamzu; its
hidden meanings drew him ever more powerfully to her as an occult force.
Her diapasons and phrases served to hypnotize and intoxicate him, thus
increasing her hold over his world and cutting him off still more powerfully from the everyday domain (Neumann, "Dynamic Aspects of the Psyche"). Unlike the Sirens of old (as depicted by Homer, Aristotle, Pliny,
Ovid, Heine, etc.), Gemulah had no intention of catching the unsuspecting
Gamzu in her web. Rather, it was Gamzu who succumbed to the
numinousness of his vision and the subtle rhythms and tones of her song,
when gazing at her "poised on a rock at the top of a mountain which not
every man could climb, with the moon lighting up her face while she sang,
"*Yiddal, yiddal, yiddal, vah, pah, mah.*" Likewise, according to the
Kabbalists, did the Shekhinah in exile sing songs and hymns to her beloved
husband, God (Scholem, *On the Kabbalah and its Symbolism*, 148; *Zohar*,
2:195b).

Amazed, transfixed, Gamzu likened Gemulah to one of the angels of the
Divine Presence who unites with the Divine Being. The image before him
worked on his conscious judgment like a narcotic, nullifying it to the point
where instinct alone dominated.

Gamzu was *blind* to the fact that Gemulah was a collective figure and
immune to any personal relationship. As her name indicates, "the reciprocal or the reciprocated one," she cannot give of herself; nor can she fulfill
Gamzu's unrealistic expectations of her. His lack of psychological development, his utter inexperience with nonpersonal eros, makes him fertile field
to the power she exudes when standing on the mountain peak bathed in
the luminosity of moonrays (Harding, *Woman's Mysteries*, 119). So taken
was Gamzu by Gemulah that he immediately went to her father to ask for
her hand in marriage.

Why should Gamzu have acted so precipitously? Several factors may
serve to explain his affective reactions. He connected the feminine figure
he saw etched against the heavens with paradise and the primordial
experience of oneness. The intensity of his feeling of belonging and of
being enveloped in the divine sphere, when heretofore he had felt at loose
ends, unrooted, and homeless, enabled him to experience the sense of
blissful unity a child knows: that *participation mystique* that is the
avowed enemy of any developing ego. His archaic vision of Gemulah,
bewitching, alluring, and instilling him with a sense of great joy and

comfort, is also death-dealing. If one is caught up in its seductive and devouring nature, regression and stagnation could readily ensue (Neumann, "Fear of the Feminine," 11).

To be submerged by admiration, to be bewitched by a spell or an illusion, debilitates the power of reason and of evaluation. No confrontation with the feminine principle, which could be instrumental in detaching Gamzu from his vision's impress, is forthcoming, nor can any development of his own individuality be expected. As long as he remains mesmerized by what he perceives to be the most sublime of beings, his incipient ego remains vulnerable to destruction. Important as well is that his ungoverned unconscious and his uncontrollable emotionality allow archetypal imagery—the dominance of a Moon figure—to flood his psyche (Neumann, "Fear of the Feminine," 11).

Mountain symbolism, on the other hand, reveals the presence of a counterforce in the personality; Gamzu's need for the patriarchal realm and for ego-development. Heights, by their very verticality, convey transcendence, spirituality, sacredness; a mountain's mass expresses a power principle. In many religious traditions, mountains have been identified with theophanies and hierophanies: Olympus, Meru, Tabor, Olives, Kaf, Fuji, etc. The mountain peak on which Gevariah stands may be viewed as the closest point of contact between heaven and earth, and as an example of a human being's ascensional needs. Gamzu's sense of urgency, albeit unconscious, indicates a need for finding some figure associated with the heavenly sphere, who would not only accept and care for his wandering soul, but would endow it with wisdom. Unwilling to bind or limit himself to earthly matters alone, Gamzu, like Dr. Ginath, had rejected a life of enslavement to a world of commitment. Their search kept taking them elsewhere.

Gemulah and her father seemingly fulfilled all of Gamzu's needs. They belonged to their landscape and they experienced their attachment to their distant mountains as David had: a stronghold of security and comfort in time of trouble. "Lord, by thy favor thou has made my mountain to stand strong: thou didst hide thy face, and I was troubled. . . . Thou has turned for me my mourning into dancing . . . and girded me with gladness; . . . To the end that my glory may sing praise to thee" (Psalm 30: 7, 11, 12).

Unlike most women identified with the moon, Gemulah did not live in a grove, spring, or grotto: areas where water trickles down. Nor, as is the case of many of her predecessors, is she associated with moisture or fertility. Her habitat is the mountain. Her constellation is the moon, referring not to the body but to the spirit. Let us recall in this connection that Mount Sinai, where God gave Moses the Tablets of the Law, is translated as Mountain of the Moon (Harding, *Woman's Mysteries*, 54).

In ancient Hebrew tradition, the changing aspect of the moon was equated with a nomadic and continuously modified itinerant existence. Its association in Agnon's tale, then, with members of the tribe of Gad and other biblical figures, is analogous. Adam, let us recall, was the first to begin a life of wandering (Gen. 3:24); Cain, the builder of the first city, was destined to the life of a vagabond after his crime (Gen. 4:14); Abraham received God's commandment to leave his father's land and home (Gen. 13:1). The lives of these and other religious exiles, prefigurations of the Diaspora, may be likened to Gamzu's peripatetic existence (Scholem, *On the Kabbalah and Its Symbolism*, 105).

That Gamzu identifies the feminine principle with the moon is also in keeping with the religious beliefs of multiple nations from time immemorial (Hathor, Isis, Artemis, Astarte, Mary, etc.) To associate a constellation with a human being, however, is to endow that person with spiritual and nonearthly qualities, and with collective and nonindividual attributes. As already suggested, Gemulah, as experienced by Gamzu, has no identity, no ego, and is not flesh and blood. She lives in Gamzu's psyche as an aspect of matriarchal consciousness. In that the moon passively reflects the sun's rays, it stands for the indirect, unmanifested, and occult side of knowledge as well as for the cold, impassive, feminine nature. Gemulah is just that. Her connection with the moon transforms her into a measurer, not of abstract quantitative but of qualitative time, with its periods and rhythms, its waxings and wanings. The mysterious connection between the lunar cycle and the woman's biological rhythms (twenty-eight-day cycle), which conditions to a great extent physical and psychological life, has both positive and negative, or light and chthonian, aspects. Equated with the unconscious, the moon, like the dream, represents that pale, barely illuminated side of life that emerges at night.

The "ambivalent" or dark side of the moon, when associated with the Shekhinah, is, as has already been seen, also identified with the notion of exile. Whereas, in the Talmud, God is present wherever the Hebrews are driven, in the Kabbalah, when persecution forces them to wander, "*a part of God Himself is exiled from God* (Scholem, *On the Kabbalah and Its Symbolism*, 107). Such an exile within the Godhead, as represented in mystical texts, is virtually personified: it is tantamount to the banishment of the queen, or the daughter of the king by her husband or father. The abyss between the feminine and masculine principles within the Godhead, as previously suggested, indicates a projection of the duality existing within the hearts and minds of those forced out of their lands. The Shekhinah's exile, during the waning moon, further indicates a degradation of status, a robbing of her light to the point of becoming the "lightless receiver of light" (Scholem, *On the Kabbalah and Its Symbolism*, 108). For this reason, prior to the birth of the new moon, prayers of repentance and fasting were called for by the pious; after its rebirth, prayers of joy. When God was once again reunited with his Shekhinah, the inner division gave way to a condition of original unity and harmony, which then flowed unimpeded throughout the cosmos (Isa. 30:26).

On a psychological plane, God's separation or exile from his Shekhinah, or his feminine principle, suggests a deprivation or rejection of his *anima* (an autonomous psychic content or inner woman in man). To reject an *anima* or soul force is to divest oneself of one's guide or inspiration. Living in a strictly patriarchal sphere, both Gamzu and Dr. Ginath had obliterated any workable eros force, any capacity to relate, to feel deeply for another human being. When Gamzu sees Gemulah on top of the rock, with moonbeams shining all about, he experiences her as a function: a sublime, idealized, untouchable abstraction. As *anima*, she takes on the allure of a mysterious autonomous force projected onto spatial heights. Looking up to her, he is drawn away from his earthbound connection and distracted from his own focus in life. His idolization of Gemulah encourages him to lead an increasingly passive and withdrawn existence, thus trampling and crushing whatever remains of his individuality and creative élan.

That Gamzu equates Gemulah with an angel, an evanescent creature fluttering about in the air, is yet another indication of his atomization of his *anima*. He has an unconscious fear of being trapped by an earthly woman and desires to flee all commitment such a relationship demands. Angels, traveling from the heights to the depths of astral spheres, are messengers, as the Greek word *angelos* suggests. Their functions are multiple: they are destroyers (2 Sam. 24:16); interpreters of God's messages (Job 3:23); and protectors (Gen. 19). Gemulah is, for Gamzu, a mediating force between celestial and earthly spheres, an invisible transformative principle.

That Gamzu equated Gemulah with Virgo, one of the twelve signs of the zodiac, suggests a transformation of primordial energy from unity or the nonformal (within God or an individual), to multiplicity or the formal (as constellation in the heavens). Virgo's visibility, then, indicates her fall into matter or existence, her exile from the Godhead, and her yearning to return to the world of the absolute.

Gemulah, as Virgo (virgin), *anima*, or soul image, must remain unblemished, ethereal, and sublimated. She can, therefore, thrive only as a projection, never as an earthly woman. Like the Shekhinah when exiled from God, so Virgo, if banished from her habitat, will either die, or become a negative power, or both.

The Archetypal Spiritual Father

Gevariah, Gemulah's father, could have been a positive archetypal father-figure for Gamzu. But Gamzu had been unable to objectify his reaction to this sublime, formidable, and awesome figure. Instead, he was transfixed by Gevariah, a spiritual force, particularly when standing, as had Gemulah, on the highest of mountainous peaks: "a sky-blue turban on his head, his complexion and beard set off by his flowing hair, his dark eyes shining like two suns, his feet bare and the color of gold." Gevariah had, Gamzu said, the face of a *lion*, the strength of a *bull*, and the light-footedness of an *eagle* in flight. The three Biblical epithets with which Gevariah is endowed reveal the incredible energy constellated by this figure in Gamzu's psyche: the lion, a sovereign solar-symbol, known as the king of animals, is identified with Judah (Gen. 49:9); the bull, with strength and power (Jer. 50:11); the eagle, with the masculine, spiritual, and fiery nature of the sun-image (Job 9:26; 39:27).

Gevariah[3] has multiple virtues: he leads his people in prayer; he heals the sick; writes charms; teaches the young girls the dances and songs of their people; and forges the weapons for the tribe. Gemulah is Gevariah's mainstay. After his wife died in childbirth, he took no other, preferring to pass his esoteric knowledge down to his daughter. The father-daughter identification experienced by Gamzu was so powerful that his weakly structured ego was overwhelmed by its energetic charge. Frozen, as if caught in a spell, Gamzu was incapable of coping with anything remotely connected with the empirical domain. His inner world was transformed into a blank space, immobilizing whatever healthy instinctual reactions might have helped him. Had Gamzu undergone a numinous experience, an epiphany, unconsciously envisioning the Father-Daughter complex as God and his Shekhinah?

The day Gamzu asked for Gemulah's hand in marriage, Gevariah took him to the highest of the steepest mountains, then dug beneath a certain rock, lifted the stone that blocked access to a cave, went inside and removed a bundle of dry leaves from an earthenware jar, saying,

> There is magic in them . . . as long as they remain in your hands you may control Gemulah's steps so that she will not go astray. . . .
> So, when the nights of the full moon come, take these plants and set them in the window facing the door, and hide them so that no

---

[3]*Gevariah* has two parts in Hebrew: *gever*, meaning man, strength, power; the suffix *iah* is the name of God. *Gevariah*, then, might be translated as the "strength of God."

man will notice them, and I assure you that if Gemulah leaves the house she will return to you before the moon returns to her proper sphere.

Strange characters had been written on these leaves, Gamzu noted. As for their colorations, they were unrecognizable: mixtures of gold, azure, purple, and the primary colors of the rainbow, all of which altered with silvery moon strands and tones of seaweed as if drawn from the depths of the sea.

Before Gamzu's marriage took place, he went to Vienna to see if his blind eye could be made to see. It could not. Upon his return to Gemulah's mountain region, he sensed that something had changed. What it was, he did not know. He had been told, nevertheless, that a holy man, a Hacham Gideon of Jerusalem, had stayed with Gevariah's tribe for six months, that he had healed the sick, alleviated much suffering, and had recorded Gemulah's songs and conversations in his notebook. Then, one day, as Gevariah walked to the mountaintop in an attempt to learn from the eagles how they renew their youth, one of the birds of prey attacked and mauled him with his talons. Neglecting his wounds, Gevariah grew steadily worse, remaining alive only to witness and direct the seven nights of dancing, singing, and feasting celebrating his daughter's wedding.

Gemulah: The Shekhinah in Exile

Only after a year of mourning did Gemulah agree to leave her land and make the long, hard journey, by caravan and ship, to Israel. Gamzu's return to Jerusalem indicated a step toward wholeness; for Gemulah, it meant exile. Excision from her native soil, could only lead to catastrophe. Her ancestral home, symbolizing for her sustenance and support, had suddenly vanished. As if standing high on thin air now, Gemulah's rock of generations, which had endowed her with the solidity and energy needed to pursue her work as her father's daughter and as inspiration for her tribe, had suddenly been withdrawn. Undone, divested of her original roots and function, she no longer felt a sense of continuity. Her ancestral soul had been banished, the spiritual power she had inherited from her father and his father before him, giving her life dignity and purpose, had been drained. Dissociated with the archetypal foundations of her psyche, she no longer had a collective role to play for her people, nor was she the bearer of her father's secret wisdom. What remained? To be an incompetent wife.

Because of the father-daughter identification, Gemulah related, psychologically, to paternal *logos:* the spiritual male force within her (*animus*), characterized by cognition. As a female replica of paternal spiritual knowledge, she had been endowed, as had her father, with intense energetic tension, that is, with numinousness. Because she had been her father's helpmate, she had been looked upon as a kind of high priestess for the tribe of Gad, a community of lost souls (Jung, *Collected Works*, 1:5).

Once she had relocated in Jerusalem, Gemulah was incapable of facing her now-empty existence. A vast and fearful void opened up before her. Divested of her spiritual mission, and with no love or sexual longing for her husband, nothing could fill the seemingly infinite vacuum that cannibalized her being. Depression and illness set in; song and speech were withheld (Franz, *Creation Myths*, 206). Inwardness and motor aphasia led to depression. The withdrawl of libido from the empirical world and its introjection into the unconscious, led to a concomitant loss of interest in any and all activities in the empirical domain. Blackness prevailed in her silent, cold, remote, and unfathomable inner realm.

Always her father's daughter, Gemulah had never been able to develop into an independent woman. Tied as she was to the patriarchal sphere, she had always adjusted her individuality to the will and needs of the collective. Regression is implicit in such a relationship, based as it is on an unconscious self-renunciation, and perhaps even a suicidal tendency. That Gemulah passively accepted to play such a role in life indicated her ego's fascination with her father's mythical world.

Just as struggle and confrontation were lacking when Gamzu projected the form of Gemulah onto his *anima*, so the same may be said to have happened to Gemulah, dominated as she was by her *animus*, represented by her father. As such, she was contained in the collective world of the tribe and therefore was and would always be her father's daughter.

Both Gamzu and Gemulah reacted to their unconscious condition of psychological stasis instinctually and affectively. Gemulah, however, adding inertia to an already passive and weakly structured ego, and a fear and inability to relate to the outside world, was continuously driven back to the spiritual domain of the father archetype. No transition to independence could come to pass, nor could there be any progressive development of the ego without struggle or fight. Because she never developed her own feminine side, she existed as an extension of her father: *logos*, spirit, sublimation, etherealness.

When Gamzu, married and living in Jerusalem at the time, discovers that the precious leaves Gevariah had given him are lost, and that Gemulah, on the night of the full moon has not returned home, he tells the narrator that not long ago he had sold some ancient texts, and he thinks that the precious leaves may have been mixed with them. Just as they had disappeared, so had his power over Gemulah's somnambulism vanished.

As Gamzu informs the narrator that his wife is nowhere to be found, his facial features alter: they resemble "formless clay," as if he had suddenly been divested of his soul. As if unconsciously propelled to do so, he turns his head toward the door, the window, and the wall. Voices are heard. A strange language is being spoken. Gamzu rushes to Dr. Ginath's anteroom. The narrator follows. Both are greeted by an incredible sight: moonlight fills the room as Gemulah, wrapped in white, in a somnambulant trance, speaks to her spiritual lover—Dr. Ginath—in her esoteric tongue. He, seated at a table, takes down her every word.

Reminiscent in some ways of Wagner's motif in *The Flying Dutchman* and of Ibsen's *Lady From the Sea*, in which heroines await the arrival of the "stranger" to experience their great love, so Gemulah serves her beloved as she once had her father: as *logos*. Had she lived out her passion concretely, she might have detached herself from her father's image or transferred its archetypal power to that of her lover. In a somnambulant trance, however, she was not conscious of what she was doing or speaking. In love with Dr. Ginath, the Hacham Gideon who had visited her land when Gamzu was away in Vienna, the vulnerable and inexperienced Virgo side of her character prevailed. Like Gamzu, she is acted upon, not actor (Harding, *Woman's Mysteries*, 120). Panic-stricken by what he sees, and fearful of losing his soul or what he considers to be his love, Gamzu rushes towards Gemulah and flings his arms around her waist. She draws back, calling to Hacham Gideon—Dr. Ginath, in reality—who tells her she must follow her husband. She begs to be allowed to remain with Dr. Ginath, maintaining that she is no one's wife, and promising to sing the song of the Grofith bird, which can only be sung once in a lifetime, after which it dies. He still refuses. Gamzu grasps her weakened body and takes her home.

There she remains, but only until the moon has completed its cycle. Once it shines anew and in all of its radiance, she, like the Shekhinah, seeks to unite with her Beloved. The reader learns that tragedy ensued from an article that the narrator happened to read in a newspaper. An eyewitness account reports the death of Dr. Ginath, who had gone out of his room to rescue a woman climbing to the roof. When he rushed up to her, however, the parapet collapsed and both fell to their death.

Neither Dr. Ginath nor Gemulah could have met a different fate in Agnon's parable. She existed for her scholar-lover as she had for her father and for Gamzu: as *logos*. In exile, like the Shekhinah, she had been divested of her function as inspiration to her people; thus she was cut off from her purpose and goal in life. Attempting to resume her role as *logos* for her lover-scholar, and failing to do so, she felt bereaved. Spirit had been cut off from its lifeline. Gemulah, who had never existed as a flesh-and-blood human being, but only as a disembodied voice going back to the beginning of time, never died because she never lived. Redeemed, like the Shekhinah, she has returned from her exile and united with her Beloved, in the written word. Gemulah is *voice*; Dr. Ginath, *transcriber*. The books resulting from their oneness have been disseminated throughout the world: "Anyone who is not blind, anyone who has the power to see, readily makes use of his light."

6 Kawabata's *The Master of Go:* Game as Ritual of Exile

Yasunari Kawabata's[1] *The Master of Go* (1954) concentrates on the game of Go as a ritual of exile into death. The events, based on a real Go match that began in Tokyo on 26 June 1938 and concluded on 4 December at Ito, were written up by Kawabata for Osaka and Tokyo newspapers. His narrative version of the match appeared in book-form more than a decade after the defeat of Japan in World War II.

In *The Master of Go*, labeled a combination of reportage, memoir, chronicle-novel, and autobiography, names are fictionalized, except for that of the "invincible" Go Master (Shusai), who is also a Zen Master. The championship match, lost by the old and ailing Master, lasts fourteen sessions—nearly six months—with a three-month respite from August to mid-November. The Master's death from heart failure follows shortly thereafter. His defeat may be looked upon as a metaphor of the Japanese military defeat (which took the lives of many of Kawabata's immediate

---

[1]Yasunari Kawabata (1899–1972) was born in Osaka, Japan. Having lost his parents in infancy, he lived his early years, marked by extreme loneliness and melancholy, with his grandparents. He described his grandfather's last days in his earliest extant work, *Diary of a Sixteen-year Old* (1925). He received his degree from Tokyo Imperial University in 1924. The setting for many of his works during the 1920s was the Izu peninsula (see, for example, *The Izu Dancer*, 1926). In the 1930s he focused on Asakusa, the center of Tokyo's underworld (*The Scarlet Gang of Asakusa* was serialized in 1929 and 1930). The hot-springs resort in the mountains of central Japan was the setting for *Snow Country* (1935). Kawabata lived in Kamakura and its environs from 1936 on, distancing himself from nationalist war hysteria. Solitariness and a sense of homelessness marked his life. Kawabata is also noted for *Thousand Cranes* (1951), and *House of Sleeping Beauties* (1960–61), among other works. He developed many young talents, notably that of Mishima, and was the first Japanese to be awarded the Nobel Prize (1968).

relatives) as well as the end of both a moral and aesthetic aristocratic tradition.

The game of Go, which originated in China, was imported into Japan around the tenth century. It was in its adopted country, however, that it "flowered . . . elevated and deepened," writes Kawabata. An infinitely complex game, Go is not to be confused with chess or checkers. Going beyond the diversionary nature of contest per se, it invites participants to undergo a deeply spiritual experience, so profound, indeed, as to take them out of their ego-oriented world and immerse them into the intricate patternings and interrelationships involved in the transpersonal experience.

That Kawabata chooses a game as the pivotal force around which to construct his chronicle-novel is significant. Games are metaphors of struggle: a means of pitting one's actions and reasoning powers against another's, a way of determining one's place in life, and an example of one's need to risk the security of an established position. Games may also be viewed as structures able to bring order to anarchical situations, substituting a thinking and objective realm for a more primitive and instinctual world. Go, even more than chess or similar games, calls for extreme cerebralness rather than spontaneity, abstraction instead of concreteness.[2] Played on a square wooden board with Black and White stones, the complex combinations of plays and modes are, for the Japanese, also dependent upon intuition and the chance factor. The game may, therefore, be viewed as a world unto itself: a microcosm within a macrocosm, or an expression of mankind's limited freedom within an unlimited universe.

"The Master Filled in a Neutral Point"

Kawabata begins his chronicle-novel with the protagonist's last play: "The Master filled in a neutral point." The psychodrama, starting at the end, that is, after the Master's death, reveals the intense connection existing between the old player and the White stones he places on the wooden Go board. In successive flashbacks, readers learn how he slowly effaces himself from empirical reality while immersing himself more deeply in his game of Go. Because each successive move increases his sense of exile, the Master finally ceases to exist as an independent person. Psychologically, we may say that his libido (psychic energy), like blood, is being withdrawn from his body and poured into the White stones. The progressive imbal-

---

[2]Analogies may be made between the Oriental's notion of the game and Occidental works such as Stéphane Mallarmé's "Never will a Dice Throw Abolish Chance," Aleksandr S. Pushkin's *Queen of Spades*, and Jean Cocteau's *Children of the Game*.

ance, while diminishing his vigor, strengthens the magic link established between the Master and each of his succeeding plays.

This highly cerebral contest, awakening the Master to a new life and a different reality, also functions as a ceremony leading to a ritualized exile and demise. The intense absorption and concentration required of the players during the match, lasting nearly a year, drains all participants of that very power that entices to life.

That Kawabata writes "The Master filled in a neutral point" is not only a psychological commentary on the interaction between human and inanimate factors during the game process, but a metaphysical appraisal as well. The "neutral" symbolizes the Master's slow but final disengagement from the game of life. The "point," or unity, existing in the Origin, or Beginning—that is, prior to the opening of the game—as opposed to the diversity in the differentiated world, or an already started match, suggests a subtle return to the nonformal stage (Void). For the Buddhists, the Void, a progressive concept that varies depending upon the sect to which one belongs, suggests the absence of ego and dualism and the existence of a transpersonal sphere of infinite luminousness in which the interdependence of all phenomena and concepts reigns. The Void, also referred to as the "Great Emptiness," is, paradoxically, the source of all things, or, as Jung noted, a complex of opposites.

The neutral space on the Go board, if viewed as a Void, no longer exists linearly, but beyond time and space. Zen Buddhist painters have illustrated such a concept in their brushing of a few lines onto paper, surrounded and interlaced by empty areas. The image of vacuity succeeds in conveying a profound sense of cosmic loneliness (Izutsu, 182–83). The "neutral point," understood as both Origin and Ultimate, alpha and omega, or the life-and-death experience, is implicit in Zen Buddhist, Taoist, and Shinto traditions. Viewed as a totality and not, as in the West, in terms of a loss or gain, past or present, life and death are part of a process, as attested to by a fifteenth-century Zen Buddhist monk: "I take a rest as I switch from the path of suffering to the path of enlightenment; if it rains, let it! If the wind blows, let it!" (Awakawa, 28). What the Westerner considers to be polarities or antithetical situations (life and death), the Oriental understands as being multitiered and having various spheres and levels within a cosmic totality. Life and death are contained one in the other, each being experienced in the other's realm in relative degrees of purpose and power.

Life is considered metaphorically by the Japanese as a journey between the world of illusion—implying the full range from suffering and conflict to plenitude and serenity—and death, viewed as a release and the awarding of freedom. In keeping with this transformatory notion of flux is the epithet ascribed to Kawabata ("the eternal traveler") because he was in the habit of wandering about Japan composing his works. So, too, is the Master of Go a wanderer and "rootless" in the metaphysical sense: he is deeply entrenched in Go, as a game, but also as a paradigm of Zen Buddhism, Taoism, and Shintoism.

The notion of flux at the heart of these philosophical concepts is expressed in the temperament of the Master, Shusai, and also, although less so in his younger and more modern opponent, Otaké. The old man is at one with nature and with the cosmic flow, each echoing the other's merging into the other, thereby fulfilling the circularity of the exilic design: the transformation from one sphere of being to the other. The Master faces old age, therefore, not with fear or desolation, but as part of the natural growing, evolving, expanding ritual of exile, to be performed until he attains, as closely as he can while still living, the experience of nirvana or enlightenment.

During the lengthy months the game is being played, the Go Master never feels sorry for himself, nor does he express terror or any other emotion at his defeat or approaching death. Unlike the Westerner's carpe diem, which suggests that one should live life to the hilt as it will terminate anyway, the Master, in keeping with Zen Buddhist views, believes that every episode in the life process must reach its own plenitude, one event having no more importance than another. Implicit in the eternal transformatory process is that no event has a beginning or an end in the circular coming and going. To fear death is to be bound to a host of superstitions. It is to be paralyzed, to be unable to live life fully in each of its manifestations. Once perturbation imposes itself upon a human being, the very notion of cosmic fluidity is shattered. Detachment, such as the Master knows, allows him to divest himself of emotional hindrances that might otherwise prevent him from being in tune with the impalpable and palpable universe. The burden of such hindrances would deprive him of the power of concentration needed for the playing of Go.

Because the Master in both the game of life and of Go is filling "a neutral point," thus experiencing the notion of perpetual flux, nature, glimpsed by him throughout the contest, is neither concrete nor fixed; rather, it is motile, timeless, the "mystery of being-becoming and becoming-being" (Awakawa, 254). Because the Go Master does not consider his existence as a series of disparate moments, nature appears to him rather as part of a cosmic landscape in an eternal unfolding. The outer world is an integral part of himself, physically and spiritually, an aspect of his own fullness/emptiness/neutral point/void.

Since the continuous exiles inherent in the life/death experience are viewed as an infinite number of progressions within the universe, they also reflect the Oriental's traditional views as manifested in Zen Buddhism, Taoism, and Shintoism. Life, then, is not ego-centered as it is conceived to be by the Westerner. Nor is the sine qua non of the individual's earthly existence focused on the continuous construction and strengthening of a personal identity. The Oriental's world is cosmic-centered, diffused rather than unified or synthesized. Life consists of a series of parts, or, as in the game, a group of stones, isolated in space or on a board and not bound together according to Western rational patterns. Intuitive and not syllogistic or logical thought processes are the bases for the Master's world-view. Existence is a series of fleeting moments. Life and death are implicit in the rotating patterns of universal flux. Mind, matter, and time are conceived by the Westerner as something tangible and concrete: they are real; past, present, and future are the bases for his everyday activities. The Zen Buddhist considers time as unreal. Nothing is permanent for him because continuity and duration do not exist. Cyclical and nonlinear time-frames predominate. Life, like a game, is a series of agglomerations: after the game has been completed, the board lies empty, ready for another scheme. Time, as we know it, is a concept devoid of meaning for the Oriental. It is a figment of the mind. For him, and for the Master of Go, there is no past, no future. The only concrete reality is the *moment* or actuality: the experience of playing Go.

The Master, therefore, neither disavows nor fears the aging process. It is conceived, as are youth and childhood, as part of a pattern in the complex cosmic experience. Like the Black and White stones to be placed on the board, physical age is approached in a detached manner, in terms of flux or nowness, no more to be conquered, rejected, or reviled, than nature itself. Each state in life, as in the game, lives in its plenitude, arouses wonderment or sorrow, contains its own dignity, and inspires the compassion or admiration befitting it. The phenomenon of humanity, whether revealed in a young and beautiful body or in an old one, even a dead one, conveys a human being's close connection with nature as part of the cosmos. No distinction, therefore, is to be made between one form of life or another: "the plants and trees, the land itself, shall all attain Buddhahood" (Awakawa, 23). The Master, as well as the stones with which he plays his game of life and Go, are metaphors of sequential exiles. Like a flower, tree, mountain, or spirit, each manifests itself to humanity, then exiles itself from its sight, returning into the void.

Both the Master and the challenger are imbued with Japanese religious traditions of Shintoism, Taoism, and Zen Buddhism, which will now be most briefly described in order to acquaint the reader with the emphasis placed on inwardness in Kawabata's work.

Shintoism, "the way of the Gods," is an animistic religion with no official scriptures. It teaches that a life force exists in all things, animate or inanimate. Everything in nature, including the Black and White stones with which Go is played and the simple wooden board on which moves are made, is endowed with spirit or soul. Shinto nature-worship is based on the simple feeling of "awe" for nature. Particular phenomena, such as a waterfall, a crag, a tree, an interestingly shaped mound of gravel, a flower, or an insect, are imbued with an essence, a force that inspires awe. Whatever inspires such a feeling is called a *kami*, which has been translated as "God" or "above," that is, "superior" to mortal beings. Shinto deities, or kami, are many and may include the spirits of trees, mountains, flowers, deified ancestors, emperors, heroes, the sun, the moon. Humans approach the kami without fear and in friendship. Before doing so, however, they must purify themselves by washing their hands and taking part in devo- tions, such as standing in a sacred enclosure, in a grove or shrine on a mountain. Once the ceremony is completed, they are worthy of entering the shrine and experiencing a sense of awe: that dynamic force of liv- ingness, that incredible energy which allows the worshiper to feel (a para- doxical notion for the Westerner) oneness or Nonattachment with nature.

The notion of Oneness or Nonattachment is readily discernible in every page of Kawabata's chronicle-novel. The game ends in autumn, when gardens are already cold and color tones are "at the edge of darkness," setting the mood and the mystery of the Master's lonely and reflective approach to Go. His detachment is manifest when he is taken to a hotel at Kawana with its beautiful garden, broad lawn, golf courses, and sea. There, the Master "sat in silence, as if not even aware of the view before him." When Kawabata describes the old man bent forward climbing a short slope, the one blends into the whole:

> I could not see the lines on the palms of the small hands he held tightly clasped behind him, but the network of veins seemed to be complex and delicate. He was carrying a folded fan. His body, bent forward from the hips, was perfectly straight, making his legs seem all the more unreliable. From below the thicket of dwarf bamboo, along the main road, came a sound of water down a narrow ditch. Nothing more—and yet the retreating figure of the Master some- how brought tears to my eyes. I was profoundly moved, for reasons I do not myself understand. In that figure walking absently from the game there was the still sadness of another world. The Master seemed like a relic left behind by Meiji.

Nature for the Shintoist is a hierophany: a manifestation of sacrality that may be experienced aesthetically through an intuitive sensitivity. To stand or walk through beautiful and pure surroundings, as does the Master in the above quotation, indicates an inner awareness, an awe for the sacredness of nature of which he is a part.

Japanese Zen Buddhism is modified Indian Buddhism, divested of most of its theology. A philosophy for the most part, it seeks to transmit the Buddha-Essence of the Buddha-Mind to humanity through silent meditation and abstract contemplation. If properly experienced, *Satori*, or enlightenment, may result: "the immediate esthetic perception of reality" which makes itself known through flashes of intuition that reveal "the truth about the universe." At such moments the acolyte may transcend his individuality (i.e., ego-consciousness), and know Self-consciousness (i.e., cosmic-consciousness). Unity of existence underlies the meditative practice: the mind becomes vacant and detached from worldly problems while at the same time absorbing the universe into itself. No longer disturbed by the vicissitudes of daily life, it remains serene when faced with adversity and thus is able to know the is-ness or now-ness of the world. There is no God in Zen, no rational or syllogistic reasoning. Zen is an intuitive, not an intellectual experience. It cannot be taught. It is a way of life (Suzuki, *Zen and Japanese Culture*, 4–16).

Tao is an energetic force in the universe that generates everything. The individual, even after Cosmic Oneness was divided into two forces—*yin* (feminine) and *yang* (masculine)—is implicit in nature. Taoism preaches silence, meditation, inwardness, the nonexistence of fear, replaced by a kind of serenity. The level of concord known to an individual may be increased through the practice of contemplation. Taoism is a mystical acceptance of an incorporation into nature, which allows the psyche to unfold and become integrated within cosmic consciousness. Lao-tzu's *Tao-te-ching* (*The Book of the Way and Its Power*, sixth century, B.C.E.) opens the way to transcending the mundane and artificial nature of empirical existence, favoring an intuitive and spontaneous rapport with Tao in nature and in oneself. *The Book of the Way and Its Power* also reveals a path in which heart and mind find harmony or unity within the sacred modes of consciousness.

Because religion is lived out in its natural and cultural forms by the Master, and on a lower level by the young Otaké, both are able at times to establish an emotional and spiritual rapport with natural forces: a glowing sun, or the misty moistness of its dim shadows cast rapturously upon the black earth. Storms also replicate inner feelings, not as a technical device, as used by Western novelists to heighten atmosphere, but rather as a manifestation of nature's own personality: her capricious, rambunctious, playful, angered side, frequently followed by a tenderly loving and caressable aspect.

> The white stones, reflected on the mirrorlike face of the board,
> became one with the figure of the Master, and the violence of the
> wind and rain in the garden seemed to intensify the stillness of the
> room.

Kawabata's protagonists and the world from which they emanate come
through in *The Master of Go* as clusters of intuitive visions and as sequences of exiles and awakenings.

> When the play began, however, the sky was lightly clouded over
> once more. There was a strong enough breeze that the flowers in
> the alcove swayed gently. Aside from the waterfall in the garden
> and the river beyond, the silence was broken only by the distant
> sound of a rock-cutter's chisel. A scent of red lilies wafted in from
> the garden. In the almost too complete silence a bird soared
> grandly beyond the eaves.

Should a protagonist touch a pebble, finger a cherry blossom, or look out
upon a mountain in the distance as it breaks through a cloud, the opaque
becomes transparent, inviting that which lies beyond human vision to
enter into understanding. For Kawabata's protagonists, immersed in
Shinto, Zen, and Taoism, to drink a drop of seawater is to have imbibed
the waters of all the oceans in the universe.

The Way of Go: Black/White

Go is played with Black and White stones on a normally plain wooden
board. In Kawabata's work, however, the board is greatly prized for its
brilliant lacquer finish, intersected into 361 crosses by 19 lines. A work of
art in and of itself, the glowing board represents a living monument to the
aristocratic taste the Master values so highly.

Lacquer (*maki-e*) technique was developed during the Heian period
(794–1185). At that time colors along with gold and silver dust or particles
were sprinkled onto sticky lacquer and allowed to dry, after which the
surface was sanded to bring out the luster. The process was repeated over
and over again, depending upon the kind of luster that was desired (Baker,
105). Because lacquer is a toxic gum and difficult to work, only a highly
skilled craftsman is capable of achieving the wanted effects. Even he
works slowly, particularly when introducing other materials and colors
into whatever he is making. Equal caution is required during the drying
process, which requires a very humid atmosphere (Swann, 121).

The goal of the Go player is to fill the board with as many stones as he can, thereby occupying his opponent's corner. A very special kinetic faculty, as some have called it, is needed to become a Master of this excessively intricate game. Like Noh and Sumo wrestling, among other Japanese arts, one usually begins its study at nine or ten years of age, thus blending intellectual and metaphysical disciplines.

The stones used in Go have psychological as well as spiritual connotations. In that we are dealing with an object in the phenomenological world, we may suggest that each piece contains both ego and the wider notion of Self. Attempting to give psychological perspective to certain Zen Buddhist notions, Jung writes: "In the same way as the *ego* is a certain knowledge of my *self*, so is the self a knowledge of my ego, which, however, is no longer experienced in the form of a broader or higher ego, but in the form of a non-ego [*Nicht Ich*]" (Foreword to Suzuki, *An Introduction to Zen Buddhism*, 13).

The concept behind the use of Black and White stones in the game of Go indicates the Zen Buddhist's "negative attitude" toward color as an aesthetic experience. These sober hues, perhaps better than anything else, convey the thought of the utter loneliness and sadness in human existence. As the Zen Master Sengai (1750–1837) wrote in his *Song of Solitary Life:*

> I come alone,
> I die alone;
> In between times
> I'm just alone day and night.

> (Izutsu, 175)

One of the principles of Zen Buddhist painting involves the elimination of colors, except for black and white, which, strictly speaking, are not considered colors in that they are composites of all other hues. Nature's limitless shadings and tonalities are reduced to their austere components. This is the best way to convey a mood of sobriety, quietude, and stillness. Such willed poverty of colorations, in contrast to the brilliant tones used during the Heian period (794–1185) and the sumptuous splendors of the Momoyama period (1573–1615), achieves the deepest strata of beauty in the sublimation and consummation of an individual's solitariness during the course of his or her earthly journey (Izutsu, 175).

The austerity of colors, allowing the Go participants to live in the absence of all ornate hues, divests them as well of their accompanying energy charges. Existing alone, in seemingly vacant space, the players are made metaphysically aware of the eternal Void. Such a colorless or monochromatic state also renders concrete the unlimited nature of colors: within black and white exists the echo of all hues, thus paving the way for the Zen Buddhist's positive aesthetic.

Just as sobriety of color exists in the Black and White pieces used in Go, so Kawabata eliminates all flamboyant colorations in his prose. Moderation and restraint serve to enrich his palette in the Zen Buddhist sense, allowing for noncolor to activate the inner world of his protagonists. The unstated and the unseen exist within the monochromatic touches splashed here and there in the text. They are sensed as desolate twilight tones, along with pearls, greys, shadows, reflections, reverberations, blacks, and whites capable of arousing tension, but also of subduing and sublimating feelings of anguish.

The prevalence of black and white hues and the paucity of strident tones throughout the book create a climate of loneliness and also of emptiness, so dear to Zen Buddhism. Because black and white include all other colors, and vacancy (the Void) contains all dissolved phenomenal forms of being, one might suggest that each time the Master and Otaké move their stones spiritual energy pours from the players into the pieces. The consciousness of such an event releases contestants increasingly from what Westerners term the "I-ness" of consciousness (ego), enabling them to see things from a different perspective: only what is actually there being perceived (Jung, Foreward to Suzuki, *An Introduction to Zen Buddhism*, 21).

Each of the Black and White stones as well as the brilliantly lacquered board is imbued with its own emptiness, spiritual energy, and aura of sacredness. Such objects, charged with the energy the players invest in them, may be considered as hierophanies. The game, therefore, cannot be flippantly thought of as a mere pastime; it must be approached as a ritual, with veneration and solemnity.

The players experience the awesomeness of Emptiness in the spatial intervals between the stones. The sacred moves about freely within these open areas, interacting and intersecting with visible forms. Inside and outside of the squares, viewed as harsh and aggressive boundary lines, or as harmonious coalescences, life is affirmed or depleted, as nonbeing emerges (Ellwood and Pilgrim, 144).

Whenever the Master or Otaké touch the Black and White hierophanies, these newly energized objects become the recipients of intense thought, and of energy waves: mute actors participating in the cosmic flow. The motility of the players' perceptions or ideas, as decanted into the Black and White stones, replicates the philosophical notion of perpetual transformation: "the Master seemed to be lost in vast distances." In this regard, the game of Go becomes both a rite of exile (the manner chosen by the Master to exit from the empirical world into another realm) and a rite of entrance for his opponent, who will be assuming the position of Master with the responsibilities such a title implies.

White and black, like two opposing cosmic forces, two energetic powers pitted against each other in battle array, are not dead matter but objects invested with livingness. "The unmoving stones," Kawabata wrote, "as I gazed at them from the side of the board, spoke to me as living creatures. The sound of the stones on the board seemed to echo vastly through another world." Each play of the stones is an expression of an anonymous process, harboring its own overtones and nuances, sustaining an infinite number of atoms, stirring intuitive experiences by means of gestures.

What do white and black symbolize? The former, a diurnal force, represents the manifest world, the dawn of life, the prebeginning. For the Oriental, white is also linked to death, because death exists prior to life. White is the Master's color. He uses this hue, the absence or sum of all colors (nothingness or everythingness) with "appetite," obsessively, as if he "were giving himself up to the fangs of gaming devils" and penetrating "the deeper recesses of a strange Japanese tradition." As in a Noh drama or a Zen tea ceremony, he builds his stones in White triangle formation. "It perhaps told of his age and experience, the fact that like the flow of water or the drifting of clouds a White formation quietly took shape over the lower reaches of the board in response to careful and steady pressure from Black."

Otaké's color is Black. A replica of night, shadow, the earth force, it suggests growth and fertility, the nondifferentiated *prima materia*, an expression of the beginning and end of all things. Black is "aggressive," as is Otaké; it is "diabolical," mirroring his bold and uncontained instinctual world. Black spreads rapidly from stone to stone, throughout the board, replicating the "ferocity" for which Otaké is known. During the game, the sky suddenly turns an inky hue, unleashing a downpour. Trees, flowers, bushes, reflect their reactions to the atmosphere of disquietude within the Go board, the pieces, and the contestants. However, the storm soon abates.

> The Master stood firm and averted a crisis. He retreated a pace and forestalled disaster. A magnificent play, it cannot have been easy to make. Black had charged into a headlong assault, and with this one play White had turned it back. Black had made gains, and yet it seemed that White, casting away the dressings from his wounds, had emerged with greater lightness and freedom of action.

The sky brightens, the clouds break, the sun emerges beyond the valley, and the shrill sounds of locusts are heard. Moments later, tranquility again impresses itself upon the happenings. The now-ness and the is-ness of the world outside is but an echo of nature's capriciousness.

White and Black are as different as the Master's and Otaké's approaches to Go. The younger contestant, an ultrarational man for whom science, rules, and regulations are uppermost, lacks the "grace and elegance" associated with Go as art. "The finesse and subtlety of the warrior's way," which flourished during the Meiji period (1868–1912), is foreign to him, but not to the Master. Otaké is unaware of the older man's desire to turn every undertaking into a "masterpiece" and a thing of beauty. Nor does he pay due respect to his elders, as has been traditional since earliest times in Japan. Otaké conducts his campaign as if he is battling only to win, without recalling "the dignity and the fragrance of Go as an art."

Go: Exile as Art

As the Zen artist carves out a figure from a piece of wood or from an inorganic material, so the Master and Otaké reconstruct in the game a domain in keeping with their vision. Alone, aloof, solitary, exiled in a world of their own, the participants reach out, by means of the stones, beyond dualistic notions into transpersonal spheres. These mediating powers into which the players have decanted their libido are instrumental in helping them attain higher spheres: the unknown, that giant emptiness that may lead them to satori (Suzuki, *Zen and Japanese Culture*, 16ff.). Jung describes such a spiritual happening in terms of a breakthrough of "a consciousness limited to the ego-form in the form of the non-ego-like self." According to Jung, satori may be viewed psychologically, as "a release of the ego through self, to which 'Buddha-Nature,' or godly universality, is added" (Foreward to Suzuki, *An Introduction to Zen Buddhism*, 14).

Nearly every chapter of the forty-one in *The Master of Go* begins with a specific move or refers to one or more. The highly developed intuitive sense of the participants succeeds in destroying the blockage imposed upon them by consciousness, allowing the invisible to be visible. Such displacement of libido, allowing an unlimited flow into the collective unconscious, serves to increase activity in the subliminal sphere, leading to a breakthrough of content into consciousness. Because the unconscious is the "matrix" of creativity, the impact of these tremulous pulsations heightens awareness, and in so doing, expands consciousness. Both the Master and Otaké experience such interaction and fluidity metaphysically as participants in a game, enabling them to know the fruit of exile in the work of art (Jung, Foreward to Suzuki, *An Introduction to Zen Buddhism*, 22).

The breakthrough into timelessness and cosmic harmony implicit in Go is likewise unequivocal in many Japanese sculptures, such as *Myoe Shonin meditating*, by the thirteenth-century Enichibo Jonin (Baker, 92). So, too, the configuration of the game is like an art object: a means of transcending the empirical sphere and reaching Buddhahood. Go, as a meditation, enables the player to be in touch with his own Buddhahood, his own essence, bringing him to a new level of understanding in his perpetual quest for enlightenment. Go, the medium most suitable to the Master's temperament, invites him to experience a breakthrough and know that unanalyzable creative power which transforms a game into art (Ellwood and Pilgrim, 33–35).

Although seemingly disconnected, the moves of the Go pieces, around which Kawabata's chronicle-novel gravitates, are at the core of the artistic process. Whether the move is made by the Master or Otaké, it is described as expansively as possible: physically, spiritually, and psychically. Even more important, the participants are depicted as connected progressively to the White or Black stones, not only in keeping with their inner and outer states, but also as part of an immediate environment within the larger framework of a universal experience.

Because the various stages of the Master's progressive exile from life are delineated in each of the chapters and, simultaneously, Otaké's exile from a lesser to a higher degree of mastery, great care is given to mood and pace. The Master's eyes, eyebrows, lips, strands of hair, are elliptically and objectively alluded to as living components of a body. Each is viewed both as a separate power and as part of a complex totality.

The Master's eyelids, for example, are "swollen"; his speech slow, "as if to relieve the heaviness of the air"; his voice "low but intense"; when rising to his feet, he holds a folded fan in his hand, reminiscent of "a warrior readying his dirk." He is a *samurai*, heart and soul, prepared to carry out the precepts of the "Way of the Warrior." Very much of the Zen Buddhist and Taoist inwardness and strength are visually conveyed in the way he holds himself when seated: his left hand buried "in the overskirt of his kimono" and "his right hand tightly clenched," as "he raised his head and looked straight before him." Each move he makes takes him through the vastness of eternal time, in seconds, minutes, hours: youth is an active state; age is slow. Whenever the Master's eyelids close, linearity yields to long meditation. Listening inwardly to the Lotus Sutra, the Master sways slowly and gently to the rhythms of the monotonous incantations inhabiting the very fiber of his being, now welded to the Great Nothingness. Whatever his activity, whether slow-paced or rapid, inner or outer, multiple layers are touched upon, sources of energy tapped, and mysterious harmonies unfold.

The old hermit, Basu-sen, in a work of art by Tankei (1173–1256), stooping forward, his right shoulder protruding, and holding a sutra scroll in his right hand, though physically frail and gaunt, discloses an indomitable strength in the intensity of his faith (Baker, 112). Likewise, the Master, his asceticism revealed in the little flesh left to his body, resembles an "undernourished child." His skeletal form, like Basu-sen's, is pure dross, shorn of ornamentation and other superfluities. What is left out or removed in the description of the Master's body creates the impression of progressive Emptiness. Like the reticent form of poetic expression in haiku, also an ascetic art, a reduction of all external factors takes place during the Master's last match. What remains is the *essence*.

Fluidity is implicit in Kawabata's imagery depicting the Master's progressive physical diminution. When seated, for example, next to the Go board at the outset of the game, when his prospects seem so favorable, he gives the impression of actually growing in dimension and power. His prestige and experience, the confidence he has in the knowledge of his art, his active mental acumen, the strength and discipline enabling him to endure the protracted periods of concentration needed for the struggle, seemingly endow him with an increase in physical stature. His jaw seems stronger, his trunk longer, his face wider. He is a man in possession of himself and in harmony with both his inner and outer worlds. Kawabata's use of flashforward and flash-backward cinematographic technique throughout *The Master of Go*, allows him to either increase or decrease the Master's dimensions, intensifying the drama of his proximity to defeat—to exile.

Photography: The Art of Mystery

What also adds to the fascination of Kawabata's chronicle-novel is the author's use of photography. The narrator says that after the Master's demise, he took a snapshot of the corpse's face. He studies this image at the outset of the novel, touching upon a different level of reality and concept of art. We are no longer presented with a verbal black and white ink painting, reminiscent of those accomplished by Zen Buddhist monks, in austere black outlines, watered-down tones, and vaporous greys, appealing to the most refined of sensibilities.

The camera, a mechanical device and a paradigm of the modern age, is able to depict the object/person it shoots. Yet something else is also at stake. As the narrator peers at the photo, he seems to be penetrating an obscure, suggestive, and mysterious world. Configurations are not cut-and-dried, like markings on a geographical map. Rather, the physical forms he observes take on depth with each delineation, breadth with every curve of the eyebrow or line of the lips. Like a Noh mask, an art object created with such infinite care and a work so precious that many are handed down from one generation of actors to another, the snapshot is striking, artful, and elegant, and it is filled with the respect due an exiled Master.

> I would have liked to take pictures from all sides and angles, but out of respect for the dead man I could not bring myself to wander through the room. I took all my pictures from a single kneeling position.

Because of the narrator's veneration for the Master, had the photos of his face been offensive, he would have been prepared to destroy them, unwilling to diminish the reputation of one he held in such high esteem.

The photographs, like the Black and White stones and the exquisitely lacquered Go board, are art objects. Each virtually takes on the stature of a hierophany: it is as if flesh had been cleansed away and the sacred allowed to appear in all of its purity and beauty. The poses of the Master captivate the narrator. Some are reminiscent of a man sleeping in quietude; others reveal the mystery embedded in the very heart of the phenomenological world. The Master has an eloquent expression of serenity, the coarseness of life having been removed and supplanted by impressions of fresh, new overtones of a vaster world.

The narrator is absorbed in the outlines, forms, details, angles, and lighting effects revealed in the photographs. His attention is arrested by what he takes to be "a certain intensity of feeling," which may be interpreted as a reflection of inner pulsations originating from a deeper and incomprehensible mental level.

> The face was rich in feeling, yet the dead man himself had none. It seemed to me that the pictures were neither of life nor of death. The face was alive but sleeping. One might in another sense see them as pictures of a dead face and yet feel in them something neither living nor dead. Was it that the face came through as the living face? Was it that the face called up so many memories of the living man? Or was it that I had before me not the living face but a photograph? I thought it strange too that in pictures I could see the dead face more clearly and minutely than when I had it before me. The pictures were like a symbol of something hidden, something that must not be looked upon.

The narrator has a momentary change of heart. He regrets having taken the photographs: "Dead faces should not leave behind photographs." Yet something else about the Master's being comes to life in these very stills: a heretofore undiscernible "power to quiet his surroundings" as well as a "deep sadness in the lines of the closed eyelids, as of one grieving in sleep." Once again scrutinizing the photographs, the narrator has the distinct impression that the Master has shrunk back into fetal position: a body, tiny, withered, "quite weightless," except for the head, which is so large in comparison with the rest of the frame as to appear "gruesome." A strange irreality is embedded in these images. Perhaps they disclose, better than anything else, the Master's readiness for exile: the completeness of the circular route of existence.

The lighting effects in the photographs heighten their sense of mystery and beauty. Depending upon the angle from which the picture is viewed, the lights serve to accentuate or suppress black and white tonalities; to underscore grief, pain, or irresistible longing; or to convey metaphysical qualities, such as the fleetingness of life, its loneliness, or the unobtrusive nature of a person withdrawing from the empirical world. The interplay of black and white shadows interspersed in the photographs also reveals the unfolding of the Master's game and personality.

Distortion is also a factor in the narrator's photographs. Was the camera telling the truth? Or was it exaggerating certain parts of the Master's body? "For a lens there was neither living nor dead, there was neither man nor object, not sentimentality or reverence." Viewing a photo from one angle, the narrator recalls the Master differently from what the lens now shows.

> The absence of a pillow was the mark of death, and the face was tilted ever so slightly upward, so the strong jaw and the large mouth, just perceptibly open, stood out even more prominently. The powerful nose seemed almost oppressively large. There was profound sorrow in the wrinkles at the closed eyes and the heavily shaded forehead.
>
> The light through the half-opened night doors came from the feet, and the light from the ceiling struck the lower part of the face; and, since the head tilted slightly backward, the forehead was in shadow. The light struck from the jaw over the cheeks, and thence toward the rise of the eyebrows and hollow eyes to the bridge of the nose. Looking more closely, I saw that the lower lip was in the shadow and the upper lighted, and between them, in the deep shadow of the mouth, a single upper tooth could be seen. White hairs stood out in the short mustache. There were two large moles on the right cheek, the farther from the camera. I had caught their shadows, and the shadows too of the veins at the temples and forehead. Horizontal wrinkles crossed the forehead. Only a single tuft of the short-cropped hair above caught the light. The Master had stiff, coarse hair.

A sense of mystery pervades the very ambiguity associated with the concept of photography: the stilling of flux and the retention of exact replicas of no-longer existing forms. There is, the narrator remarks, "something hidden, something that must not be looked upon," something existing in another sphere of being. Are these photographs of the Master hierophanies, as were the White and Black stones and the Go board? Further scrutinizing the snapshots, the narrator again feels the same sensations he had when the Master was alive: the wasting away of the life force, "as if from the waist he dwindled away to nothing"; he "seemed quite weightless save for the head." The photographs, though they were said to translate reality, were really unreal. The camera's eye perceived a portrait, taking the viewer perhaps beyond the world of phenomena, disclosing

> the ultimate tragedy, of a man so disciplined in an art that he had lost the better part of reality. Perhaps I had photographed the face of a man meant from the outset for martyrdom to art. It was as if the life of Shusai, Master of Go, had ended as his art had ended, with that last match.

The Contest

The House of the Autumn Leaves, in which the Go match is being played, befits the Master's serene countenance. Its sliding doors and openwork, the panels decorated with maple leaves, evergreens, and dahlias in the Korin style; the outer view with its smoothly raked garden; its clumps of bushes, each inhabiting its specific spot: all seem in their rightful place.

Once tensions build, the Master's breathing grows increasingly rapid and his shoulders rise and fall in rhythm with his labored respiration.

> Yet there was nothing to suggest disorder. The waves that passed through his shoulders were quite regular. They were to me like concentration of violence, or the doings of some mysterious power that had taken possession of the Master.

Nevertheless, the Master's mind is free, roaming about, alighting at will here and there, seemingly unaware of the rest of the world. Unfettered, unobstructed, he sits silently observing the stillness and the vast emptiness of his being. Virtually enclosed within his own circumference, the Master remains uncommunicative; his face is expressionless. When his breathing resumes its normal pace and diapason, the change marks another "point of departure, the crossing of the line, for the spirit facing battle."

Then, suddenly, the Master seems to retreat still further from the empirical world. Was a thought or intuition perceived, growing and swelling within him, calming him, endowing him with the wealth of quietude, with the sensation of timelessness? It was as if it touched upon its own eternity. A mood of repose envelops the surroundings. The Master's face is at ease again. His stance, facial expressions, gestures, are all manifestations of an inner topography, a soul glimpsing the vastness of the unconscious, that inner ocean within the psyche from which inspiration takes root. The Master's eyes now seem to dance; his physiognomy conveys an inner *scintilla*, a prismatic vision. Is he experiencing that exquisite moment when enlightenment makes itself felt and the soul casts off "all sense of identity and the fires of combat [are] quenched?"

Otaké, seated opposite the Master, closes his eyes every now and then. To interiorize his moves requires him to shut out the world around him so that the intensity of his concentration may be directed toward the game. There are times during the long intervals between moves, however, when Otaké casts his eyes toward the ground, suggesting another way of isolating himself from others, to reach into those inward folds of the mind. During other intervals he is "tight-mouthed and almost sullen, shoulders back," pacing "the halls defiantly," his narrow eyes sending "forth a fierce light." When planning ahead, the narrator writes, Otaké gave

> himself over to his next assault, a slashing one of the sort that characterized his game. Having dispatched a spy against the White forces below, he returned to the upper part of the board. There was an aggressive impatience in the click of the stone.

Otaké's outward stance, however, belies a physical tension, and a gnawing anxiety that causes him to empty his bladder frequently.

In contrast to the Master's reserve, restraint, and silence, there are periods when Otaké moves about, jokes, and indulges in conversation. Younger men are glib, given to peculiar habits such as reading a story while waiting for the opponent to make his move or even deriding the adversary. The extreme reserve inherent to the Master would perhaps never be acquired by the new generation. Otaké has not experienced his own center; thus he is unable to become integrated into the universal flow. Nor has Otaké's mind attained the fluidity of the Master's. He still feels hindered by emotions such as fear, joy, and passions of all sorts. He has not yet learned to interiorize these powers, to adapt them to his needs through meditation. Unlike the Master, he has not yet succeeded in transcending the dualism of the phenomenological world, nor has he experienced the emptiness and fullness of being.

When the Master has "sunk himself into a session," he does not stir from the board. The "heaving" of his shoulder indicates, at times, the "secret advent of inspiration, painless calm." At such moments he resembles a certain statue of the Amida Buddha (1252 c.e.), in deep meditation. Like a Zen monk, the Master has been trained in the ancient art of rigorous self-discipline; he knows the meaning of loyalty and dedication, to his art and to his game. Like the samurai, he is forever ready to encounter exile in death at any moment. He has learned to still the mind during periods of difficulty, as during his game of Go, thus overcoming subject/object polarities intrinsic to the empirical world.

As the stones move from square to square, thus journeying from one corner of the Go board to another, modifying their natures in so doing, the game also changes locations: from Atami to Koyokan to Hakone. Like the ancient itinerant monks, or the haiku poet Basho (1664–94), also wandering and evolving in his essential loneliness, the Master and Otaké penetrate different spatial and metaphysical dimensions.

During the course of the match the Master's body and mind, like all mechanisms, become enfeebled. His breath becomes increasingly labored. He suffers palpitations, bathes in perspiration. Hospitalization for a short period of time follows. Yet the Master does not let go. Not only does he continue his match, but he plays other games—chess, mah-jongg, and billiards—during the intervals between moves. His mind is forever active and full; only when his mind is occupied can he quiet his nerves. Then not a single thought can disturb the precarious balance hovering between the empty and filled squares.

The match pursues its course: attacks and counterattacks; parryings and dodgings; frontal, side, and rear confrontations. The board, filled with stones in one corner, empty in another, transfers spatial configurations, and moves energy patterns into a variety of visual arrangements, reflecting the players' inner energetic spasms: swirling, undulating, clashing, then dispersing, like so many mesons and quarks.

> The Master had put the match together as a work of art. It was as if the work, likened to a painting, were smeared black at the moment of highest tension. That play of black upon white, white upon black, has the intent and takes the forms of creative art. It has in it a flow of the spirit and a harmony as of music. Everything is lost when suddenly a false note is struck, or one party in a duet suddenly launches forth on an eccentric flight of his own. A masterpiece of a game can be ruined by insensitivity to the feelings of an adversary. That Black 121 having been a source of wonder and surprise and doubt and suspicion for us all, its effect in cutting the flow and harmony of the game cannot be denied.

Go, personified and humanized, has become in the Master's and Otaké's hands an organic and living instrument, an extension of the human being, a surface upon which each of the players projects his life force. The last few moves prior to the finale are enacted with heightened awareness, greater order, more determined perseverance: that "of a precisely toothed machine, a relentless mathematical progression." Never do the Master's eyes leave the center of action. Increasingly anxious, he declares, "I think I would like if possible to finish today." As the two press on in combat like archetypal images, nerves are raw.

The Master's struggle is condensed; his breathing grows halting. The most minute nuances of facial expressions and gestures are contained and stilled beneath his mask, as if nature were immured and imprisoned. Soon his attention span lapses; intense inner anguish predominates. An observer comments that "White" is having difficulties making his moves. As age struggles against youth, as the patina of antiquity opposes modernity, age is exiled.

That Kawabata, in the act of *seppuku*, put an end to his own life is understandable to a reader of *The Master of Go*. His ceremonial suicide, steeped in Japanese tradition, was executed according to samurai notions of virtue and purity. As Yukio Mishima wrote in *Runaway Horses*:

> Purity, a concept that recalled flowers, the piquant mint taste of a mouthwash, a child clinging to its mother's gentle breast, was something that joined all these directly to the concept of blood, the concept of swords cutting down iniquitous men, the concept of blades slashing down through the shoulder to spray the air with blood. And to the concept of seppuku. The moment that a samurai "fell like the cherry blossoms," his blood-smeared corpse became at once like fragrant cherry blossoms. The concept of purity, then, could alter to the contrary with arbitrary swiftness. And so purity was the stuff of poetry. (120–21)

Kawabata, like the Master of Go, was ready to experience exile, the gateway to the ineffable and timeless universe. Without the arrogance implicit in Stoic doctrine, his act of seppuku was reasoned and tempered by the feelings of one who had experienced life in all of its plenitude. He and his Master of the game left this world in a ceremonial rite of passage, experiencing the infinite in the finite of each instant, both looking deeply into the spotless mirror of eternity.

7 Levi's *Survival in Auschwitz:* Exile and the Death-Machine

Primo Levi's[1] *Survival in Auschwitz* (1947) is a factual account of his abduction from his native city of Turin and his ten-month exile in a Nazi death camp. His memoir may be viewed as a testament to his heroic capacity for endurance when "crushed against the bottom," in the face of death. That he was not selected for the gas chamber, as were millions of others at the Auschwitz complex of camps, was perhaps due to a combination of factors: chance; his degree in chemistry, which gave him the technical knowledge and training to work at the I. G. Farben Company at Auschwitz; and a parahuman desire to survive. Although emotional anguish and intense physical pain accompanied him during all of his days at Auschwitz, his conclusion to his ordeal is rare: "no human experience is without meaning or unworthy of analysis, and . . . fundamental values, even if they are not positive, can be deduced from this particular world."

The comparison Levi makes between his experiences and Dostoevsky's as recounted in *The House of the Dead* (1862) gives pause for consideration. Although the similarity of "features" in the Russian and German camps is recognizable, Levi writes in his "Afterword" to *The Reawakening* (1965) that Dostoevsky's imprisonment is a paradigm of "czarist absolutism,"

---

[1]Primo Levi was born in Turin in 1919. He received a doctoral degree in chemistry from the University of Turin; was arrested as a member of the anti-Fascist resistance, and was deported to Auschwitz in 1944. The author of seminal works on his experience in the death camp and his travels through Eastern Europe, his writings, in addition to *Survival in Auschwitz* (first published as *If This Is a Man*), include *The Reawakening, Moments of Reprieve, The Periodic Table, If Not Now, When?* (the latter won the Viareggio and Campiello prizes), and *The Monkey's Wrench*. Dr. Levi retired as manager of a Turin chemical factory in 1977, devoting his time thereafter to writing. He committed suicide in 1987.

whereas the "German camps constitute something unique in the history of humanity . . . they set a monstrous modern goal, that of erasing entire peoples and cultures from the world." The Nazi "deathmachines," beginning to operate even before 1940, "were deliberately planned to destroy lives and human bodies on a scale of millions." Auschwitz, Levi continues, broke the record: in a single day in August 1944, 24,000 people were exterminated. Death, in Dostoevsky's time, was "a by-product of hunger, cold, infections, hard labor," whereas "one entered the German camps, in general never to emerge. Death was the only foreseen outcome" (208).

Although the facts included in *Survival in Auschwitz* are harrowing and Levi's suffering great, the sobriety of his account, the restraint with which he narrates the events, make it that much more powerful and unforgettable a document. His writing fulfilled an inner necessity: "the need to tell our story to 'the rest,' to make 'the rest' participate in it, had taken on for us, before our liberation and after, the character of an immediate and violent impulse." Levi expressed no feelings of hatred or of revenge toward the Germans; this reaction so surprised many of his readers that he felt it necessary to explain.

> My personal temperament is not inclined to hatred. I regard it as bestial, crude, and prefer on the contrary that my actions and thoughts, as far as possible, should be the product of reason; therefore I have never cultivated within myself hatred as a desire for revenge, or as a desire to inflict suffering on my real or presumed enemy, or as a private vendetta. Even less do I accept hatred as directed collectively at an ethnic group, for example, all the Germans; if I accepted it, I would feel that I was following the precepts of Nazism, which was founded precisely on national and racial hatred. (*Reawakening*, 196)

"Exactly because I am not a Fascist or a Nazi," he continued, "I refuse to give way to this temptation" to hate (*Reawakening*, 196). That Levi refrains from hating in no way suggests forgiving the perpetrator of evil

> unless he has shown (with deeds, not words, and not too long afterward) that he has become conscious of the crimes and errors of Italian and foreign Fascism and is determined to condemn them, uproot them, from his conscience and from that of others. Only in this case am I, a non-Christian, prepared to follow the Jewish and Christian precept of forgiving my enemy, because an enemy who sees the errors of his ways ceases to be an enemy. (*Reawakening*, 197)

Nevertheless, because there are "certain aspects of the human mind," Levi writes, that defy understanding, they must be explored. The very existence, for example, of the death camp must be looked on as "a sinister alarm-signal," a malfunctioning of the mind and psyche that must be analyzed so that it may be rectified, reoriented, and redirected before such an infection sets in anew, suppurates, and spreads. The Nazis, with their scientifically ordered logic, succeeded in destroying six million Jews, not to mention countless other religious groups. The scale and the manner in which these continuous annihilations were carried out in a world that had reached, so it was thought, the pinnacle of "civilization," defies the imagination. Is the creation of the highly organized and brilliantly functioning death camps and crematoria and the rigor with which massacre and genocide were carried out to be regarded as a tribute to a most finely tuned mind?

Not only is *Survival in Auschwitz* a study in heroic endurance, it is an exploration of sordidness and beauty, of the extremes of human nature. So urgent was Levi's need to write what he had been unable to articulate that he composed *Survival in Auschwitz* in a few months, shortly after his return to Italy.

> My need to tell the story was so strong in the Camp that I had begun describing my experiences there, on the spot, in that German laboratory laden with freezing cold, the war, and vigilant eyes; and yet I knew that I would not be able under any circumstances to hold on to those haphazardly scribbled notes, and that I must throw them away immediately because if they were found they would be considered an act of espionage and would cost me my life. (*Reawakening*, 195)

Unbeknown to Levi, *Survival in Auschwitz* may also be an answer to the wishes of the eighty-one-year-old Jewish historian Simon Dubnov, who, before he was shot and killed by the Nazis (December 1941), cried out to his fellow Jews during the evacuation of the Riga ghetto, "Write and record!" (Marrus, 13).

Jewish/Hebrew martyrdom is not new. Examples are many, including the Exodus from Egypt, when Moses led the Hebrews out of bondage; and exile in Babylonia, when Nebuchadnezzar brought the Kingdom of Israel to its end, and took 20 percent of the population into captivity (597 B.C.E.). With this displacement was born the Hebrews' permanent desire to return to their homeland: "If I forget thee, O Jerusalem, let my right hand forget her cunning" (Psalms, 137:5) Upon their return (538 B.C.E.), exiles and killings continued: among them was the siege of Jerusalem by the Roman emperor Titus and his conquest of the fortress of Masada (70 C.E.), leading to the mass suicide of the garrison, the prototype for future collective suicides by Jews (some of which occurred during the Crusades). The Fourth Lateran Council (1215) established the Papal Inquisition, which spread throughout Europe, most notably in Spain, leading to burnings at the stake, imprisonments, and torture of Jews and heretics. A unique phenomenon, the Inquisition has been alluded to as the first example of "brainwashing" in history. Nor can the pogroms in Russia and elsewhere in Eastern Europe, encouraging the killing of entire populations, be omitted. The slaughter of Jews reached its apotheosis with the advent of National Socialism and Hitler's Nazis. "In the course of two thousand years," writes Simon Wiesenthal, "no people has been persecuted or had to face death as often as the Jews" (Wiesenthal, 4).

Archetypal Violation/Kidnapping

An archetype for the psyche is comparable to an instinct for the body. Both are unknown motivating dynamisms that determine human psychological and behavioral patterns. Because an archetype is a psychological factor, it is invisible; it cannot be represented except in metaphors or other apprehensible figures of speech. Let us explore the nature of the archetype of violation/ kidnapping, which was operational in Levi's arrest at age twenty-five.

As archetypally experienced, by victims, the unleashing of destructive energy pockets that lead to the theft of a being, and thus a plundering of what is most sacred—human life—is a universal motif in history and is also implicit in myths, legends, and fairy tales. Violations are encountered in the legendary rape of Persephone, Deianira, Europa, and the Sabine women, as well as in the tribute, exacted by Minos, of seven Athenian maidens and seven youths forcibly taken to Crete to be fed to the Minotaur. The fairy tales of Little Red Riding Hood being eaten by the wolf and of Hansel and Gretel being imprisoned by the witch are additional examples.

To despoil or carry away a person by force is tantamount to a divestiture of soma and psyche: a robbing of one's identity and of one's capacity to function as an individual. Such a hostile act pits the agressor against a weaker force, thus enabling the stronger to appropriate to himself what is not rightfully his. To acquire dominion over another individual not only indicates a condition of inflation, that is, an exaggerated belief in one's own importance, but is also an example of *shadow projection.*

When characteristics of the shadow (the unconscious part of the personality, usually containing traits unacceptable to the ego) remain unconscious and unacceptable to the individual, they are frequently "projected" onto others. Instead of analyzing one's own feelings of inferiority, or those factors in oneself considered reprehensible, thereby bringing them into consciousness and so transforming what is negative into something positive, the individual (or nation) attempts to exterminate these by destroying the object of the projection.

The Nazis, remaining unconscious of their shadow, projected it upon others in acts of hatred, persecution, and war, as a way of killing those very factors they despised in themselves. By exterminating their alleged enemy, the carrier of their shadow projection, they saw themselves as heroes, cleansing and purifying the world, when in effect they were repressing their own negative characteristics (Neumann, *Depth Psychology and a New Ethic*, 57).

In ancient times the collective shadow (the evils of the community) was projected or heaped onto a goat by a priest; the animal was then sent out into the wilderness and the clan was ostensibly purged of its sins. The negative characteristics of the community supposedly disappeared along with the animal; so, too, however, did the tension needed to face and try to resolve the problems in question. To reject a painful situation by blaming it on others is to escape the very conflict that could lead to greater understanding.

Archetypal violation and kidnapping, which had become a way of life under the Nazis, was a living-out, to a great extent, of an unconscious shadow projection. To survive such a condition required, on Levi's part, not a passive approach, but a declaration of war. Militancy, as conveyed in the *Bhagavad Gita*, requires action: the death of one mode of existence so as to give birth to another.

Engulfment, imprisonment, physical and emotional torture, awakened in Levi aspects of his psyche about which he had been unaware. Dormant until now, for example, was his instinct for self-preservation. Reacting to his dilemma triggered expanded consciousness, enabling him to think of ways and means of preserving soma and psyche. Cognizance of his own shadow brought understanding and acceptance of his vulnerability as well as recognition of the need to be immoral (e.g., stealing within the prison camp) in order to survive. The terror he fought against during the many harrowing moments he endured made him aware of the depth of his own resources; it also helped him structure a modus vivendi.

Levi's own innate emotional order, along with his equilibrated personality, facilitated his thinking out a course of action during this traumatic period in his life. Because reason and feeling cohabited in harmony within his psyche, he was able to discipline his will and his ways, within the limitations of the death-camp environment. In so doing, he created priorities, the first of which was survival. Levi's accepting his violation/

kidnapping passively could have led to the dissolution of his ego (center of consciousness). His struggle to deal with the powerful archetype was so intense, however, that the libido (psychic energy) he expended in his battle prevented it from invading and dominating his life. He composed behavioral patterns for himself early on in his imprisonment. Although Levi had, four years prior to his abduction, experienced racial laws under Mussolini's dictatorship—which caused him, he wrote, "to live in an unrealistic world of my own, a world inhabited by civilized Cartesian phantoms, by sincere male and bloodless female relationships"—the thought of deportation never entered his mind. Not in Italy.

Levi, a man who had always lived deeply within himself, was guided in his activities by his thinking function. His mind was the supreme consciousness, regulating the laws that would order his inner life and dictate his outer behavior. Unlike the top-heavy minds of many intellectuals living in an ivory tower, Levi's was functional not only in the empirical domain but also with regard to his feeling world. He was never all head and no body. Neither took possession of the other, despite the harrowing moments when physical suffering was so intense that thought receded into the background, but never disappeared.

Thinking for Levi, then, was a function of consciousness; to be aware every minute, to learn, to appraise people and situations was his behavioral plan. He studied events and his own actions and reactions to these, never omitting the feeling function. "He who errs but once pays dearly," he wrote. To understand the dangers involved in unconscious behavior was essential.

Discernment and discrimination, instrumental in guiding his conduct, did not cut him off from his primitive or natural self. The sense of violation, injury, and mutilation he felt, worked positively for him: they forced him to fortify himself against evil, while always remaining vigilant against the impairment of his integrity or consciousness (Jung and Franz, *The Grail Legend*, 242). Slowly, and with mistakes (like so many heroes of old, Parsifal being a case in point), Levi became not a master of knightly arts, because these had gone out of style, but of the accompanying characteristics of fortitude, valor, fearlessness, constancy, and loyalty to personal codes of ethics. Because his ruling principle throughout his ordeal, as previously mentioned, was that of consciousness, the depth of his reflections increased his ability to judge situations and people. This approach diminished his vulnerability, because he could read into events. Neither an instrument of arrogance nor a mechanism of defense, his intellect operated with openness, searching always for relative truth. Thus did he exercise his free will: as master of his destiny, he could consent or refuse to act within his extremely limited environment. In the face of fate's possible intervention to select him for the gas ovens, Levi's psychological attitude at the time revealed an inner drive toward survival and wholeness.

Let us examine Levi's activities prior to his kidnapping in order better to assess the magnitude of the powers he put to work when called upon to test his ego. Although inexperienced in warfare, Levi had, nevertheless, prior to his kidnapping, been a member of a loosely organized, ill-directed, and virtually nonexistent Resistance organization called Justice and Liberty. When, in January 1944, it became known that he was a Jew and a partisan of Justice and Liberty, he was sent to a large detention camp at Fossoli, near Modena. The Jewish detainess, he was told, were to leave on February 22. For where? No one knew. He understood, nevertheless, the gravity of his situation. "Only a minority of ingenuous and deluded souls continued to hope" that they would not be sent to a death camp.

The immediate question facing Levi, and others experiencing archetypal violation/kidnapping, was how best to deal with death at this particular juncture. Most people reacted by denial: the day prior to their departure, mothers prepared food, diapers, and toys for their children. "Would you not do the same? If you and your child were going to be killed tomorrow, would you not give him to eat today?" Others resorted to prayer, solitude, candle-lighting, lamentations, weeping, and whatever ceremonies were needed to comfort them. The "six hundred and fifty 'pieces' of human cargo" were loaded into buses, then onto the "notorious transport trains" with the traditional "absurd" Germanic precision—on "a journey towards nothingness." Upon leaving Italy, "everybody said farewell to life through his neighbor. We had no fear." Unlike the journey of the Jews of the Exodus, who left Egypt for the Promised Land, Levi's departure was accompanied by "grief without hope."

The Death Syndrome

Auschwitz was not one camp, but the administrative capital, housing 20,000 prisoners in a complex of some forty camps. The other camps included Birkenau (60,000), just outside of which functioned four huge gassing-cremation installations, where more than 4,000,000 people, mostly Jews, were annihilated. The record was 24,000 exterminated in one day in August 1944. The Vrba Westzler report (1944) describes one of these killing centers as follows:

> It holds 2,000 people. . . . When everybody is inside, the heavy doors are closed. Then there is a short pause, presumably to allow the room temperature to rise to a certain level, after which SS men

with gas masks climb on the roof, open the traps, and shake down a preparation in powder form out of tin cans, . . . a "cyanide" mixture of some sort which turns into gas at a certain temperature. After three minutes everyone in the chamber is dead. . . . The chamber is then opened, aired, and the "special squad" [of slave laborers] carts the bodies on flat trucks to the furnace rooms where the burning takes place. (Wyman, 289)

Monowitz, the largest of the work camps, where Levi was interned, was located seven kilometers to the east of Auschwitz. Two fences of barbed wire, the inner with high-tension current, surrounded the sixty huts, referred to as "Blocks," which included kitchens, latrines, showers, an infirmary and a clinic. Block 49 was reserved for the kapos, who sometimes beat the prisoners out of pure "bestiality and violence." Jews wore a yellow, six-pointed Star of David, criminals a green triangle, political prisoners a red triangle. Isolation from the outside world increased the atmosphere of doom, and "malevolent clouds" completed the task of cutting Levi and the other deportees off from the warming sun. Pain, bathed in this abysmal atmosphere, cohabited with hostility and evil. Levi would have to learn to deal with the Teutonic mentality: warlike, fierce, cold, antithetical to his own Italian psyche.

No matter how conscious he was of his situation and the continuous threat of his imminent death, he understood despite his youth that the elimination of life signified, psychologically, the eradication of a whole unlived part of himself. Until the death-camp experience, Levi had taken life virtually for granted: it functioned normally, like the "running down" of a clock, until the time came when it was heard no more. The ever-present reality of death in Auschwitz gnawed at him, sending wave upon wave of sensations that caused him to shudder. Such emotionality, however, abated when he explored the notion of his own mortality: he faced the unknown, that hidden realm lying beyond the bridge between life and death. He accepted his helplessness and perhaps even the meaninglessness of it all. Taking this strong stand may have been instrumental in encouraging Levi to approach his fate with wisdom and dignity.

The reality of his situation became clear when he witnessed the first selection made between the fit and the unfit: more than five hundred of those chosen were no longer living two days later. So gruesome were these acts that Levi felt himself elsewhere, perhaps in limbo, a domain beyond the credible. Or was it, he questioned, a dream sequence? When the impact of what he had witnessed had been assimilated, he understood that he would have to learn to approach death in a paradoxically positive manner if he were to survive.

Because death had to be faced each moment of every day (in selections, beatings, torture, thirst, cold, starvation, bleeding sores and wounds), Levi could not submit to feelings of defeat. Consciousness had to intervene; reason and evaluation of the precarious nature of his situation had to point the way to a positive course. Resignation and apathy would have to be buried so that the instinct for life would trigger sufficient energy to overcome "the void of bottomless despair" (Jung, *Collected Works*, 8:405).

To help him survive the terror of death, Levi tried to wipe out past and future, living only in the present, the moment. The concept of death as an abyss and as an immeasurable space existing beyond human comprehension generated, as is to be expected, a *horror vacui*. The formlessness and irreversibility of the void Levi faced encouraged him to take countermeasure: along with his pragmatic determination to live in the present there developed a deep recognition and acceptance of that other side/death, rather than avoidance of it. Only in this manner could he begin to assimilate the terror that might or might not be his (Herzog, 27).

Levi's success in achieving his goal, as attested to by his ability to adapt to the reality of his situation and the acceptance of his fate, revealed his strong ego. Expending an astonishing amount of energy, he avoided passivity, lethargy, and despondency. His understanding grew of the customs and laws of the kommandos and the kapos in the concentration camp, and of the necessity of establishing a kind of nonaggression pact with the other deportees.

Analogous in some respects to the mythical David who fought Goliath, the little Levi eventually triumphed over the creatures that would destroy him. Within him there existed a creative and persevering individual, one endowed with an exceptional will to survive. His mind, like the instinct of an animal, had the power to sniff out danger. Rarely, if ever, was ego-consciousness suspended (Jung, *Collected Works*, 8:405).

Daily, Levi set his goals. The purpose of life, he wrote, "is rooted in every fibre of man" and is "a property of the human substance." His guiding principle was to reach the next moment, the next hour, the next day, week, month, spring. The intensity of the energy needed to reach out, to extend his activities and bring about the next time sequence, superimposed itself on what could have been a plethora of negative ideas. The limitations he imposed upon his thoughts prevented them from wandering from the focus intended and annulled any possible indulgence in self-pity or thoughts of destruction. The present was his reality. How best to cope with it and go on were his by-words.

As a student of human nature, Levi also understood that hierarchies, constructs of the mind, have therapeutic value. Grief and pain, for example, although experienced by him simultaneously, were, nevertheless, different in their repercussions upon the psyche. They "do not add up as a whole in our consciousness, but hide, the lesser behind the greater, according to a definite law of perspective." Different kinds of physical stress were also categorized according to the need to deal with them at the moment. When, therefore, Levi was ordered to work in his light prison garments in the unbearable cold of a Silesian winter, he was much too preoccupied in preventing frostbite to anguish over his hunger. The moment the spring thaw was felt, hunger took priority: "The Lager *is* hunger: we ourselves are hunger, living hunger."

Levi's clear perception of his goal of survival made him more acutely aware of the constant dangers he faced. He kept vigilant watch for ways of protecting himself without endangering the lives of others. In certain situations, as we shall see, he called upon his intuitive function to become operational together with his thinking and feeling principles, mustering the energy needed to help him cope with death while fighting for life. During moments of agonizing stress, he experienced a coalescing of instinct, as heart, spirit, body, reason worked not at odds with each other but as a cohesive whole. Displacement, therefore, did not create chaos after the initial trauma of the death-camp experience; on the contrary, it served to reinforce a steady inner course, enabling Levi to cope with what for others were insurmountable odds, in this necropolis that was Auschwitz.

"My Own Body is no Longer Mine"

Until Levi's deportation, body and psyche had seemingly lived in harmony. Because no real problems had faced him, his physical being had not cried out for attention; the physical suffering endured at Auschwitz, however, made him conscious of his body and its needs.

Upon entering the death camp, Levi had considered the body a self-contained system and mechanism used for the living of the life-process, as always available and possessing a seemingly continuous source of energy. Levi's first test, like that of Tantalus, was of unappeased thirst. Water was denied him from the time he and the rest of the human cargo left Italy to the end of the first five days of his internment. Such deprivation compelled the body to voice its needs in its own language: sensations of dryness of the mouth, parched tongue, feelings of weakness and dizziness. Somatic dehydration, a lethal condition, made obedience to the rules and regulations ordered by the Germans more difficult than they would have been ordinarily.

Water, as the source of life, spells fertility, as all potentialities are contained within this fluid element. Because it purifies and regenerates, it divests the drinker of impurities while also, symbolically, restoring the cleanliness and sanctity of a primordial past. It allows a person, symbolically, to reform, to relive, to reconceive life in an ever-new manner. Thus does it inspire hope.

Let us note that water and fountains played an important role in Teutonic mythology. Mimir ("he who thinks"), the giant water divinity and keeper of the well of wisdom, for example, was a figure of veneration. With the welling-up of water from Mimir's fountain, there came an increase in self-knowledge and strength and ability to deal with the outer world, bringing the sense of rejuvenation and of rebirth.

It was these very energy patterns that the Nazis attempted to annihilate in their death-camp victims. To deprive them of water would not only weaken soma, but psyche as well, to the point of death. Levi's reason again came to his aid. When his body cried out its need for liquid, his parched tongue and listlessness becoming virtually unbearable, he better understood the danger at stake. Like the ascetics of old, he attempted to meet the body's demands, but on a higher level: by superimposing the discipline of patience. When, by the sixth day, water still had not been given him, he happened to notice an icicle outside the window; he broke it off, intending to put it to his mouth, but a guard outside saw him and "brutally" snatched it away. Although Levi would have wanted to resist the thievery, he understood that physical and emotional control were of crucial importance at this juncture. Having been denied water for so long, Levi's view of it altered. It became a hierophany: a sacred entity and not to be treated lightly or casually. Water, then, became a benediction, in the world of reality and symbolically as well. Like the magic brews of old, when finally he obtained some, it saved him from drying up and wasting away.

Cold, as mentioned earlier, was another factor with which Levi and the other deportees had to contend. The frigid conditions during the winter months spelled death for many; others were able to summon up the body's energy (associated with fire) to stay alive, putting this combustible entity to work through rigorous motions, exercises of all types. Levi's body, then, become a barometer for measuring the degree to which he could adapt to the climate, and helped him to cling to life.

Levi looked upon the congealing, ice, and snow of the long, dark winter months as a dangerous omen: a prelude to the disappearance of life, when nature withdraws her foliage and lives within the earth. Such an approach is also in keeping with ancient Nordic myths and their realm of darkness, cold, and fog, which they called *Niflheim* ("Mistworld"). The abode of the dead, Niflheim was a somber, damp, and glacial underworld, inhabited by giants and dwarfs. Its entrance was guarded by the monstrous dog Garm.

Levi, like the other deportees, so dreaded the arrival of winter that he sometimes personified it; he wrote of fighting with "all our strength to prevent the arrival of winter." The prisoners desperately clung to the warmth of daylight as greedily as possible, to the last vestiges of leaves and yellowing grass, for they knew that between October and April, seven out of ten of them would die.

> Whoever does not die will suffer minute by minute, all day, every day: from the morning before dawn until the distribution of the evening soup we will have to keep our muscles continually tensed, dance from foot to foot, beat our arms under our shoulders against the cold.

Discipline had to prevail even more forcefully in winter than in summer. On the coldest of days, the prisoners were ordered to run naked from their hut to the showers and back again; at other times, they were driven out into the freezing cold of an icy dawn, either bare or in their "unrecognizable rags," barefoot, carrying their wooden-soled "broken-down boots." No longer did they resemble real people. When looking at each other, they seemed to have been "transformed into the phantom . . . reflected in a hundred livid faces."

Cold, thirst, hunger, fear, and pain contributed to "the demolition of man" by the Nazis. Unable or unwilling to express the feelings of agony he suffered, Levi conveyed his own personal struggle cosmically: as a climactic war waged by summer against winter, by fire against ice, by civilization against barbarism.

The value of food was another aspect of life that Levi had not considered prior to his incarceration. So minute were prisoners' rations of watery soup and bread that they scraped the bottoms of their bowls for whatever tiny morsels might be left and ate their bread above the bowl so as not to lose a crumb. "Chronic hunger" settled in on Levi's limbs. His belly grew swollen, his face hollow, his countenance deformed and wretched. Although many had become apathetic, Levi's intense instinct for self-preservation was so powerful that it acted as a catalyst.

There was so little bread, sometimes only half-rations of the minute amounts supposedly given daily, that as soon as reveille sounded, everyone rushed out into the icy cold, half-dressed, urinating while running just to save time, to be present when the "holy grey slab" of bread was to be distributed. Sometimes bread was money, used as barter for a cup, a spoon, a button, a rag or a piece of dirty paper, the latter used under a garment, though forbidden, to protect against the cold.

During the ancient Hebrews' first exodus, when the supply of bread had been depleted and starvation was in the offing, God said "I will rain bread from heaven for you" (Exod. 16:4); when Elijah was in the wilderness, he was fed bread by ravens (Kings 17:2–6). The fantasies to which Levi was subject, revolving around bread and hunger, seemed to dance before his eyes. There were days and nights when he thought and dreamt only of eating cooked spaghetti and meals at home, in warmth and in love. There were other times when he and the other prisoners were so desperate for food that they prowled around the camp like scavengers, "with lips half-open and eyes gleaming, lured by a deceptive instinct to where the merchandise shown makes the gnawing of their stomachs more acute and their salivation more assiduous." Nerves were taut as strength ebbed and exhaustion set in. Nevertheless, these dehumanized beings expended their last bit of energy ferreting here and there, in some out-of-the-way place, for an extra potato peel or a crumb.

Nor had Levi understood until Auschwitz the agony that could be caused by feet: "Death begins with the shoes . . ." instruments of torture which marching accentuates, causing painful sores to become "fatally infected." His wooden-soled and ill-fitting clogs, which he wrapped around with "precious" rags he had found or traded for bread, made his feet numb with sores. During the many long marches, his will forced him to walk erect and not drag his feet. It was the only way to "remain alive, not to begin to die."

By exercising his will to its capacity, Levi overcame excruciating pain when an iron weight fell on the back of his foot and cut it. Nor did he allow the swelling under the boot, which he did not remove for fear of not being able to put it back on, to disturb his work or his balance. When the pain was accompanied by a humid feeling around his foot he realized that his blood had congealed, "kneaded into the mud and rags of the cloth" he had put into his boot as a footpad a month before.

Unlike Hephaestos, born with deformed feet, Levi refused to reveal his deformity; nor, like Achilles, would he expose his secret vulnerability. To do so would encourage the Nazis to consider him unfit for work and select him for the gas ovens. Everything had to become an appendage of his will, the single power exercising its position of authority. Outwardly, at least, he would maintain an attitude of strength, a balanced, mobile, and erect walking stance. The shoe as well as the foot within it was his property, as was his ego. Both were his responsibility as were his acts and their outcome.

Physical and psychological suffering was designed to reduce the human species to its lowest denominator. Further divestiture was experienced when hair was shorn and personal possessions removed. No psychological mutilation was so traumatic for him, however, as the stripping of his name and its replacement with a number. Levi carried his number, 174517, tattooed on his arm to the end of his days. No deportee was deemed worthy of a name, of an identity, of a life. Emptiness reigned inside Levi's psyche. Facelessness. But were he to have succumbed to indifference, his already starving and fatigued body would have given up its search for any source of nourishment.

Levi understood the importance of following the wisdom and rhythms of his body. No longer taken for granted, the body had become as important a part of his being as the psyche and the intellect. Working together, they held in a cohesive whole what could easily have been dismembered, and restructured what could have been dismantled or corroded beyond recognition. In his lust to survive, he used the "instinctive astuteness of wild animals" in addition to his intellect. It might be said that he was parahuman.

Because Levi had begun to experience the topography of his body, directing it in the most healthful ways possible, his unconscious responded to its needs through specific patterns of behavior as revealed in his dreams, which he describes in fascinating detail.

Dreams

Levi's dreams reveal the method used by the unconscious to deal with the environment. That the inmates were forbidden to talk among themselves made the intensity of Levi's dreams that much more important for his psychological well-being. The Babel-like atmosphere of his Block 30, where Hungarian, Polish, German, French, Greek, Czechoslovakian, or other languages were spoken, also made communication virtually impossible, except on the most rudimentary level of sign language or bits and fragments of a mediating tongue. When he or another prisoner found the orders given by the Nazis incomprehensible, obedience might not be immediately forthcoming, resulting in additional floggings, torture, starvation, and increased workloads, frequently leading to death.

Levi's inability to communicate with others compelled him, and fortunately so, to listen to his inner voice as manifested in the dream. The inner voice could convey its needs in scenarios and metaphors, catalyzed by an inner energy and speaking in resonating tones, pointing the way and indicating what action should be taken. It was as if some unrecognizable, unknown, or autonomous power from his subliminal depths had come to his aid when the need was most pressing.

Levi's first mention of the subliminal sphere reveals, as is to be expected, deep fear of the ever-present enemy. The dark side of the psyche manifested itself at times in the form of an unseen, fearful, monstrous train threatening to crush him at any moment. The power of this negative energy in the dream could be stopped neither by him nor by his fellow prisoners, threatened with instant annihilation by the ever active enemy. "I feel myself threatened, besieged, at every moment I am ready to draw myself into a spasm of defence. I dream and I seem to sleep on a road, on a bridge, across a door through which many people are passing."

Levi's feelings of continuous dread, coupled with the phrase "spasm of defence," suggest a desire to stay alive and a need to activate psychological antibodies that would come to his aid. Although there is no sense of abdication in the dream, there is a sense of pause. His situation requires thought, not haphazard action. He must, therefore, sleep on the road, despite the dangers involved, so as to be able to meditate upon the right course to take.

The condition of sleep is a signal given to him by his unconscious as an option. A metaphor for biding time, it suggests that inaction is the best course at this point. Indwelling, or introversion, indicates the direction. At this juncture, Levi finds himself unable to act, incapable of deciding upon a road to take, a bridge to cross, or a door to open. The dream tells him not to venture forth at this time; to do so might jeopardize his future. Unprepared, still disoriented, he has not yet found the equilibrium required to proceed. His unconscious, the dream tells him, is not yet prepared to come to the aid of his conscious orientation. It has not yet sufficiently assimilated the shock of his displacement.

The archetypal image of sleep is crucial for Levi. So overwhelmed is his consciousness by the catastrophe of abduction from his homeland that inaction alone can perhaps save him from the perils awaiting him. Sleep suggests a need to transcend the dismembering effect of his present experience and attempt to unify what has been divided. He must, as the saying goes, sleep on it. That his unconscious in the dream reveals an emotionally and physically helpless human being, unable to act as he views the world passing by, sets him apart from others. He is isolated among the crowd, and at a crossroads. His intellect, always his governing principle, is no longer operational.

In a second dream, we find Levi experiencing an even more precarious psychological condition. He sees himself climbing into a train and hiding in a corner under a pile of coal and remaining there until dark, listening "endlessly to the rhythm of the wheels, stronger than hunger or tiredness." When the train stops, he finds himself able to get out and joyfully immerse himself in the warm air of his native land, smelling the hay, bathing in the sun, and then with rapture kneeling down to "kiss the earth." A woman passing by questions him in Italian: "Who are you?" After telling her his story in Italian, although she sympathizes with his martyrdom, she can

hardly believe his tale of woe. Only when he shows her his number tattooed on his arm does his story become credibile to her. She offers him
food and shelter.

The image of the train in Levi's dream evokes his profound need to
travel back to his homeland to find again all its warmth and nurturing
qualities. That he hides in a corner indicates a need for concealment and a
fear of opening himself up to others. That he chooses coal, a combustible
substance representing potential fire buried within the earth, represents
potential energetic material and spiritual elements existing within him.
These warm and illuminating powers, when properly fed, become operational. In that coal must be lit by some outside element suggests that if life
is to exist, that is, to become flame, it must be fueled, catalyzed, so as to
burn with sufficient ardor to light the way.

The rhythm of the wheels, as a metaphor for the human heart, indicates
a need for soothing and for compassion. It also offers, when identified
with the beating of a clock or other mechanical instruments, order, organization, and punctuality. The lulling of the wheels allows him to regress to
a joyous past. That he yearns to bathe in the warm sun, smell the aroma of
hay, and breathe the balmy air of his land underscores his attachment to
Italy and also singles out the pain he is suffering by being severed from
what he loves.

The immensely comforting images derived from his contact with
Mother Earth and his motherland, which he kisses in utter rapture, trigger
in him feelings of rebirth and revitalization. Contact with this power
endows him with strength and encourages a positive outlook.

That the woman, an *anima* figure (the autonomous psychic content in
the male personality or inner woman), is a warm, nourishing, and loving
power, and also speaks Italian, inspires him with feelings of contentment.
Because the *anima* figure brings him joy, she activates his will to live; she
filled his world of deprivation with feeling, his aching inner emptiness
with a nurturing warmth. Of supreme value is her capacity to listen to his
agony. Let us recall Levi's preoccupation with his inability to communicate with others: first, because of an interdict; and secondly, because of
the many foreign languages spoken. The woman's capacity to relate, to
communicate with him in Italian, his mother tongue, answers one of his
most desperate prayers: to be able to confide in someone, to fill the void
within him, to share his grief and dread with another gentle-hearted soul.
"Alas for the dreamer: the moment of consciousness that accompanies the
awakening is the acutest of sufferings. But it [dreaming] does not often
happen to us, and they are not long dreams."

The next dream was probably experienced during a particularly difficult
moment in Levi's adaptation to the rigors of his new world. It may be

classified as a panic dream, its magnitude being of such proportions that with but few variations, it was dreamt over and over during Levi's internment. Levi sees himself sleeping on a railroad track just as the engine (the same one he unloaded daily during his work period) is about to arrive. The train is panting, puffing, and snorting as it comes nearer and nearer. Instead of running over the dreamer, however, it simply never arrives.

The train—a gigantic, powerful force, like a beast of prey, a leviathan, or a bull, huffing and puffing its way toward its prey on the track— represents the overwhelming Nazi industrialized power machine as it makes its thunderous mechanical way toward him. Ruthless in its capacity to crush, it continues, unerring and unimpeded, to pulverize anyone or anything in its way. Like Donar, the Teutonic God of thunder and of war, a deeply feared divinity who rode a wheeled chariot on the vault of heaven, casting his thunderbolts in the form of an axe, stone, or hammer at an enemy's head, the train in Levi's dream is ready to dismember anything on its path.

Levi is paralyzed, defenseless, against this unassailable and never-satiated Teutonic death-demon. Dread increases with each breath taken by this giant machine, reminiscent of the fire-breathing dragons of ancient times. Levi, however, sees himself neither as Jason, killer of the dragon guarding the Golden Fleece, nor as Hercules, destroyer of the dragon guarding the Garden of the Hesperides, nor even as a dragon-killer like St. Michael or St. George. Weak and unaggressive, living within himself, he simply awaits destruction by this crushing power. So acute is his terror at this juncture that he tries to rip off the veil of sleep, so as to find the necessary energy to steer clear of the danger.

> My sleep is very light, it is a veil, if I want I can tear it. I will do it, I want to tear it, so that I can get off the railway track. Now I have done it and now I am awake: but not really awake, only a little more, one step higher on the ladder between the unconscious and the conscious.

Although he succeeds in partially awakening himself from the dream, he is not yet ready to face the harrowing world outside. His eyes, therefore, remain closed. That he can now hear the whistles and notes of actual camp trains, and distinguish their rhythms and keys, gives him a clue as to their direction. He can do no more: merely hear and observe, but not act. Feeble and insecure, his virtually lifeless form awaiting death, he is conscious of a transpersonal power beyond anyone's control. The blind, unfeeling, mechanical, dark, murderous train, which he recognizes as the one he had been unloading that very day during his working hours, is an expression of the Germanic community, viewed as a death-father, a negation of life. For some reason beyond his ken, it never arrives.

Another image appears: the dreamer's sister with a friend whom he does not recognize and some total strangers. All listen to his story about the hardships he has endured. Although the pleasure of being at home is intense, he is surprised by the fact that his listeners are "completely indifferent" to what he is saying. It was as if he were not even there. His sister looks at him, gets up, and leaves without saying a word.

The *anima* figure now appearing is no longer the warm and understanding mother-image of the second dream. Rather, it is his sister, accompanied by people he does not know. That he cannot communicate the depth of his feelings of humiliation and suffering to any of them is understandable; only a nourishing force, an older person who has experienced the viscissitudes of life, can *feel* the hopelessness of his condition. His sister's lack of understanding and of sympathy, as well as friends and strangers' indifference to his plight, causes him untold grief. Her departure, a severing image, isolates him from what he had always looked upon as a helping force and is a mirror image of his own immense solitude. The abrasive lesson this dream teaches Levi is that no one can know the anguish of another (except, perhaps, a mother) unless he or she has experienced it; even then, the knowledge is incomplete. The dream warns him that solitude will be his for the rest of his days, even upon his return home to his family. Nothing can breach the gap. He will have to suffer the pain of being different from others. This dream, then, is premonitory, in suggesting that although danger is everywhere, Levi's life, for some inexplicable reason, is to be spared.

Nightmare upon nightmare invaded Levi's sleep throughout his Auschwitz experience. The image capacity of his psyche frequently produced the presence of Tantalus: a mirror image, perhaps, of the hungry, cold, exhausted, suffering, and tortured being that he was. "Frozen with terror, shaking in every limb," he lived with the expectation of imminent outbreak of violence, killings.

Work and the Killer Ethic

The *Buna*, where Levi and other deportees worked, was a large factory city. Because the soil was impregnated with poisonous saps of coal and petroleum, it was shorn of grass and other natural growth. The only living entities in the Buna were the forty thousand or so foreign slaves, whose number varied with the months and years. The Buna's goal was to produce synthetic rubber. Not a pound of it was made.

Levi worked in a squad of kommandos lorded over by a kapo, under a system where "the privileged oppress the unprivileged." Work lasted from dawn until dusk, and the elements had to be fought: fierce winds coming from the Carpathians, the snows, and rain. Particularly difficult for Levi, untrained in physical labor, was carrying enormous weights from one area to another. Were he to fail in his task, he would be considered unfit and sent to the gas chamber.

As a chemist, Levi resorted, not surprisingly, to numbers or equations in the continual formulation of his behavioral system. He had done so with regard to his approach to death and was to rely upon this method when carrying out the Nazi's commands. When forced to carry enormous weights, for example, he would, during his first trajectory, count the number of steps to be taken from one area to another. He would then begin the hauling task; each time he felt his strength ebbing he would force himself to take just one more step, intentionally minimizing the pain of exhaustion. On the occasion when the falling piece of iron cut the back of his foot, although he was blind with pain and overwhelmed by dizziness, Levi stood his ground, refrained from any overt act, holding himself ready for the punishment meted out for mistakes and inefficiency. At other times, he accepted his distribution of kicks, punches, and abuse from the kapo as a matter of course.

When, on another occasion, Levi was to "carry the sleepers" used to build a path in the soft mud on which a cylinder could be pushed by lever into the factory, his heart sank. Each sleeper weighed 175 pounds. After only one try, Levi's shoulder bone was maimed. "I am deaf and almost blind from the effort," he wrote. His partner, taller and stronger than he and aware of his dilemma, tried to help him, bearing the great part of the weight. Nevertheless, Levi's knees almost buckled under him. His shoes, sucking into "the greedy mud," made him nearly lose his balance. To make matters worse, the snow coating the sleeper knocked against Levi's ear as he walked, then slid down his neck, icing him, though he perspired with fatigue. When finally the goal had been reached, the "negative ecstasy of the cessation of pain" was complete, as was the exhaustion, the stiffening of the body with its empty eyes, open mouth, hanging arms. No time for the body now. The work began anew.

When Levi was later selected to work in the Buna's chemical plant, he answered the questions posed as required, rapidly and to the point. He had taken his degree at Turin in 1941, *summa cum laude*. During the interrogation, he permitted his thoughts to wander back to the period of his studies and his past. Only momentarily, however, just long enough to experience sensations of inner joy: "this sense of lucid elation, this excitement which I feel warm in my veins, I recognize it, it is the fever of examinations, *my* fever of *my* examinations, that spontaneous mobilization of all my logical faculties and all my knowledge."

Levi's work in the chemical factory had deleterious side effects. The fumes not only burnt his eyelids and coated his throat and mouth with the taste of something like blood, but the phenylbeta with which he was working permeated his clothes, sticking to his limbs and abrading and chafing his skin, which first took on the color and blotchiness of a leper's and then began peeling off his face in "large burnt patches."

On those rare occasions when Levi was sent to the *Krankenbau* or *Ka-Be* (infirmary), he had to make certain that his illness would not be diagnosed as "organic decay," in order not to be shipped to the gas chamber. When examined, even when he contracted scarlet fever, he minimized his illness. Others did likewise, whether they had diphtheria, typhus, erysipelas, tuberculosis, or illnesses in which the sufferers simply wasted away. Some with severe diarrhea preferred to remain "contorted in the pain of keeping in their precious evidence another ten, another twenty minutes" so as to give the impression that their health was improving. "In this discreet and composed manner, without display or anger, massacre moves through the huts of Ka-Be every day, touching here and there," the inmates never knowing where or when their number would be called.

By August 1944, after the landing of the Allies in Normandy, the bombardments of Upper Silesia began. Labor at the Buna "degenerated into a disconnected, frantic and paroxysmal confusion."

As predicted in the "Volupsa," a poem in the *Eddas* (eleventh–twelfth centuries), and re-created in Wagner's *Ring* cycle, the gods, giants, and demons of evil and their world were doomed to collapse. Odin, the chief god, the "All Father," faced his end resolutely while watching the violent warfare of his men, giants, and gods in the final catastrophe known as "The Twilight of the Gods." The Nazis, however, unlike Odin, fought on. The ferocity and ruthlessness of civilians, military men, and guards in Auschwitz and elsewhere was unparalleled. To crush any and all deportees was the order of the day. One explanation for such behavior: the fury of the secure man who wakes up from a long dream of domination, sees his own ruin, and is unable to understand it.

On 26 January 1944, just prior to the liberation of Auschwitz by the Russians, Levi wrote of his captors: "The work of bestial degradation, begun by the victorious Germans, had been carried to its conclusion by the Germans in defeat."

A statement made by Jung also gives pause for meditation on the subject of responsibility and guilt for the unheard-of atrocities committed in the death camps and elsewhere prior to and during World War II: "What are we to say to an Indian who asks us: "You are anxious to bring us your Christian culture, are you not? May I ask if Auschwitz and Buchenwald are examples of European civilization?" (Jung, *Collected Works*, 10:196).

8 Garro's *Recollections of Things to Come:* "Exiles from Happiness"

Elena Garro's[1] novel, *Recollections of Things to Come* (1963) sketches certain events in the lives of a community of Mexicans during the politically difficult 1920s. Not only are the families involved cloistered in their small town of Ixtepec, and therefore exiled from the rest of their country, but they are cut off from the other members of their community and themselves. Alienated, they are "exiles from happiness."

Surrealistic in style, Garro's episodic narrative has banished rational and logical systems. Instead, spasmodic glimpses, flashbacks, and flashforwards into events revolving around a variety of lives are offered the reader. In keeping with the dictates outlined in André Breton's *Surrealistic Manifesto* (1924), Garro explores hidden and neglected areas of the psyche in poetic images, forms that seem to have been molded from the very substance of her native Mexican landscape. (Like Breton's protagonist in *Nadja* [1928], Garro's is schizophrenic.) Although seemingly incongruous at first glance, in keeping with surrealistic technique, Garro's spontaneous combinations of unrelated objects disclose associations and implications that lead to a deeper understanding of the personalities involved and the forces at stake.

Analogies are, therefore, key to an understanding of Garro's literary technique. The prevailing and most significant object used throughout

---

[1]Elena Garro was born in Puebla, Mexico (1920). After graduating from the National Autonomous University of Mexico, she became interested in theater and choreography; later, in journalism. She started writing films in 1954 and plays in 1957. Her play *A Solid House* received rave reviews from the critics, as did her collection of eleven short stories, *Week of Colors.* Garro's marriage to the poet and essayist Ocatvio Paz ended in divorce.

Recollections of Things to Come is the stone. Readers, however, would not be well served if they were to attempt to ferret out rational reasons for Garro's inclusion of this image at the beginning and conclusion of her novel. Nor should they try to justify the author's grounds for endowing the stone with a feminine voice. What is intriguing is the frequency of the stonelike lamentations issuing forth from this inanimate object. Transpersonal or archetypal in dimension, its increasingly powerful tones take on amplitude because it exists "outside of time." As if emanating directly from within the ancient sculptures and friezes adorning Olmec, Toltec, and Aztec palaces and pyramids, the impact of its message is timeless.

Exile into Stone

We learn at the very outset of the novel that the narrator, Isabel Moncada, whose voice we hear emerging from a large stone on top of a hill, is already dead. It is from the world beyond the grave that she not only articulates the events which come to pass, but also depicts the topography surrounding her native town of Ixtepec, "the spiny mountains and yellow plains" and valleys. At the novel's conclusion, we are told gratuitously that following Isabel's demise, she was "transformed into a stone."

> Only my memory knows what it [stone] holds. I see it and I remember, and as water flows into water, so I, melancholically, come to find myself in its image, covered with dust, surrounded by grass, self-contained and condemned to memory and its variegated mirror. I see it, I see myself, and I am transfigured into a multitude of colors and times. I am and I was in many eyes. I am only memory and the memory that one has of me.

Exiled from the world of the living in death, Isabel had been equally alienated from the realities of life during her earthly days. Austere, static, and secretive in her ways, she lived through events that had been carved out of pain. No free-flowing communication existed between her parents and herself any more than it did with anyone else in the community. She walked, talked, and comported herself in a stonelike manner, as if detached from her environment.

The stone images in *Recollections of Things to Come* are used with felicity. They reinforce the separateness of individual existences, as well as the novel's restrained and slow-paced sequences. Their timelessness gives the impression of drawing deeply from a collective past: the very fundaments of Mesoamerica. The characters, be they the dark-skinned autochthonous Indians, the white-skinned invaders, or the mixture of the two in the mestizos, seem to step out directly from the unfriendly and isolated terrain of Garro's ancestors, all having been molded in one way or another from its basic material, which was used by pre-Columbian artists and craftsmen. Symbolizing immobility and solidity, stone images and associations, as used by Garro, also underscore the sameness of the human personality.

That Garro identifies the stone with death is not unusual; Mixtec and Toltec artists also carved their numerous stylized sculptures of death in stone. Indeed, in many pre-Columbian cultures, life and death were represented, to the right and to the left, respectively, in a single face or mask (Castedo, 20). In keeping with a culture in which violence and blood predominated, the place of honor is accorded to the Aztec goddess Coatlicue, deity of Earth and death: she who wore a necklace of skulls and a serpent skirt, was the mother of the gods of war, of the moon, and of the southern stars. Isabel's brother, at the novel's conclusion, refers to his sister as "the avenging goddess of justice."

Isabel as stone is witness to events, memories, the vagaries of climate and political and religious dominations. Be it covered with dust, grasses, or shrubbery, or with the sands of time, concealing palaces, pyramids, raised causeways, cities, and empires of ancient civilizations, the stone for Isabel is a self-contained entity: a microcosm of the macrocosm. Inanimate and animate, it functions, as does the containing capacity of a uterus, like the collective and personal unconscious: "I am only memory and the memory that one has of me."

Isabel as stone is not, like biological entities, subject to rapid change. As such, she symbolizes a kind of continuity and indestructible strength within nature itself. She and her stone, therefore, may be alluded to as an archetypal image, thus transpersonal. As a collective voice existing from time immemorial, it/she represents a magnetic field and energy center within the nation's and individual's collective unconscious. In her capacity as archetypal image, then, Isabel reveals inherited and recurring patterns of behavior within the Mexican psyche, like the "mnemic deposit"existing in life itself (Jacobi, 48).

Throughout her narration of events, however, Isabel is continuously rebelling against her stonelike world: her separateness and solitude. She seeks to forget her past; she would like to fragment, splinter, disintegrate, turn into dust, vanish with the wind. As stone, she cannot escape her memories; she is imprisoned in the continuous recollection of her past/future, which, from her vantage point of nontime, is one and the same.

As she looks down from her stone onto the bone-dry valley below and the arid lands unfolding as far as the eye can see, memories of bygone civilizations and historical events intrude. While divesting Isabel and her voice of her individual existence, they emphasize her existence as a collective figure speaking out her dirgelike words: "I was founded, besieged, conquered, and decked out to receive armies." The nomadic tribes that first peopled her land were followed by the Olmecs Zapotecs, Mixtecs, Toltecs, and Aztecs. Although they and other ancient cultures drank her blood during their wars and in their ritual human sacrifices, things were no better, perhaps even worse, after the Spanish conquest. Hernán Cortés (1519) ordered six thousand throats cut in less than two hours in Cholula. Destroyers not only of humans, but also of artistic wonders, the conquistadores had the monumental sanctuary and palace of Tenochtitlan, with its unique carvings and architectural wonders, reduced to rubble; its inhabitants were slain or taken into slavery. Nor did government and church officials' taste for blood diminish during the centuries to come.

That Isabel depicts her landscapes in mathematical and geometrical configurations, also viewed as archetypal, allows her to cross centuries and peoples, thereby adding a transpersonal note to the visual design of her narrative.

> And as the memory contains all times and their order is unpredictable, I am now in the presence of the geometry of lights that invented this illusory hill like a premonition of my birth. A luminous point determines a valley. That geometric instant is joined to the moment of this stone, and from the superimposition of spaces that form the imaginary world, memory returns those days to me intact.

Her descriptions of the squat houses and stone churches of the Ixtepec of her day, a palimpsest for the ancient religious sanctuary of Tenochtitlan and the pyramids of Teotihuacan, lend a syncretistic note to her novel. Like the steps of a pyramid or the various stages in the construction of a palace, the imposition of layerings of religious beliefs and governmental practices on a people underscores the constancy of human instincts, needs, and yearnings. Like the stone of the landscape, names and ideologies may alter, but the fundaments remain the same.

Garro's archetypal geometric images (triangles, squares, circles, quincunxes) underscore the stylized and sculpturesque nature of her characters; they also codify their traits, adding yet another collective note to *Recollections of Things to Come*. Automatons of sorts, not one protagonist is a flesh-and-blood person; not one descends into himself or herself. Like isolated stone forms on a checkerboard, they seem to be pushed hither and yon by some outerworldly will or transpersonal force. Egos (centers of consciousness) are nonexistent. The transpersonal Self (total psyche or higher order) dictates their acts, relationships, and comportment. Enigmatic, mysterious, Garro's archetypal creatures are conjunctions of various time-frames, glimpses of reminiscences emerging from within the infinite memory of the cosmic flow (Jacobi, 65).

Geometric configurations and allusions in the novel also bring order where there is volatility and unpredictability, limitation to where there is vastness of spirit. Squares, circles, spheres, axes, and the like, endowed as they are with a numinous quality, appear frequently in works of art or religious tracts when individuals or the collective suffer from some psychic disorder or anguish. Not invented by the conscious mind, geometric forms and numbers emerged from the unconscious spontaneously as archetypal images when the need or desire arose (Jung, *Collected Works*, 8:456).

Garro's literary technique of using geometrical figures to articulate the meanderings of the deeply introverted Isabel underscores the fragmentation of her psyche, the irrationality of her behavior, and the potential tragedy of her situation. As containers for her chaotic and continuously turbulent emotions, the figures help her function in the real world, at least temporarily, thus compensating to some extent for her psychologically confused and bleak existence. On a broader level, Garro's orderly configurations are devices intended to help her protagonist restrain the emotions of terror activated by the continuous collective threat of bloodshed triggered by both governmental and church officials.

Isabel's search for psychological order, continuity, and serenity, as symbolized by her geometric references, is evidence of her intense personal need for organization and regularity. It is also evocative of the systematization implicit in many pre-Columbian cultures, as revealed by the ancient king-god Quetzalcoatl (the Plumed Serpent) to his worshipers, when he told them that the greatness of mankind emerges from the awareness of spiritual order.

The pyramids consecrated to Quetzalcoatl at Teotihuacan, said to have been built by the gods at the outset of the world, were in keeping with his injunction to adhere to regularity and uniformity, and thus were constructed with incredible mathematical rigor and knowledge. The friezes of bodies and heads of serpents ringed with feathers, the stylized carvings of Tlaloc, the god of rain, with his eyes depicted in symmetrical circles, the long stairways, the straight and parallel holy avenues of Teotihuacan trod upon during Olmec, Toltec, and Aztec times with profound solemnity: all remain as a fundament, a primordial image within the collective unconscious of the Mexican people and of Garro and her verbal transcriptions (Séjourné, 87).

That Garro should use stone as well as geometric or archetypal forms as part of her creative process suggests the powerful role these active energy centers play in the psyche of her protagonists. The Aztec Law of the

Center, for example, according to which conjunctions of opposites hold antithetical forces together, is ever sought but never achieved by Isabel, her brothers, her parents, or the other creatures in her fantasy. Unlike the mathematically oriented Aztecs, the inhabitants of Ixtepec live divested of a center. They are splinter personalities, each impulsively acting out his or her fragmented vision. They do not face their inner worlds. No questions are asked; no psychological growth comes into being. Nevertheless, although exiled from the empirical domain, some find solace in a world of fantasy, in dream or non-time.

Exile into Non-Time

Isabel's loneliness, her stone-voice intimates, has caused her to seek solace in nonchronological memory. In so doing, she has not only ushered into her mind's eye individual recall, but recollections of an inherited or archetypal past comprising mnemic deposits that dwell within the collective unconscious.

Defined by Jung as a suprapersonal matrix, a storehouse of typical behavioral patterns and "inherited potentiality of psychic functioning," the collective unconscious contains accumulations of contents millions of years old (Jacobi, 20, 59). Looked upon as an inner cosmos or ocean, this neutral or objective sphere contains undifferentiated values and notions. Divested of judgmental views, (which are products of the conscious mind with its prohibitions and injunctions), the collective unconscious not only includes, but fuses what the empirical domain divides into past, present, and future. Jung wrote:

> In my experience, the conscious mind can only claim a relatively central position and must put up with the fact that the unconscious psyche transcends and as it were surrounds it on all sides. Unconscious contents connect it *backwards* with physiological states on the one hand and archetypal data on the other. But it is extended *forward* by intuitions which are conditioned partly by archetypes and partly by subliminal perceptions depending on the relativity of time and space in the unconscious. (Jung, *Collected Works*, 12:132)

That Isabel's memory has been transformed into sensations, that her minutes, hours, and days are depicted by her as shapeless accumulations, is understandable in view of Jung's definition of the nature of non-time as experienced from the vantage point of the undifferentiated collective unconscious.

Unhappiness, like physical pain, equalizes the minutes. All days seem like the same day, acts become the same act, and all persons are a single useless person. The world loses its variety, light is annihilated, and miracles are abolished. The inertia of those repeated days kept me quiet as I contemplated the vain flight of my hours and waited for the miracle that persisted in not happening. The future was the repetition of the past. Motionless, I let myself be consumed by the thirst that rankled at my corners. To disperse the petrified days all I had was the ineffectual illusion of violence, and cruelty was practiced furiously on the women, stray dogs, and Indians. We lived in a quiet time and the people, like the actors in a tragedy, were caught in that arrested moment. It was in vain that they performed acts which were more and more bloody. We had abolished time.

Isabel's ego (center of consciousness) has been inundated by the flood tides of the collective unconscious. Never has she asserted her independence; never has she cut out on her own, broken the umbilical cord: the act that would pave the way for increased understanding and maturity. Rarely if ever does she distinguish between various value judgments except in the broadest of terms. Incursions of her unconscious, of that non-time, obliterate any possibility of clarification concerning her own acts: her ability to discriminate, to analyze, even to order her world.

Isabel's nonchronological experience is not of her invention. It came to her naturally: from her father, Martin Moncada. It is, therefore, an inherited mode of psychic functioning. His entire life—and subsequently, that of his wife, Doña Ana, and his children, Nicolas, Juan, and Isabel—revolved around the non-time–oriented attitude. Every evening at nine o'clock, Felix, the servant, "obeying an old custom of the house" unhooked the pendulum of the clock. The clock was silenced and time stood still. At this point, "the room and its occupants entered a new and melancholy time where gestures and voices moved in the past." The entire family was instantaneously transformed into

memories of themselves without a future, lost in a yellow, individual light that separated them from reality to make them only personages of memory. That is how I see them now, each bending over his circle of light, engrossed in forgetfulness, outside of themselves and outside of the feeling of sorrow that came over me at night when the houses closed their lids.

The nonchronological approach to life adopted by Martin disclosed his inability to adapt to the present; it also encouraged him and his entire family to regress or reintegrate into a past where events and relationships, after taking on the patina of time, became bearable. In the non-time of the collective unconscious the future had already become past. Living as they did in an eternal present, the Moncada family looked upon each day as had the primitives of old: as a cycle or circle to be understood and experienced in eternal patternings without beginning or end. The concept of past, present, and future had been abolished. Like archaic people who live close to nature, Isabel and her family also placed themselves within the endless series of cycles, but only after nine at night and until the next morning. During those sacred hours no consciousness of themselves as separate entities, no split between them and the forces of nature, existed.

Eschatological or linear time for the Moncadas did not consist of "an avalanche of days pressed tightly together," but of a "multitude of unlived memories." In his childhood, Martin's memory had always played tricks on him. Unlike the memory of other five-year-olds, his memory was a composite of reflected shadows, colors, and rhythmic reliefs of lived and unlived sensations. Snow, for example, was experienced as "a form of silence"; odors to which he was unaccustomed disoriented him. The intense crimson colorations of bougainvilleas terrified him, so convinced was he that they were "possessed by a white mystery, as certain to his dark eyes as the roof of his house."

When Martin married and became the father of a household, he extended his dislike of linear time to calendars. They were looked upon as imprisoning devices designed to limit individual and collective existences to schedules and chronologies, thus obliterating atemporal memories and the magic such memories arouse in certain individuals. Thanks to Martin's insistence, his wife and children developed that "marvelous" faculty of being able to slip not only into non-time, but into landscapes, colorations, and incorporeal presences. Such power bewitched them. Glitter, excitement, and the joyful fiesta spirit could at times dominate what was otherwise a world of sadness.

When they were old enough to work, Juan and Nicolas left for the mines of Tetela. Although only four hours away from Ixtepec, this mountainous region was difficult to reach in the 1920s. Once her brothers moved away, Isabel saw little of them. Her mood turned melancholy: her house was viewed as "an empty shell." Her estrangement from everything and everyone grew increasingly pronounced. Even her parents were virtually transformed into ghosts. Their voices, like those of the servants, seemed to emanate from disembodied powers. Alienated from the world and from himself, she felt detached, aloof, lost, divided, and insensitive to the feelings of others.

Isabel had developed a schizoid personality. Unwilling to form social relationships, preferring to remain alone, self-absorbed, and daydreaming excessively, she could at will sever herself from her surroundings while moving back in time and losing herself in space. By indulging in such activity, Isabel was courting danger.

Isabel's ability to divide herself between the workaday world and subliminal realms, to traverse "space like a meteor, and fall into an unknown time," cut her off still more powerfully from her ego, from whatever conscious elements remained. Although suffering from a precarious psychological imbalance, particularly during those periods when the split-off portions of her psyche led their own independent existence, she felt progressively disoriented. At certain times her condition filled her with dread and panic; at other times she was able to assess herself coolly:

> There were two Isabels, one who wandered through the rooms and the patios, and the other who lived in a distant sphere, fixed in space. Superstitiously she touched objects to communicate with the apparent world and picked up a book or a saltcellar as a support to keep from falling into the void. Thus she established a magical flux between the real Isabel and the unreal one, and felt consoled.

During her adolescent years, Isabel and her brothers had wanted to rebel against their parents' exiles into non-time. To withdraw into an unreal and invented world, they felt, was alien to life. Valiantly, at first, Isabel sought to put an end to the destructive fantasy existence that prevailed at home. After a while, however, particularly after her brothers' departure, her attempts to alter conditions ceased. Pity took their place: pity for her misguided parents who had Felix stop the clocks every evening. They were in their way, she realized in her more lucid moments, captives: exiles from life. Having refused to become engaged in either political or religious affairs, Isabel's father with the passing of years found even reading newspapers depressing. He saw through people's hypocrisy, their manipulations, and their vested interests: "And while the peasants and the rural priests prepared for atrocious deaths, the Archbishop played cards with the wives of the atheistic leaders." To take part in the workaday world, he reasoned, was to no avail: the sameness in life's constant struggle for land, food, and housing made every act futile.

As the years passed, Isabel's depersonalization so aggravated that her periods of withdrawal into the non-time of her collective unconscious increased in length and her lack of interest, even in members of her own family, gave her parents cause for alarm. When Mrs. Moncada attempted to arouse her daughter from her prevailing apathy, or stupor, through talk, rarely if ever did Isabel reply. She listened, fatigued and inattentive. Nor could her father understand his daughter's continuous discontent, loneliness, lethargy, and what he considered to be her self-centeredness. Because he had lived in loneliness, he erroneously thought he could relate to his daughter.

> He had entered the subterranean world of the ants, complicated by minuscule tunnels where there was not even room for a thought and where memory was layers of earth and roots of trees. Perhaps that was like the memory of the dead: an anthill without ants, only narrow passages through the earth with no exit to the grass.

Let us glance at the symbolism involved in the above statement. The ant, known for its incredible activity and industry, lives in an ultraorganized society. For each insect to fulfill its multiple activities, thus assuring the continuation of the harmonious society, requires the expenditure of great quantities of energy. The "subterranean world of the ants," when identified with Martin's unconscious, suggests that enormous amounts of libido are being generated, but only subliminally. As such, the intense inflow of electric charges into Martin's unconscious leaves little power left to work out problems facing him in his daily activities.

The "minuscule tunnels," like narrow passageways within the lobes of the mind or the unconscious, taking thought or feeling from one sphere to another, one inner chamber to another, indicate an increasingly desperate search for some kind of answer. As if digging for the roots of a specific tree, or the folds of the cerebral cortex, Martin's process is ever inward, back to the beginning, to prenatal time, to non-time.

That there is "no exit to the grass" suggests no egress: no alternative method of living out his existence. Grass, representing the greenness of fertility, of yearly death and renewal, has been obliterated from Martin's world. Closure, imprisonment in darkness, exile into infinite inner space, although looked upon by some as positive, can only end in tragedy for an individual who is unendingly entrapped. To live in an undifferentiated world; to act and interact only in the inner chambers, corridors, and tunnels of the mind is to yearn for death: to exist in a necropolis of one's own fashioning.

Given the kind of father Isabel has, her schizophrenic personality may certainly be viewed as both the product of her upbringing and an inherited mode of psychic functioning. Despite her difficulties, however, she is still able to live in two worlds, and she is convinced that were her brothers to return to Ixtepec to live, she would succeed in surmounting all odds. Hope, then, is still present. The crisis has not yet come.

Exile into the Hetaera

Besides Garro's interweaving of the stone symbol and of non-time, another important image to be found in *Recollections of Things to Come* is that of *hetaera* (courtesan). It emphasizes the pronounced surrealistic climate in Garro's novel and underscores yet another form of psychological exile.

The hetaera archetype has existed since time immemorial. Beautiful, entertaining, and charming, she was associated with worship of Aphrodite and was introduced into Greek society by an ordinance of Solon. Her function was to see to the pleasures of unmarried men, thereby preventing any threat to the structure of marriage. Many hetaerae were well known for their refined and exquisite ways and attracted men of renown. Aspasia of Miletus drew to her the most extraordinary men of her day, including Socrates and Pericles; the latter abandoned his legal wife to marry her. There were many other hetaera types: Semiramis, Cleopatra, Diane de Poitiers, Jeanne d'Aragon.

The hetaera occupied an important place in Aztec society, where she was "valued" as the helpmate and companion of warriors. Unlike the Christian world, which rejected the courtesan on the surface yet sought her favors clandestinely, the Aztecs were open in their attitude. Although their culture was patriarchal, they neither denigrated nor looked down upon the hetaera; nor were women in general subjugated or oppressed (Soustelle, 184).

In *Recollections of Things to Come*, Julia is the hetaera. She lives in the Hotel Jardín along with the other kept women of Ixtepec. Her lover, the tall and violent General Francisco Rosas, has been sent there by the government to impose order in the area. Sad and sullen, he sometimes drowns his sorrows in drink or gambling the whole night through. Nevertheless, he has been bewitched by Julia's alluring, silent, and mysterious ways. Although able to carry out his military duties, he has little taste for anything but his obsessive passion for his hetaera. General Rosas is a prisoner of Julia's ungiving and sensual ways: an exile from the world.

The general's fixation on the hetaera archetype is understandable. As a collective figure, she is the source of pleasure, energy, and life for the man. Archetypally, she has come to encompass an ideal because it is by her charms that a man indulges in the sexual act, which he regards as creative, and yields to the illusion of being forever young and eternally reborn. The hetaera type does have positive attributes: when acting as a man's helpmate or *femme inspiratrice* on an intellectual, spiritual, or sexual level. But she may also be a destructive force in a man's life, as was the case with Pygmalion, who fell in love with his statue of Galatea. So is it to be with General Rosas. Julia, the seductress, attracts him away from his true destiny and his realistic frame of reference.

When not preoccupied with his passion for Julia, General Francisco Rosas, chief of the garrison of Ixtepec, walks through its streets "striking his leather boots with a riding whip," looking coldly at its inhabitants, and speaking to no one. His presence imposes fear on the town, abolishing the "art of fiestas" and dance. Significant are the images Garro uses to describe him: he has "*tigers* within him"; the pistol he carries is decorated in gold letters enlaced with eagles and doves. Each in its own way reveals elements of his personality.

The tiger and eagle images are characteristic of Nahuatl Indian motifs. Every night the earthly sun, when traveling through the subterranean world to the center of the earth, takes the shape of a tiger; every day, upon rising in the brilliant heavens, it becomes transformed into an eagle, reverting to its tiger shape with twilight. Daily, during the sun's circular trajectory, the warlike and fiery nature of eagles and tigers is put to the test. The sacred battle waged by this igneous mass against its enemy—the darkness of matter—reveals the terrifying archetypal image under which the Aztecs lived: the ever-constant threat of annihilation. Without the sun, life would cease. Being, then, is viewed as forever struggling against the Void. The goal of the important Aztec military Order of Knights, Eagles, and Tigers attests to the continuous tension of waging this "blossoming war" (Séjourné, 112). The Christian dove, embossed on General Rosas's pistol, is antipodal to the warlike tiger and eagle of the Aztecs. It represents that other side of human nature: the soul and spiritual power of sublimation. The Holy Ghost is frequently depicted in the form of a dove as well as in the image of a tongue of Pentecostal fire.

Psychologically, the sun's descent into the subterranean world in the Aztec myth suggests a concomitant descent into the realm of the unconscious. That the image of the tiger, popularly believed to be a violent, vicious, and destructive animal, is identified with this trajectory reveals the potent conflicting forces at work in General Rosas's unconscious. So powerful and so carnivorous is his pulsating libido, that it overwhelms his rational sphere; or, to continue the metaphor, eats up his ego. On a conscious level, Rosas has an eagle personality: like that of the diurnal bird of prey noted for its strength and size, and identified with the fulminating power of war. Rosas, who preys on the weak, is noted for his cruelty. The dove, or self-effacing side of his personality, is manifested only in the presence of Julia, the hetaera.

General Rosas is a programmed individual: always acting true to type. When, for example, Julia avoids him or in some way arouses his jealousy, he takes out his rage on the poor and the feeble: the Indians, the peasantry, and the rebels. He is always present to see to the summary hanging of cattle thieves, or anyone accused of infringement of rules or regulations. As previously mentioned, General Rosas also takes out his sense of defeat in gambling or drinking to excess.[2]

General Rosas spends as much time as possible with his hetaera in the Hotel Jardin. Life within this temple of passion is filled with beautiful and flamboyant women, mistresses of the other officers. Differences exist, however, between the devotion to the pleasure principle as enjoyed by the twentieth-century Spanish officers and their paramours and the practices of those in Aztec society. A hetaera in ancient days, companion to her warrior, encouraged and helped her lover in arranging for the ceremonies of warfare that played such a significant role in his society (Soustelle, 84). To enhance her beauty, thus her role and power, the Aztec hetaera took time to prepare herself: she "grooms herself and dresses with such care that when she is thoroughly ready she looks like a flower" (Soustelle, 131).

Unlike the Aztec hetaera, Julia does not dress with infinite care to receive her lover. On the contrary, whether lying in a hammock or on a bed, her appearance reveals her utter indifference to General Rosas. She wears pink most of the time, be it a negligee or a dress, and her unkempt appearance—"her hair hanging loose and several strands caught in her golden earrings"—in addition to her languid ways, her carelessness, and her apathy, makes her all the more alluring to her paramour. That she is a master at the art of dissimulating her feelings, or that she feels nothing for this outwardly virile man, transforms her into an irresistible power.

From the moment Julia got off the troop train at Ixtepec, she was considered a danger to any and all men: an "alien presence" and different from all other women. The very way she talked, walked, and looked at a man left her imprint forever engraved in his mind. So captivated was General Rosas by this unattainable femme fatale that he allowed no one to go near her. In the evening, however, when she strolled with him on the plaza, he could not prevent all eyes from converging on her. She "wore a pink silk dress covered with white beads, put on her gold necklaces and bracelets. . . . She looked like a tall flower brightening the night, and it was impossible not to stare at her." But if a man approached her to talk or

---

[2]Unlike the strict Aztec law governing drunkenness (a dignitary, official, or ambassador found inebriated in the palace was put to death; if discovered outside the palace, he would, and without scandal, lose his office and be stripped of his titles), infractions of this nature were tolerated under Spanish rule (Soustelle, 157).

even to look at her for any length of time, the general's fury would mount. Once back in the safety of the imprisoning Hotel Jardin, he would bombard her with questions. The more adamant he was in extracting an answer from Julia, the more elusive she became, and the more unrelenting grew his accusations.

Julia was no novice. Indeed, she was well versed in handling such a type. Her method: she would simply break away and withdraw without uttering a word, lie down on her bed, and close her eyes. Her silence, her unwillingness to communicate with her lover, cut him off still further from her world. At times General Rosas was virtually driven out of his mind. The tiger in him reached the point of explosion, whereupon he ruthlessly whiplashed her. Unafraid, and perhaps to arouse his anger still further, Julia would remain behind her wall of indifference. Her listless and aloof comportment revealed better than words her feelings of estrangement from this man she not only did not admire, but could barely endure. Impassible and silent for the most part, she never betrayed any feelings, either through her gestures or her facial expressions. Nor did she ask for anything. When he gave her gifts of jewels (taking government money away from the poor to do so), thinking these would arouse her passion, she remained unimpressed and unreachable. "He gazed into her eyes, tried to find what she was hiding behind her eyelids, beyond herself. His mistress evaded his eyes, tilted her head and smiled, looked down at her naked shoulders, and withdrew into a distant world, noiseless, ghost-like."

Although hetaera types can relate to men on several levels, Julia's power over General Rosas was sexual. What made her invincible was her utter indifference. A seductress par excellence, she was, psychologically, the bearer of his *anima* (the autonomous unconscious feminine side of his personality), or soul figure. As a product of nature, she lived out what she was, relating to herself and her own instincts. General Rosas, on the other hand, suffering from an undeveloped, undifferentiated, and weak ego, could not but be held captive, and increasingly so, by this enigmatic, sphinxlike archetypal power.

In that General Rosas projected contents of his unconscious onto Julia (not a real woman but an *anima*: a collective figure colored by his own subjective reactions), he was blind to her motivations and personality. Even more deleterious to his psychological well-being was that by projecting his subjective contents onto her, the contents remained unrecognized as his. What he viewed in Julia, then, were attributes that he assigned to her and that he claimed to love. Unaware of the process of projection, he could never develop or integrate what he saw in her into his own psyche. Thus did he divest himself of what lived inchoate within him and become

increasingly incapable of coming to terms with his *anima* as hetaera
(Harding, *Way of All Women*, 9).

By secreting her in the Hotel Jardin, Rosas thought erroneously that he
would force her to express her true feelings of love for him. So great was
his inherent arrogance that he could not conceive of her not being passionately attracted to him. His inability to see clearly into himself and into his
hetaera reached such a peak of frustration that he was not only jealous of
her present lack of interest in him, but grew jealous of her past and the
other men who had been in her entourage.

> No word, no gesture could extricate her from the streets and days
> that were part of her former life. He felt like the victim of a curse that
> overpowered both his will and Julia's. How could he abolish the
> past? That shining past in which the luminous Julia floated in mis-
> shapen rooms, jumbled beds, and nameless cities. The memory was
> not his and he was the one who had to put up with it like a perma-
> nent and badly-drawn hell. In those alien and incomplete memories
> there were eyes and hands that looked at Julia and touched her and
> then took her to places where he himself got lost trying to find her.

Although cloistered in the Hotel Jardin, Julia escaped General Rosas emotionally: they lived in different worlds, each inaccessible to the other.

How dissimilar had been his life, he believed, prior to his meeting Julia.
A power, he commanded everyone's attention when riding horseback
across the mountains of Chihuahua; when, for example, he betrayed Villa
by siding with Carranza. "The day he met Julia he had the impression of
touching a star from the sierra sky, of crossing its luminous circles and
reaching the girl's intact body, and he forget everything but Julia's splendor." He was very much aware of the fact that their liaison had changed
him into "a lonely warrior in the presence of a besieged city with its
invisible inhabitants eating, fornicating, thinking, remembering, and he
was outside of the walls that guarded Julia's inner world." Exiled from her
world, and, paradoxically, from his own, he was a man lost to himself.

Still, he could not resist her. She was the center of his magic circle: of
every man's. He had had ample evidence of this psychological fact whenever he took this personification of seduction for a walk on the plaza. "She
moved among the people like a somnambulist, dazzling us with her trans-
lucent skin, her dark hair, holding her fan of finest straw in the shape of a
transparent bloodless heart." Her secret? She never gave of herself, escaping from Rosas "shining and liquid, like a drop of mercury," slipping away
"into nameless places, accompanied by hostile shadows."

As previously stated, the hetaera is archetypal and a projection of the man's unconscious contents; she is not real, but rather the product of a fantasy world. When, therefore, General Rosas described himself as "spinning in a vacuum" with regard to Julia, his assessment was perfectly justified. She was not grounded.

> She didn't walk in this town. She didn't touch the ground. She wandered around, lost in the streets of other towns that had no hours, no smells, no nights: only a bright powdery substance into which she disappeared each time it touched the transparent streak of her pink dress.

The general's world was slowly being dismantled by this indifferent transpersonal force. Drawn inextricably into her orbit, caught in her remote world, he was haunted by her every moment of existence.

> Julia, like an icy rose, gyrated before Francisco Rosas' eyes, then vanished in the frigid wind of the sierra and reappeared floating above the tops of the pinyon trees. She smiled at him through the hail that hid her face and her frosty dress. Rosas was not able to reach her, nor could he touch the cold sound of her footsteps as she crossed the frozen sierra.

Yet this seemingly silent, frigid, and unreachable vamp could, were the right man to come along, become passionately involved. Her distancing from General Rosas may have been used as an unconscious shield: armor protecting her from any confrontations and obligations (Harding, *Way of All Women*, 20).

Taking advantage of the general's absence from Ixtepec, Julia ventured forth from her imprisonment in the Hotel Jardin. Her goal was to warn a mysterious stranger, Felipe Hutardo, of the danger he was in by remaining in town. He had incurred the general's jealousy by staring at Julia on several occasions. He was a marked man.

Upon reaching the home in which Felipe was staying, Julia exchanged virtually no words with the stranger. Her eyes, nevertheless, filled with tears, and he, too, was visibly moved. It seemed as if they had been drawn together by some inexorable power, "as if they belonged to another order." Because Julia and Felipe transcended the world of reality, they managed the miracle of leaving town, despite the general's eagle eye; of crossing the border between "light and darkness." No one heard of them again.

Exile into Schizophrenia

Isabel, from within her stone and living "outside of time, suspended in a place without wind, without murmurs, without the sound of leaves or sighing," recounted her impressions of General Rosas and Julia with, perhaps, a twinge of pain. She had to admit that Julia's presence in Ixtepec had made such a powerful impression upon everyone, men and women alike, that she had taken on the dimensions of a Divinity. Never would her presence be forgotten.

> Her beauty increased in our memory. And those eyes that no longer saw us—what vistas were they looking at now? What ears were listening to her laughter, what stones of what streets resounded as she passed, on what night so different from our nights did her dress sparkle?

After Julia's departure, Isabel's shapeless and empty days pursued their meaningless course, every dawn and dusk resembling the preceding ones. Everything in the time-ridden differentiated world seemed useless, divested of interest, alien to her. Her increasing apathy and detachment from her surroundings and her family intensified her already extreme reclusiveness.

Alone and silent, she lived in a closeted world of her own manufacture. Unbeknown to everyone, "The face that appeared in her dreams was a face that had never looked at her." She, like General Rosas, the object of her love, experienced the secret agony of one who loves but is not loved. Although she intuited only ominous results of her efforts to attract his attention, she decided to wear a red dress to a party given in honor of General Rosas.

Red, indeed, was a felicitous choice. An intensely passionate color, that of blood and fire, it conveyed Isabel's inner climate, thus obliterating momentarily her seemingly apathetic exterior. Inciting to action, red sparkles and radiates incandescent and powerful energetic charges; it provokes and arouses a whole sexual realm. Symbol of the "red light" districts, its tones invite pulsations to surge forth, instinctual activity to flare and burn.

When Isabel approached General Francisco Rosas and asked him to dance, he was, understandably, surprised. As the two twirled to the music, Isabel's "cheeks rouged and her eyes, riveted on the General, seemed to be roaming through a bloody world." That it was only a matter of time before she became his mistress was not surprising; that she should have done so knowing that Rosas had had one of her brothers killed and the other imprisoned during a political uprising, was disturbing.

No one understood Isabel's reasons for moving into the Hotel Jardin. Was she hoping, perhaps, to erase Julia's memory in her lover's heart? Impossible. Just as Julia had felt nothing for her lover, so General Rosas was uninterested in Isabel. They were not even sexually compatible, and "in bed he found himself with a strange body that did his bidding without saying a word." As soon as it was light, he left the room. Isabel remained. At night, upon his return, he encountered her "obstinate eyes." Whereas Julia's way had been indifference, Isabel's presence "asphyxiated" him.

> He had tried to imagine that it was not she who waited for him but the other one, and disconsolately he put out the light and went to bed. The young girl did the same and the room was filled with lianas and fleshy leaves. There was no space for him, or for his past; he was choking. "She takes up the whole room," he said to himself.

Rosas realized too late that he had made a mistake by taking Isabel as his mistress. Each time she mentioned her brothers, he felt trapped and stifled. The situation grew virtually unbearable after Nicolas, who was in prison, was tried for having attempted to rescue Father Beltran and Don Roque. The people of Ixtepec, and certainly those of the Hotel Jardin, thought that Isabel would finally take a stand and speak out on behalf of her brother. It was not to be, for there were, indeed, two Isabels living within her: the one who had loved her brothers and the other who accepted deceit. Each lived in its separate and incompatible dimension.

Isabel's exile into schizophrenia was irreversible. Attempting to live the life of another—Julia—so as to secure a love that was never to be, she became increasingly divested of what little ability to communicate remained. Gone was any pretense at an interpersonal relationship. Maladaptive reactions and their antisocial and nonconforming patterns dominated. Indifferent to reality, estranged from herself, she found even her fantasy life growing dull and grey.

General Rosas did not attend Nicolas's trial. His discomfiture at the idea of imprisoning the brother of his mistress had aroused his long-buried sense of right and wrong. When he returned to Isabel after the trial but before the verdict had been pronounced, fear took over as her "red dress shone beneath her dark eyes by the oil lamp." Disoriented by the sight, "he was lost, treading on unknown nights and days, guided by the shadows that the brothers and sister had cast over him."

Nicolas, who wanted to die, confessed to all the accusations. When he was sentenced to be hanged, still protective of his sister, he alluded to her with pride as an "avenging goddess of justice." At the cemetery, after

Nicolas was buried. General Rosas rode out of Ixtepec never to return. Isabel, rushing after him, got lost in the endless desert and mountains. Her body, found down the hill, had already turned into stone. In death, as in life, she felt nothing: "From her heart stones sprang forth; they ran through her body and made it immovable." As she looked out into the past that was her present and future, she understood: "We were exiles from happiness!"

9 Beckett's *That Time:* Exile and "That Double-Headed Monster . . . Time"

"That double-headed monster of damnation and salvation—Time" is the antagonist in Samuel Beckett's[1] play *That Time* (1976) (Beckett, *Proust*, 1). The mutant and miscreant Time is the enemy that forces that protagonist's exile and slow deterioration. Time, unceasingly and eternally, eats voraciously into every second, hour, day, year, decade, century. Past, present, and future in *That Time*, like three black holes in the heavens, expand when called upon to articulate thoughts and feelings, only to contract seconds later, in what becomes a final gravitational collapse at the play's conclusion. (Capra). Because of Time, life is viewed by the protagonist as a loss and an insult; a dominating, enslaving, imprisoning, and torturing indignity. Worst of all, it feeds illusions; it breeds the fossilization of ideologies, dogmas, and behavioral patterns, forever luring and alluring mortal minds to grasp at deceits in their attempt to arrest the nonapprehensible.

Because the story in *That Time* begins at the end, audiences are not imprisoned in linear time as in traditional drama, waiting and wading through an accumulation of sequences, observing the inexorable march of decrepitude in an increasingly helpless and hopeless protagonist. As humanity's foe, Time has already eliminated, pulverized, reduced Beckett's

[1]Samuel Beckett (1906–89) was born in Dublin. He studied and taught in Paris, and settled there in 1937. His first novel *Murphy* (1938) was followed by *Watt* (1942–44) and his trilogy: *Molloy* (1951), *Malone Dies* (1951), and *The Unnamable* (1953). Humor as well as pathos, an increasing sense of metaphysical anguish are implicit in his theater: *Waiting for Godot* (1952), *Endgame* (1957), *Krapp's Last Tape* (1959), to mention but a few that captured the attention of an international public. Bilingual, Beckett wrote in both English and French, translating almost always his own works in one or the other language. His plays have been performed all over the world.

protagonist, the Listener, to virtual nothingness. Born into Time, a product of the finite universe, he has failed, as does everyone and everything else in the manifest world. Yet his mind, like that of other mortals, also attempts to fit events and ideas into a series of partitions, concepts, illusions, deceptions, catching him up in what the Hindus call *maya's web*.

Although memory gives structure to *That Time*, it does not give it meaning. Associations and suggestions pull the Listener (and reader) into the story. (Asmus, 349). Because, for Beckett, the artistic process proceeds via contraction, intuition, and perception, and not via intellectual or rational concepts, no grand construct—as in the dogmas of organized religions, or of political, social, or artistic institutions—is acceptable. On the contrary, these palliatives are viewed as blinders, illusions, traps. Only doubt is real. Thus the artist, at best, is only a translator of, or Listener to, inner murmurings. He is not a creator.

That Time. Curtain. The stage is dark. A light shines on the Listener's halo-shaped white hair. Only the head is visible: "about ten feet above stage level midstage off centre". Silent and nameless, the archetypal Listener listens to the three disembodied voices (A, B, C) emanating from loudspeakers placed to the left, to the right, and above the stage space. Identityless, he exists only in terms of the succession of voices echoing from his past. Neither affirming nor rejecting a point of view or a way of life, the Listener submits to existence: fate, death. Yet every now and then, reactions are indicated though always with reserve: by the audibility or inaudibility of his rhythmical breathing and the opening and closing of his eyes. Both are barometers able to measure the impact the voices make on his invisible interior clime. His *being there* is sufficient to point up the anguish and feeling needed to create drama.

Although there are three voices, they are one. Each, representing a period in the Listener's life, is isolated from the others, imprisoned in its own dimension, limitations, time-frames, levels of understanding. As such, each is exiled in its own world: A, the middle-aged man; B, the youth; C, the old man. The trinity's speeches are sounded four times, in a different order each time, during each of the three cycles.

While listening to three segments emerging from his past, the Listener, like an eavesdropper, absorbs the fragmented unfoldings as if from a transpersonal sphere. A supreme consciousness, he hears the words, tones, and diapasons that help him redefine his existence: viewed as a slow divestiture of free will, an expiation for the original sin that was his birth into the world of consciousness. Objective, neither rebelling against Time nor siding with it, like Job he experiences his reality, his slow decomposition, as a fact of life: "Though he slay me, yet will I trust in him: but I will maintain my own ways before him" (Job 13:15).

There are times, nevertheless, when pain becomes acute. It is then that the Listener takes comfort in precedents: musing, say, about the child that he once was or about his trip back to his hometown in his middle age. Although aware that any attempt to escape the "cancer-Time" is to no avail, the Listener's voices, nevertheless lapse momentarily into dreams, loves, and ideations. "They modulate back and forth without any break in general flow except where silence is indicated." As each voice introduces its own score, instrument, rhythm, and shading, it re-collects instances from the unending memory bank that is the psyche. These retreats are only momentary in the Listener's harrowing descent/exile from the human sphere.

Despite the fragments of past happenings given in *That Time*, the play deals in universals. The city to which the voices return in their foray into the past is Dun Laogaire, south of Dublin on the coast, but it could be any city. The stories flow into a present, they encapsulate a panoply of moods and feelings, ranging from distress to elation. When, for example, the Listener reflects on the child that he was, the flashback seems comforting at first, like a habit. In *time*, it takes on harrowing dimensions: a period that once was and is no more is viewed as a painful deception, a "great deadener," a constant reminder that life consists of perpetual deaths, each moment driving one closer to the finale.

That Time 1

The play begins. Darkness is transformed into Light fading up to the Listener's face. From death to birth: from the Void (that is, the formless, the unarticulated, the potential embedded in the collective unconscious) to the created, the differentiated articulations of the ego (the center of consciousness). From no word to the word. The miracle of transformation is perhaps best conveyed by two Hebrew words: *ain* (nothing) and *ani* (I, or something). Merely changing the position of one letter, one breaches the gap between the uncreated and the created (Scholem, *Major Trends in Jewish Mysticism*, 218).

The voice of "A," the middle-aged man, speaks: "that time you went back that last time to look was the ruin still there where you hid as a child when was that." That the Listener's eyes close during A's meditation suggests a descent into an archaic past, an exploration into absence, a slow absorption into earlier comforting, feeling tones. He has recourse, momentarily, to illusion-filled mental constructs existing in a time-riddled world. By situating or making concrete a period that had been, with such statements as "that time," "back," or "that last time," A endeavors to fill the limitless emptiness of his present, the aloneness of the Listener's old age, the meaninglessness of his individual existence in an impersonal universe. Allusions to penultimate and ultimate time-frames, although seeming to give structure to abstractions, instead further emphasize universal flux. Passing moments are incarnated into present modes with such words as "ruin," which may be interpreted symbolically, as something that has fallen, crashed, been damaged, or collapsed from age; it represents the end of an era, culture, or life.

From the very outset, the "child," running through (what had perhaps once been a Druidic temple or sacred grove of stones), puts into juxtaposition the archetypal images of young and old. Within the Child exists the Old Man; within the Old Man exists the Child. That Beckett focuses on the archetypal child in *That Time* and in so many of his other works intimates a need to emphasize fluidity, rather than rigidity, of attitudes. The child to which A alludes is special in that he is what the Listener once was. Imagination roams supreme in this child: as if inhabiting fairy tales. Everything for him, be it a stone, a picture, the sky, the sun, water, has the power to alter in form and substance. Dreams, excitement, and the impossible exist in this child's actuality. Undifferentiated, unlimited, and unimprisoned unconsciousness overflows into consciousness and vice versa, inviting unimpeded communion.

Because the child throughout history has been viewed as the hope of the future, a common and universal concept is that of the divine child (Moses, Buddha, Christ) and the child-hero (David, Roland, Siegfried). As a primordial figure, *filius ante patrem*, the child represents unity and plurality; as a messiah, the beginning and the end, *renatus in novam infantiam*. Psychologically, children represent pre- and postconsciousness. (Jung and Kerenyi, 27). Vested with infinite power, these saviors of the world are capable of establishing continuity and eternality in families. The child in *That Time*, however, is identified in psychological terms with the ego; it has never been born. It has lived its specterlike existence in an unmanifested psychic state.

That the Listener closes his eyes, descending more deeply into his meditation, allows him better to absorb the welcome intrusion of past moments—those of the child in particular—into a present reality. Although he cannot situate the precise time when he stepped into the tram on the "grey day took the eleven to the end of the line and on from there no trams then all gone long ago that time," he reacts affectively upon learning that since that time the trams have turned into ruins. The only proof of their existence is in the "old rails."

Grey, like ash or embers, suggests residue; for the alchemist, the quintessence that remains after all excess has been burned off: the death of the flesh and the retention of the skeleton, the end of linear time and the even flow of cyclical or eternal time.

Through the image of the tram, a machine adhering to a time schedule as well as to a mapped-out trajectory through space, A experiences past and present as two distinct psychological and cultural phases. While permitting communication on a collective level, the tram also imposes its impersonal laws and rhythms on the individual. What remains of a once-functioning tram are its "old tracks," its skeleton (or organizational system and methodology), divested of its livingness. Tracks, coordinators of segments of a once-viable network, may also be interpreted as visible replicas of a once-productive inner psychic organizational pattern, operating according to its own mysterious and inexorable plans. A observes these unworkable, unusable tracks as so many rusted and useless carcasses, as a metaphor for old age.

The voice of C recounts another legend: "when you went in out of the rain always winter then always raining that time in the Portrait Gallery in off the street out of the cold." In the world of analogies, the winter season represents the cold, barren, stark period when nature withdraws into the earth, seeking nurturing and warmth. So, too, does the Listener dig within for comfort against the congealing rigors. Fluidity, in the form of rain, also enters C's reminiscences. For alchemists, water solves the unsolvable by dissolving it. When a stumbling block in life is broken down through liquification (as when sugar or salt is placed in a bowl of water), a smoother, more objective, and more comprehensive attitude is created. Thus, an individual and his or her problems, when blended into the whole, may be viewed from a distance, with fewer details but with greater perspective.

That C went into the Portrait Gallery for shelter from the cold and rain indicates further interiorization, hence, distancing from an inclement outside world: "in off the street out of the cold and rain slipped in when no one was looking and through the rooms shivering and dripping till you found a seat marble slab." C yearns for protection against a stormy, grim, unpitying exterior world relentlessly dominated by Time. Designed to exhibit replicas of God's creations, the Portrait Gallery, like any museum, exists in order to arrest Time, in this case, by the re-creation of the human form realistically, imitatively, or diagrammatically. Is C oblivious to such deceptions and snares? C, like the egoless child he once was, takes the same route: penetrates the inner rooms of the Portrait Gallery, surreptitiously, unseen. Shivering and wet, he wanders through the rooms until he finds "a seat marble slab," sits down, and dries off.

Is the "marble slab" referred to by C a tombstone? a dolmen? a prehistoric monument dating from patriarchal Druidic times? Is he referring to his own past? The Irish countryside is peppered with stones that symbolize continuity, cohesion, hardness, unity, and strength, as opposed to the fragmentary, fleeting formlessness of sand. Unlike the human body, the "marble slab" is not subject to rapid change. Let us also note that the juxtaposition of stone and water ("rain") brings to mind a psychological condition. When identified with Noah and the turbulent winds and waters of the Flood, the inner oceans of the collective unconscious come to mind. During moments of chaos, when "suffering" overpowers consciousness, opacity prevails; after the waters subside and calm sets in, the treasures of the deep may be glimpsed and the light of consciousness clarified. Thus is the invisible transformed into the visible, the unheard into the heard, and unconscious into conscious contents.

Affectivity (turbulent waters) is the primal mover needed to stir the inert matter, the treasures, of the deep. But cerebralness must not be overwhelmed if consciousness is to be expanded. The inert matter of the depths, recognized as treasure as it enters consciousness, may be symbolized by the marble slab—possibly Irish Connemara stone—upon which C sat. Marble is heavy and hard to move, but may also be very valuable. Highly polished thoughts, with their veins of feeling, are as beautiful as marble.

The stone may even be sacred to C, as is the case of other legendary stones: the Kaa'bah, the Emerald Table, the Omphalos, the pillar of God's house (Gen. 28:22), the cornerstone (Acts 4:11), dolmens, and so on. Within these seemingly hard and unfeeling relics of ancient times, there lives a sacred power. Did not Orpheus's sweet tones move stones? Did not stones, equated with bones in the Deucalion myth, become a source of life? Does not the Zohar tell us about Adam's descendants who recorded in hieroglyphics astronomical data on two stone tablets, one of which Noah found at the foot of Mt. Ararat? (Eliade, *Myths, Dreams, and Mysteries,* 169). Nor should the stone tablets upon which the Ten Commandments were written be omitted from the list of hierophanies. Understandably, C takes momentary comfort in these universal and timeless traditions.

The third voice that the Listener hears is that of B, the young man, who lives in a dreamland: his future (Asmus, 346). It is no longer winter: "on the stone together in the sun on the stone at the edge of the little wood and as far as eye could see the wheat turning yellow vowing every now and then you loved each other." Another trap. Two polarities come into being: the stone is warmed by the sun, but also shaded by the little wood where Mother Nature burgeons without design as *massa confusa.* Yellowing wheat, symbolizing birth and death, as did the previous archetypal images of the child and the old man, suggests the beginning of the end of life.

Once something enters the world of Time (manifestation), it takes on mortality. The ripened wheat, ready to be picked and transformed into food, reflects the apostle John's optimistic view of eternal rebirth: "Except a corn of wheat fall into the ground and die, it abideth alone: but if it die, it bringeth forth much fruit" (12:24). Within this same image exists its contrary, the agony experienced by Jeremiah: "They have sown wheat, but shall reap thorns: they have put themselves to pain, but shall not profit" (12:13).

Rebirth is just another lure, as are the love vows to which B refers. Taken when a youth, "you loved each other just a murmur not touching or anything of that nature you one end of the stone she the other long low stone like millstone." All was purity in those days and there was faith in the future, in the legends and tales where goodness and happiness prevail. In *time*, the joy of romance turned into a "millstone," a grinding experience, a heavy burden. Love, like yellowed wheat, became jaded, dated, outmoded, a tiresome habit. And all the yesterdays are the same: clusters of unendingly ripening fantasies about love concluding as pulverized fictions and fabulous fables. With "eyes closed all still no sign of life not a soul abroad no sound," the fictions of youth slowly erode. Life, sound, and sight have atomized, sunk into the unincarnated timeless, spaceless collective unconscious: the Void, that inner cemetery, that "charnelhouse" of being.

The round of disembodied voices speaking to the Listener begins anew, with the voice of A recounting another legend: of taking his "nightbag" on the ferry and walking onto "the high street neither right nor left not a curse for the old scenes the old names" onto the wharf, where the previously mentioned old rails exist in their now-rusted condition, "when was that was your mother ah for God's sake all gone long ago." This second incursion into a past marks an even greater demolition of illusions, a more cutting mockery of religious ideations. Mother and God figures, once indispensable, are now experienced dispassionately. Assessing their damage on his spirit and psyche, the speaker regards their deceit with contempt. He now experiences the "old scenes the old names" like so many overhanging rusted and unusable tram wires. Rust. Corrosion: "last time you went back that last time to look was the ruin still there where you hid as a child someone's folly." Only in the preconscious, egoless world of the child, where connections with timelessness and spacelessness take root, can "folly" exist. Does this unevolved period in a child's life spell madness? Or, like the clowns of old, are children the only ones to speak the truth?

C again looks at his past, and life in general, but in a harsher light: "for God's sake all gone long ago all dust the lot you the last huddled up on the slab . . . in the old green greatcoat." Here, too, images deceive: the beautifying green grasses of Ireland cover ruts and gulleys, dangerous stumbling blocks. Love arouses passion, but also conceals a future of routine and boredom. C walks on; "not a living soul in the place only yourself and the odd attendant drowsing around in his felt shufflers not a sound." The impact of death, decay, isolation, and alienation takes on actuality, emphasizing a soul in exile. All returns to dust, particles of a past, diffused experiences, disparate and powdery residues of earthly life, relics and products of disintegration. As Beckett wrote: "We are alone. We cannot know and we cannot be known" (Proust, 49).

B still believes in a future of burgeoning leaves, sheaves of wheat, and love retaining the glow of its vows. Thoughts of sadness do not yet intrude, though love will dry, falter, and fall. Feelings of warmth and well-being tinge his outlook, as he rekindles the memory of the time he and his sweetheart took their vows to love each other always.

A muses on Foley's Folly, "a bit of a tower still standing all the rest rubble and nettles." Towers, constructed in the Middle Ages as lookouts for observing enemies, were protective constructs, but also took on ascensional symbolism: the tower places humans far above the madding crowds, feeding them inflated ideas. It also cuts them off from the mainstream, isolates and alienates them from society. Built in the form of a tower was the alchemist's *athanor:* the stove in which the various operations leading to transmutation of metals took place. Designed to elevate base metal (lead) to its purest form (gold), the tower may also be said to unvitiate the vitiated. That A remembers the tower, though all else has turned into "rubble and nettles," suggests the sameness of mankind's yearnings: a search for final answers, the finite's need to understand the infinite.

Linear, or historical, time associated with such constructs as towers, trams, and walls, or humanized, as in family enclaves, fragments what was once unified and connected. Stone becomes rubble, bricks tumble and crack, and mortals vanish, as the whole mass of worthless and decayed detritus piles up. The fables of faith taught to the young slowly turn to dust; pain, in the form of piercing "nettles," stings and abrades tender and vulnerable flesh. Bitterness burgeons with each succeeding laceration by those coarse herbs flourishing throughout the countryside, hidden beneath a beautiful coat of green grasses.

A can't remember where he slept: "where did you sleep no friend all the homes gone was it that kip on the front where you no she was with you then still with you then." Was it with her or not? Did it really matter, as it was for only one night and the ferry would be back in the morning? The ruin where he had hidden as a child is again mentioned, as is the stone, perhaps wistfully this time. Each is a sacred affective presence, memento mori.

C recalls peering out onto "a vast oil black with age and dirt someone famous in his time some famous man or woman or even child." The soot of an industrial life that has taken over is juxtaposed with the luster of a famous person who lived in these same environs. In the Portrait Gallery, behind the glass, pictures of "famous man or woman or even child such as a young prince or princess" peer at him, only to swivel, turn, and vanish. Did they ever exist? Or were they *eidola:* fragments, glimpses, like so many scintillae, of continuously mobile atoms?

B voices anew what he had seen, said, and felt: sun, wheat, sky, vows, love. What is love? Then archetypal figures are constellated and conflated syncretistically: Lao-tzu. Chuang-tzu, and Confucius, with the Western Christ: "suddenly there in whatever thoughts you might be having whatever scenes perhaps way back in childhood or the womb worst of all or that old Chinaman long before Christ born with long white hair."

C continues to interweave Heraclitean formulas into speech patterns: "never the same after that never quite the same but that was nothing new." The eternalness of the unknown, its sameness, and its motility in the universal flow, although nonapprehensible, is forever resurrected by memory. Similarly with words: although they sound alike, A intimates, each takes on different meaning, depending upon text and context, mood and atmosphere, the tonality and tempo of the individual voicing them. Some are spoken with more *feeling* than others.

B, near the window, "in the dark harking to the owl not a thought in your head till hard to believe harder and harder to believe you ever told anyone you loved them." He must have been blind when incarnating his feelings in words of love at that *time.* Just as the owl is identified with sadness and melancholia, so B's thoughts are painful. Even worse, the owl, according to the ancient Greeks, carried out the dictates of Atropos, cutting the string of life, and hence was identified with death. Another question arises. Was B referring to the pain caused by love for reasons of adultery? For the Welsh, Blodeuwedd, the unfaithful wife of Llew, was transformed into an owl as a punishment for her adultery and for having betrayed the secret of her husband's vulnerability. Are not these tales, segments from a collective past, also examples of a personal agony? Or are they "just another of those old tales to keep the void from pouring in on top of you the shroud"? Were they once, but no longer, true? "The aspirations of yesterday were valid for yesterday's ego, not for today's" (Beckett, *Proust,* 42).

That Time 2

After ten seconds of silence the Listener's breath becomes audible. His eyes open. He is ready to undertake the "ex-foliation" of his being. Elements of his inner world become more palpable as sound waves infiltrate the stage space. Like those mysterious eidola, vision upon vision constellates before the Listener's mind, not in accordance with Cartesian or Newtonion rational and logical processes, but following the Listener's inner network of acausal pulsations emanating from his unfathomable and suprapersonal depths.

The Listener has no illusions about the meaningfulness of the triadic dialogue, which is really a monologue, nor is he deceived into thinking that it will stem the course of his progressive decline. He knows that whatever he is, thinks, and feels is contingent upon his past, which he is absorbing and reabsorbing through the voices of a world that was. As elliptical and repetitious incantations pass into the empty caverns of the Listener's decrepit old brain, their impact on his subliminal world is evident. He closes his eyes once again, enabling his reverie to proceed. As his verbal patternings fill the moment, the paradoxical degradation endured by a virtually nonexistent ego becomes increasingly heavier to bear. He understands now that life is emptiness, and to prolong it is, as Beckett's protagonist maintained in *All That Fall* (1957), to see oneself slowly burn out under the heat of an ever-smaller flame.

Twice C refers to a "turning-point" in life, once in the singular and once in the plural ("always having turning-points"), implying mankind's obsessive need to structure and give mathematical logic to the world in a frantic attempt to grasp its meaning. There is no understanding, however, of the unfathomable. Democritus suggested: "We know nothing in reality; for truth lies in an abyss" (Hesla, 9). Are C's references to turning-points to be understood as realities in eschatological time-frames? Is he adding further to his ironies in the phrase "the one the first and last that time"? Is the unstable oceanic journey that is life also a construct of the mind, like Descartes' triangle? Are both to be understood as concrete? In his seminal letter to Sighle Kennedy, Beckett wrote: "If I were in the unenviable position of having to study my work my points of departure would be the 'Naught is more real . . .' and the 'Ubi nihil vales.' " (Beckett quotes Arnold Geulincx: 'Ubi nihil vales, ibi nihil velis' [where you are "worth nothing," you "want nothing"]) (Kennedy, 304; originally published in *transition* [March 1932]: 148–49).

C's "point" (or "points"), although determined in space and time, are dimensionless and directionless. Yet, he wants. Theologians, such as Clement of Alexandria, considered the positionless point as indicating primordial unity; for Angelus Silesius, the point contains the circle; Kabbalists view it as the space from which the hidden manifests itself; the Hindu sees the point (*bindu*) as the germ or drop from which incarnation takes root.

Because everything emanates from and returns into a subjectless "turning-point" (or "points"), C's metaphor, "that time curled up worm in slime when they lugged you out and wiped you off"—may refer to the inception, that is, the birth and death process in an endless round. Didn't Beckett write in "Dante . . . Bruno. Vico .· . . Joyce" that "transmutations are circular"? Programmed existence, or the alpha and the omega, operates prior to the point's emergence, as is implied in the image of the worm curled up in the fetal position in slime. Such viscous deposits, when associated with primordial matter and the circularity of the earth's configurations, take on womblike form; and the worm takes on the form of a phallus. Although C "never looked back" then, he does now, to that birth-day in time or in "another time."

B, once radiant in his naiveté, again refers to stone, sun, towpath, sand. All are subject to change during the course of the dramatic unfolding: "facing downstream into the sun sinking and the bits of flotsam coming from behind." No longer outspoken nor quite so sure of himself as he once was, he recalls a past that resonates and reverberates through the Listener's cavernous brain. B has begun to experience time as a "sinking" "downstream," leading to confusion and absurdity, as when making something out of nothing through projection, or when stamping one's days with meaning in a meaningless universe.

What remains of all the dreams? B speaks of "flotsam coming from behind and drifting on or caught in the reeds the dead rat." Plans, ideas, works, events, are like so much floating detritus: wreckage of ships, miscellaneous materials lumped together carried along by the shifting tide and the rhythms of the waters. Everything drifts, forced here and there by the currents, or caught, ironically, by thin, swaying, fragile reeds. The "dead rat" not only conjures up images of humanity's ultimate end, but of the sameness of its aggressive and destructive habits. Like mankind, this fearsome, nocturnal, forever famished rodent eats its way into anything and everything, killing not out of hunger alone, as do other animals, but like human beings, for blood. This chthonian creature, nevertheless, suggests duality: in the *Iliad*, Apollo's other name, Sminthee, signifying "rat," suggests both a God of vengeance (as sender of the plague) and a healer of disease. So, too, in the Orient, is the rat viewed positively and negatively: although vicious, its presence in agrarian societies is considered to be a good omen of a plentiful harvest. Thus is the initial Naught followed always by the Aught.

Like a leitmotif, the images of the ruin insinuate themselves into C's monologue with growing poignancy; C, "waiting with the nightbag till the truth began to dawn," yearns for answers. But there is no truth any more than there is a final word: just continuous comings and goings of sunrises and eventides, beginnings and endings, expectations and disappointments, "coincidences of contraries" (Beckett, "Dante . . . Bruno," 6). In the world of contingencies, affirmation is inseparable from negation, position from opposition, the visible from the invisible, the audible from the silent: all constructs of the mind. Without one there is no others. Without life there is no death.

C regresses: "not knowing who you were from Adam." Who is he? Whence came he? and when? From the flotsam of eternal duration prior to the formation of ego-consciousness, prior to awareness, to the world of contradictions, antagonisms, and oppositions. The fact of "not knowing" invites him to sink back to prototypal man, the *anthropos:* Adam (*ada-mah* in Hebrew) was fashioned from earth/dust (Gen. 2:7). So the artist, replicating the Creation, brings forth his own work from his flesh and blood, amalgamating linear and nonlinear, spatial and nonspatial frames into the incarnated mixture and animating matter.

Since C mentions Adam twice, he may be referring to the two Adams: the second Adam, although referred to as the first in the Bible, and the Kabbalist's Adam Kadman, who was really the first and the purest symbol of God in human form. Because the "fullness" of the Divine Light flowing through Adam Kadman was too great, it shattered that which contained him. Thus did the first cosmological drama, alluded to as "The Breaking of the Vessels," come to pass.

When C mentions the "skull you were clapped up in whose moan had you the way you were was that time," he may be referring to the pain following the Breaking of the Vessels. When the protective coverings of dogma and systems are shattered, and thoughts and feelings wander alone in pleromatic spheres, they are vulnerable to attack by contents in both conscious and subliminal spheres.

Alone in the Portrait Gallery again, C observes the images of those who have died, like so many black spots imprinted on sheets of paper, like so many pages in a child's picture book, or signs and codes in ancient collections of magic spells. The dirt, dust, or earth of Creation, like today's DNA, serves to link the contemporary with the ancient, thus becoming another of mankind's methods of structuring and ordering what is in the last analysis outside of its dominion. To crave order, dates, and facts upon which to base each "point of departure," is for nought as much as it is for aught. Yet, from one century to another, from one pouring rain to the next, theories evolve and dissolve, dredging up the flotsam until "closing-time," when disintegration causes everything to flow back into primordial earth—*adamah*—the first again becoming the last.

For B, there is "no sight of face or any other part." Did the invisible face ever exist? Isn't each being a product of another's projection and thus without identity? Graven images must not be made, nor must a name be allotted to that which is unnamable. Letters only—YHWH—for the name of God are acceptable, as signs of that which is infinite.

B affirms that he "never turned to her nor she to you always parallel like on an axle-tree never turned to each other just blurs . . ." The axle refers to both the world of contingencies (trams, carts) and the cosmic spheres (Tree of Knowledge, Tree of Life). The image of the axle bar (phallus) and wheels (earth, womb) conflates sexual polarities with mystical ones (and is perhaps an allusion to Ezekiel's vision of the Divine Chariot, which allowed him to glimpse God's appearance on the throne) (Scholem, *Major Trends in Jewish Mysticism*, 265–66). Once again, such images, though they structure and comfort, allow "space between." The unfathomable and unnamable will always be out of reach of the finite mind, and the inch separating the former from the latter will never be obliterated, no matter how concerted the "pawing." Memories of a dead past and the once-tender vows taken are "no better than shades no worse" and cannot obliterate the gaping Void.

"Bowed half double," A experiences life as the Stations of the Cross, as a perpetual and mounting agony. After years of prayer, hoping in vain to regain that lost paradise, A faces only the "Doric Terminus of the Great Southern and Eastern all closed down and the colonnade crumbling away so what next." Cultures have come and gone: among them the Dorian invaders of Greece (twelfth century B.C.E.), colonizers of Asia Minor, organizers of Sparta, creators of the stark columns of ancient temples. Meaningful and meaningless. The austere and striking Doric colonnade adorning the train station, a paradigm for a network of confluences, may represent evolution, but for A it spells desuetude, collapsing points of departure and returning crumblings and vanishings in the flotsam and jetsam of existence.

C recalls "the rain and the old rounds," the whirls of water moving downstream, the circular dances and songs, referring perhaps to ancient Druidic stone burial monuments in the round. Roundness may be associated with the head, and by extension with the inner circuits of the mind. Linear time-frames are hurdled as C spans, syncretistically, centuries, cultures, and religions. No longer new and dynamic, no longer creative and innovative, they have left behind stones and other residues of sacred relics, now useless old forms, like the "tottering and muttering" C. Entropy has set in.

B now stands "stock still" as he looks back again at "that time on the stone" or at "that time" in the sand and sun, observing the "blue or closed blue dark blue dark stock," still dreaming, believing in the scene of love floating up into consciousness. To be "stock still," ideationally or otherwise, is to encourage stasis with its stock mental contents, its stock phrases, its stilled cerebral constructs that in time become facile mental coordinates. Or does the "stock still" refer to the arrested notion of primordial mankind from which all others descended? As A takes stock of himself, he begins to understand that his stock, once hardy and creative, is no longer so. Development has been arrested. But for him who is so young the end is not yet in sight: "still side by side scene float up and there you were."

The voice of A remembers that he "gave up and sat down on the steps in the pale morning sun," his eyes following the trajectory of the circular fireball through the heavens. Now A is pale, seated as he is in the shade, or midway through life, no longer bathed in the glow of the sun's infinite luminosities. But in the past, he recalls, he "gave up and off somewhere else," always elsewhere, perhaps on a "doorstep" entering into another sphere of being, another time-level, another spatial dimension, forever wandering through the initiatory phases of the life/death experience. Soon, A will take the "night ferry," leaving that childhood world of hide-and-go-seek, with pain but also with anger; the past, although dead, still has the power to move him effectively. The passionate cry of "to hell out of there" allows him to abreact to the "old scenes the old names," the "passers pausing to gape": is he not, like them, just such a passerby, gaping, observing, looking in from the outside, transient but not transcending? Gaping, open-mouthed, staring fixedly, gazing stupidly: all suggest new, multiple openings of chasms, abysses, yawning maws, *vaginae dentatae*. Does A refer to the boatsman Charon, who transported the dead over the Styx, in his utterance "pass pass on pass by on the other side"?

B, still "stock still," in the sun or outside of its radiant glory, observes it sinking out of his line of vision. His thoughts are also descending, as are his feelings, which until now have rarely stirred out of the categorical confines of habit and imperatives, caught up in the blissful safety of doctrines. Somewhat between "the two knobs on a dumbbell," B seeks balance rather than intellectual exercise; such exercise displaces, brings vertigo and the terror of disorientation. Stasis is simpler; unthinkingness more comfortable; numbness more protective.

C utters his soliloquy, "always winter then always raining always slipping"—as he totters along, looking here and there, seeking to remove himself from the cold, the rain, and the solitude. His "green holeproof coat" inherited from his father, not only keeps him warm and dry, but this same cloak (*brat*) is a royal attribute, in Celtic tradition, part of a person's patrimony, handed down from one patriarchal generation to the other. Both protective and isolating, this special holeproof coat permits the wearer, like the god Lugh, to remain invisible. By donning the holeproof coat, one accepts, outwardly, the will and consciousness of the collective. Only when the seemingly solid coat is cast aside and its worn threads are examined can systems and doctrines reveal their imperfections.

Wearing the holeproof coat, C, like a shadow, passes through all the old places, such as the Public Library and the Post Office, freely, unquestioned by anyone. Yet the Public Library is the very place that breeds opposition, that arouses contention, that reveals apertures in the finest of protective garments and the most veiled of arguments. The Post Office, like the railroad terminus, is the focus of infinite networks of outgoing and incoming dialogue and activity.

A, "huddled on the doorstep in the old green greatcoat in the pale sun" on his knees, perhaps praying, yearns for direction. Increasingly depersonalized and displaced, with a slowly disappearing memory, he has forgotten the details of his beloved's meanderings, and his own. He is virtually divested of ego. The "green greatcoat" of his fathers has smothered and stifled whatever burgeoned within, crushing his very being as he passes into the nothingness of death.

Life, for the Listener, a series of "points of departure" from present to past through the mediation of voices resounding in the inner corridors of his own emptiness, has taken him through two of the three zones of life: the Light of youth and the semilight of middle age. The darkness leading into the terminus remains to be lived out.

That Time 3

Ten seconds elapse. Three more seconds, and the Listener's eyes open on to another verbal foray into an increasingly contracting anterior world. As various archetypal patterns emerge and collide in Beckett's trialogue, the ego's attempts to burgeon, to find a direction, to establish its points of departure, seem to falter. Words, such as *stone, wheat, blue, towpath, rat, floating, sunset*, although used in the first two parts of the play, take on additional affectivity at this juncture. Their varied placements in the clauses lend greater ambiguity to the Listener's plight, thus increasing the terror of a world constructed on continuously shifting quicksands.

Words, such as *ghosts* and *mules*, introduced by B for the first time in part 3, add to Beckett's thematics of time. When B states "or alone on the towpath with the ghosts of the mules the drowned rat or bird or whatever was floating off into the sunset," he is recasting the already well-worn notion of death, posited in such images as drowned, floating, etc. The

French word for ghost, *revenant*, means the soul returning or coming back from the dead. Like contents sunk beneath the waters of the collective unconscious, certain words and images now return to consciousness, peopling the Listener's world with the shades of those fallen into oblivion. The Listener sees silhouettes of memorabilia floating in his mind's eye. Visions of bygone eras, they are a whole population of ghosts embedded in an inner landscape. These invisible atomizations, materializations of sound and light waves, provoke associations and recollections, perceptions so powerful that they can redirect libido (psychic energy).

The Listener's eyes close again in an attempt to block out, as if once and for all, the whole conscious/rational world. That B refers to "the ghosts of the mules the drowned rat or bird" reinstates nonhuman patterns of behavior. The mule, a hybrid animal, implies sterility, as well as stubbornness; the bird, the tapping of spiritual, aerated, and nonearthly levels; the death-dealing, fertile rat connotes dangerous polarities. That mule, bird, and rat are dead may represent a premonitory image of mental barrenness, aridity, impassibility, and the final detachment from it all.

A continues: "none ever came but the child on the stone among the giant nettles." Although the child-image once implied youth, zest, and a world of infinite possibilities, no such meanings now prevail; staid and stunted voices have taken over. The child, as ego, has aborted. The giant nettles, like the crown of thorns, have pierced A's flesh and psyche, cutting away, slowly and incisively, the once-fixed protective walls surrounding him. Now he is withdrawn into the library, where pale, shadowy, and diffused "moonlight" penetrates onto his book, "breaking up two or more talking," thus fragmenting what once appeared to be unified and impervious. Divisiveness, fostered by the brilliant and blinding rays of patriarchal consciousness (*logos*), has not insinuated itself into the book; instead, dimmer, more subdued luminosities, echoing from subliminal spheres, have shone the light of their lunar matriarchal powers (*eros*) upon him. Such feeling forces, "moods," are allowed to flow forth with increasing abandon.

But, as C notes, the mood of openness does not last. Instead, "always winter endless year after year." Coldness. Congealing. Nature goes underground again, in search of interior warmth, while bequeathing barrenness to the outside world. Opposition, however, implicit in the world of contingencies, brings "bustle," despite the rigidity and fixity of the ghostly winter. Images of the Post Office and Christmas activate the staid atmosphere: perpetual movement (of the mail) in and out of town merges with feelings of yearly renewal and expectation of the rebirth of the archetypal divine child.

B looks back again, imagining himself alone, lying on his back on the sand, prior to or after having taken his empty vows of love. Sand, when associated with time, as in Zeno's paradox of the heap of millet, or as in Beckett's *Happy Days* (the play in which sand progressively fills the stage with every passing minute, burying the protagonist up to her neck), cannibalizes life. The cycle begins anew: as linear time gives way to preconscious levels, an "old scene" comes into view, along with time-embossed symbols of the rat feasting on the ripened wheat, or the bird gliding over the sands casting its ominous shadow over events in and out of time. Repetition and habit, like a spreading cancer, leave the once-zestful B hybrid and sterile.

A increasingly seeks to anchor time in linearity: "eleven or twelve in the ruin on the flat stone." Cause and effect are steadying powers, as are all barriers erected to stave off the floodwaters of the unknown. In a last-ditch attempt, A seeks further to clarify, increasingly to differentiate ideations within the world of the intellect in order to stay on top of things. In so doing, he lapses back into petrified schemes and formalized units of time. Yet, here, too, energy patterns remain. Eleven, the penultimate, before twelve, the number of completion; as well as the conjunction of 5 and 6, the microcosm and the macrocosm, still reveals struggle and action. So does 12: although it represents the end of the yearly cycle of months, en route back to the beginning, the number's digits taken singly indicate dynamism: 1 (unity) and 2 (duality, differentiation, in the unending birth/decay syndrome).

As childhood, youth, middle age, and old age move on simultaneously with the dimming sun, A pursues his "moonlight muttering," paralleling the continuous march of a degenerating mind and body. And "clutching the nightbag and drooling away out loud eyes closed and the white hair pouring out down from under the hat," on he walks. His imaginings feature him still wearing his hat, perhaps like the archetypal wise old man. An object used frequently by Beckett, the hat, identified with the intellect, as was the crown in ancient days, is now seen as covering for a forgetful and failing mind.

The decrepit form enclosing the faltering mind, seen by "passers pausing to gape at the scandal there" continues on. (The word "gape," indicating a wide-open mouth, like that of Kronos/Saturn when devouring his children, is also reminiscent of the medieval replicas of the Inferno, its voracious jaws open wide, waiting for the bodies of the sinful.)

Fearing "ejection having clearly no warrant in the place," C understands that he no longer belongs to this town or any other: there are no ties, no bonds, no links—but also no chains. Any relationships that he might have had, like "thin air," are no longer.

A, still walking, "making it up on the door step . . . again for the millionth time" rêcapitulates, reassesses, reviews, rethinks. The "doorstep," threshold of the inner world, leads from one time zone to the next from the known to the unknown. It must be passed if he is to pursue his initiation and step from life to death, thus confronting the two-faced Janus, the Roman God who looks east toward the rising sun and westward to its setting. Determining beginnings and endings, Janus stands guard at doorways and gates, opening and closing them *once* during the year.

C refers again to the Library, to the dust, "the big round table with the bevy of old ones poring on the page and not a sound," while B recalls the time he gazed out of the window into the dark and saw "the owl flow to hoot at someone else or back with a shrew to its hollow tree." The hollow tree, emptied of its life force, serves as the owl's protection. And "not another sound hour after hour not a sound when you tried and couldn't any more no words left." Aridity, sterility, nothing but an outer core remains.

A is anxious to leave, "not a curse for the old scenes the old names not a thought in your head only get back on board and away to hell out of it and never come back." C's last words confess to endless emptiness: "not a sound only the old breath and the leaves turning and then suddenly the dust . . . only dust . . . and not a sound only what was it said come and gone." Infinite deaths and rebirths. As Beckett noted, "In the one movement is unidirectional, and a step forward represents a net advance: in the other movement is nondirectional—or multi-directional, and a step forward is, by definition, a step back".

The Listener's eyes open. He smiles, "toothless for preference." Is he smiling at himself? at the thought that he has taken himself too seriously? Does his grin spell triumph, for having finally accepted himself and his life such as they are? Or is the rictus a sign of pain? Did not Beckett himself define the essence of his art when he wrote, "Nothing is funnier than unhappiness" (*Endgame*, 18).

Enigma faces the Beckettian explorer, confirming Roger Blin's statement: "Beckett's theater's very "ambiguity makes for its richness" ("Le froc d'Estragon," 35). To attempt to explain and define *That Time* or any other Beckettian work is to try to clarify mystery. At best, one can offer only a personal reading for one's own edification.

Beckett's sense of exile in *That Time*, his feelings of aloneness and lack of identity, of irremediable hopelessness as life pursues its continuously coruscating and abrasive struggle against the supreme antagonist time, is perhaps best conveyed by the dramatist himself. At the conclusion of a lecture by Jung that Beckett attended, he wrote:

He [Jung] spoke about one of his patients, a very young girl. . . . At the end, as the people were leaving, Jung remained silent. And, as if speaking to himself, astonished by a discovery he was in the process of making, he added:—Actually, she was never born. . . . I had always had the feeling that I, too, had never been born. (Juliet, *Rencontre avec Samuel Beckett*, 31)

10 Cheng's "The King of the Trees": Exile and the Chinese Reeducation Process

In "The King of the Trees" (1985) A. Cheng[1] narrates the experiences of a group of Chinese city-bred high school students, referred to as "intellectuals," who were exiled by their government to a remote forested region for reeducational purposes. Virtually unique in contemporary Chinese literature is Cheng's manner of fusing Taoist, Buddhist, Confucian, and shamanist concepts with the modern Communist credo. His fiction runs counter to the cut-and-dried social realism popularized after Chairman Mao Zedong proclaimed the People's Republic of China in 1949. "The King of the Trees" is deeply rooted in both the empirical world and the mysterious forces of nature. That a tree is the protagonist of Cheng's tale suggests not only a poetic responsiveness to transpersonal powers governing the universe, but a concomitant unwillingness to reduce the tangible and intangible world to the mechanistic laws of science alone. Nor, in his view, should life be geared to strictly utilitarian purposes any more than the earth should be used solely to benefit humanity. Everything, be it formed or unformed, created or uncreated, visible or hidden, circulates throughout the universe as a vital and living entity, acting and interacting with everything else in a seemingly unbroken web of movement. Endowed with its own vital essence, life, a complex of opposites, links the individual to

[1]A. Cheng was born in 1949, the son of two "intellectuals." Having read his father's entire library, he had been exposed not only to the works of such Western writers as Tolstoy, Dostoevsky, Zola, and Hugo, but to the writings of Chinese philosophers as well. After completing his undergraduate education, he was "sent to the country" for ten years in keeping with the dictates of the Cultural Revolution. Encouraged by his friends to write about his experiences during his ten-year exile, he did so in the three novellas included in "The King of the Trees."

the whole in ever-flowing and continuously transforming patterns. In that humans are both manifold and uniform, they are able to, in Cheng's narrative, participate in the world of actuality while also experiencing the natural beauties that suggest a deeper underlying reality.

Cheng's strange combinations—a hidden world of gods, demons, and ancestral spirits controlling events lurking behind a visible world with its modern political, economic, and scientific concepts—serve to kindle both tension and fascination in the reader. As noted in the *I Ching* (*The Book of Changes*, 1122–770 B.C.E.), when two conflicting situations exist in time, "they become compatible by following each other in time, the one changing into the other" (Wilhelm, *I Ching*, 3).

Although very much aware of his country's problems, Cheng is neither concerned about rectifying economic or political conditions, nor about denouncing the multiple problems facing the young in China today. He neither praises nor condemns extreme ideologies, be they utilitarian or mystical. His prose is a distillation of paradoxical elements; detachment is juxtaposed to profound feeling tones. Melodramatic and bloody events are absent from his novella. Conforming to traditional literary views, Cheng's style is imagistic when needed; meditative when linking natural and supernatural worlds; controlled when relating events; and intuitive when broaching the mysteries of nature. First and foremost, Cheng is an artist, a spinner of tales in which spiritual agencies are at work.

Exile into Remoteness

Of prime consideration for the Communist party leaders in charge of the young boys and girls exiled to a primitive country region is the transformation of a beautiful but economically useless forested mountain into a productive enterprise. Youth, the party leaders believe, must be catalyzed into action in order to wipe out the schism between past and present and to foster more drastic egalitarian reforms in the rural people's communes. An effective way of achieving such a goal is to use slogans, such as the "Great Leap Forward."

The remedying of a faltering economy, let us recall, began to be organized after a period called the "Three Years of Hardship" (1959–62), which ended in China's dispute with the Soviet Union and the launching of its Cultural Revolution (1966–76). During these turbulent years, city-bred "intellectuals" and "bourgeois" were sent to labor on the land, in an attempt to abolish whatever class differences remained between poor and rich. Cheng spent ten long years working on farms and in mountainous regions in Shanxi, Inner Mongolia, and Yunnan provinces. His tale is not fiction, but rather carved out of his own experience.

The "young intellectuals" of the novellas have never been exposed to the primitive conditions of the remote forest which they now face: thatched huts, communal bamboo beds, no lights, no amenities. One of the most outspoken of the group, Li Li, prides himself on his rational, logical, and scientific outlook. Practical and utilitarian, he comes armed with a fine library given to him by his parents: the works of Mao Zedong, Lenin, Marx, Engels, Lin Biao, and others in the Communist canon. The purveyor of but one single and rigid point of view, he believes that the future rests with the young. Not only does he undergo a culture shock upon his arrival in this far-off region, but he is immediately bent on changing what he considers to be the ignorance and backwardness of the natives. Their ways are totally unacceptable in the new, modern, and utilitarian China.

What Li Li's inflated ego (center of consciousness) has not taken into consideration is the behavioral patterns of the indigenous mountain people whose land he is visiting. For centuries they have lived in harmony with nature, fervently and zealously retaining an equilibrium that not only brings them contentment but enriches their spiritual lives. Because they believe that everything in the universe is linked, terror for them is provoked by large-scale natural disturbances such as tornadoes, floods, and earthquakes. These are regarded as signs of a greater struggle taking place among the gods and spirits inhabiting trees, streams, mountains, grasses, and celestial spheres (Eliade, *Shamanism*, 448–54).

One man in particular, in Cheng's tale, arrests the narrator's attention: the small but sturdy Wizened Xiao, whose first iron-grip handshake makes him, and the others in his group, wince with pain. Carrying the heavy luggage of the young "intellectuals" to the dormitory, the Wizened Xiao hoists it onto his shoulder with speed and dexterity, as if he were toying with a feather. Most impressive is the manner in which he cuts wood: in one stroke he severs a large tree trunk with a hatchet. Li Li cannot believe his eyes. Not to be outdone by this "primitive" man of the forest, he intends to prove his worth in the same manner, but barely succeeds in cutting through the bark. Unnerved and embarrassed, he tries again. This time he buries the hatchet so deeply into the trunk that he cannot extract it. The Wizened Xiao comes to his aid, pulls it out with ease, and proceeds to cut the tree trunk into pieces. After bringing the logs into the main hall, he lights a fire that crackles and sputters like a series of explosions. Its glow and aroma, in addition to the intense energy emanating from the conflagration, fills the entire area with warmth and feelings of well-being.

So impressed are the young boys with the Wizened Xiao's incredible skill and strength that they compare him to Prince Wen Hui's butcher, mentioned by the Taoist sage, Chuang-tzu. Because the butcher knew where the animals' natural joints were located, he could carve a thousand cattle without once having to sharpen his knife. Likewise does the Wizened Xiao approach his trees not with his eye but with his mind.

The narrator, glancing out of the window of the dormitory at the thickly forested mountainous area under lunar light, is moved by its misty and incandescent beauty. The site instills in him a sense of awesome mystery, as if he were in some way in touch with the Taoists' otherworldliness— that which exists beyond the phenomenal sphere. A barking deer gamboling about the bushes and trees for some strange reason seems to cast a spell on him. The forest, one of Mother Nature's domains, represents mystery. Because certain wooded areas give the impression of being enclosed, and because they are moist, and retain their freshness, they have been associated with the maternal womb, and are, therefore considered a source of regeneration and of secret knowledge. Within this dark and fertile realm, with its uncontrolled growth of thick foliage, shrubs, ivies, and creepers, sunlight has been banished in favor of obscurity. Because of Mother Nature's undirected fertility, forests have also been identified, psychologically, with the unconscious and the irrational.

For the psychologically unprepared, danger lurks, so to speak, behind every tree, every stone, every shadow in a forest. People unable to fathom their motivations and character traits, or to explore the nature of their fears, hates, and loves, may, like the unsuspecting and uninitiated wanderer, disregard the signs of the forest and its portents. As a result, they may be swept away and fall victim to the terrors and perils of the night world, or to a wild animal, or poisonous serpent. Inability to see into situations, people, and oneself can lead to the mutilation and cannibalization of the ego by subliminal forces. In forested regions, apotropaic rituals are not uncommon, and function with felicity in the form of tree cults. Propitiatory offerings suspended from the branches of sacred trees are ways "primitives" have of paying homage to these powers, thus warding off disaster from forest demons and enemies.

Ascending the Mountain-Forest

The day after the young people's arrival, the party leader orders them to climb the steep mountain so as to familiarize themselves with the right path to take to its summit while also becoming aware of whatever dangers they might confront. The stifling heat, high grasses, shrubs, trees, and creepers, as well as the insects, snakes, and other creatures they meet on their way, obstruct their pace, leaving them breathless every few feet. Upon reaching their goal, they are thrilled with the spectacular view: a seemingly infinite range of smaller mountains, planted fields, and clusters of thatched huts opens up before them in the distance.

The ascent of a mountain is viewed symbolically by the Chinese as a creative move upward; in ages past the cosmic mountain K'un Lun, the Abode of the Taoist Immortals, was considered by believers to be the highest point on earth. Centuries back, Taoists warned that heights, for the spiritually unprepared and untrained, can encourage hybris. To integrate a sense of loftiness into the personality, they maintained, takes time and experience. The city-bred youths, who have no understanding or feeling for sacredness or for mystery, could easily become inflated and imbued with a sense of power as they stand, so to speak, on the top of the world. Whereas for the narrator, the sight instills wonderment and awe, Li Li reasons that the mountain and the forest are to be conquered, dominated, and put to work for the people.

Likening the shape of the mountain to a human brain, the narrator is reiterating, perhaps unconsciously, Taoist belief. The K'un Lun not only corresponds to a head, but has also been identified with a nine-tiered pagoda. Each step is ascended only after preparation in mystical matters is deemed to have been completed. Such instruction, psychologically, takes an individual from a strictly one-sided, pragmatic, earthly view of life to a more transpersonal spiritual approach.

The mountain experience may, therefore, be viewed as a testing ground designed to teach the narrator and his friends how to cope with physical difficulties and how to protect themselves from harm, but also how to temper their drive for power and their zeal to convert others to their way of thinking. An example of hybris in Chinese history is found during the Han dynasty (200 B.C.E.–200 C.E.), when an ancient mountain people, founders of the Yelan Kingdom, became so filled with their own importance that they considered themselves to be the center of the world. Inflation, the Taoist, Buddhist, and Confucian canon notes, must be cut at the root.

That the Chinese government has called upon the narrator and his group to cut down the old trees, burn them, and plant new ones, with the idea of changing a sickly economy into a healthy one, is, on a psychological level, a paradigm of the archetype of transformation. The tension existing in the archetype per se may foster psychological growth from an adolescent frame of mind to mature understanding, from limited knowledge to vaster horizons. Thus, the narrator and his friends will perhaps learn to flow with time and adapt to continuously altering circumstances. When a person or the collective is unable to deal with a problem, archetypes may act as energetic compensatory devices for what is lacking or remiss, helping to mobilize counterforces to solve the difficulties at hand (Franz, *On Divination and Synchronicity*, 56).

In the case of certain archaic psyches, such as those of the Wizened Xiao and Li Li, the emotional intensity associated with their specific archetypes is so powerful that subject and object become rooted in one another. So passionately identified is the Wizened Xiao with trees in general, and with one sacred Tree in particular, that his very existence is bonded to them. The same is true of Li Li but for opposite reasons. He projects onto the archetype of transformation, which he equates with abstract political notions. The two are fused. His doctrinaire, utilitarian, and pragmatic vision is driven to override all opposition to his singleness of purpose. In each case, psychic energy is connected with either natural phenomena or dogma. Both the Wizened Xiao and Li Li live in a uroboric stage of original totality and self-containment. The former experiences a profound communion with nature, transcendental powers regulating his universe; the latter is programmed by his abstract political ideology. Their undeveloped egos exist *in potentia*, enjoying primary identity with the Self (total psyche). Neither functions as an independent or evolved force. Both cling to one way, to a rigid inner topography, rather than adapting to an eternally changing world. Confucius, in his *Doctrine of the Mean*, wrote: "Effect central harmony"; that is, maintain a flexiblé attitude in life, remain open and ready to deal with the world of opposites. Whereas contrasts exist and help usher in awareness of one's role in life, rigidity perpetuates a condition of battle rather than harmony (Wilhelm, *Lectures on the I Ching*, 4–5).

The birth of the People's Republic of China and the drastic changes effected in religious, ethical, social, educational, literary, and political values created a vacuum in the psyche of many Chinese. The long, rich, and self-contained traditions adumbrated by Taoist, Buddhist, and Confucian philosophers had not only been rejected, but, at least on the surface, had been supplanted by a functional and economically oriented system dominated by modernism, technology, and Westernism. The religious and philosophical feelings inculcated into the Chinese for over two thousand years, although seemingly defunct after Mao Zedong's revolution and its aftermath, were, however, very much alive, driven underground into the transpersonal spheres of the psyche or the collective unconscious.

What are the implications of Taoism, Buddhism, and Confucianism with regard to Cheng's "The King of the Trees"? Taoism (the Way), as conveyed in the *Tao-te-ching*, attributed to Lao-tzu (604 B.C.E.), and in the philosophical writings of Chuang-tzu (369–286 B.C.E.), approaches life in terms of a bipolar concept. Nature's cyclical processes (night and day, seasonal changes, growth and decline, etc.) indicate two complementary abstract forces continuously at work in the universe: yang (masculine) and yin feminine). Each contains its opposite: within yang there is a dot of yin; and within yin, a dot of yang. One polarity, however, is not necessarily at war with the other; rather, it is viewed as complementary to its opposite. These ordering principles, as yang and yin are frequently alluded to, interact eternally and constitute the only certainty in life: the continuously transforming elements in Tao.

While yang is identified with ethereality, light, spirituality, and the highest values, yin is equated with earth, moisture, darkness, and gross matter. It must be stressed that the intuitive mental mode of Taoism does not assign moral judgments to cosmic forces. As transpersonal powers, neither yang nor yin may be translated into empirical terms. Each has its destructive and constructive sides. A condition of aridity and sterility in a society may occur if that society overvalues the yang, or rational, function; if yang is properly diffused, illumination comes into being, the thinking function becomes productive, and cosmos replaces chaos. So, too, yin may be nutritive, warm, and healing when applied to situations and individuals in a moderate manner, or death-dealing when used immoderately. When Tao is violated and the yang or yin principle becomes overpowering, one of the polarities is seen as sinning against the other. A reconciliation of the opposites is in order.

Tao, viewed as a life principle (or breath of life) that circulates throughout the cosmos as yang and yin, was metaphorized by Lao-tzu. He saw it as a perpetually flowing force, as the source of energy that vitalized nature, and as the "mother of all things." In the *Tao-te-ching*, Tao is depicted as an operative power meandering about the universe, allowing psychic energy to flow from patriarchal to matriarchal spheres. Because it is universal and eternal, activating and determining the path individuals and societies take, it may be said to be archetypal.

The humanistic rationalism of Confucius (551–479 B.C.E.) preached a family-style morality based on the ethical wisdom of "superior men," on character-building, learning, virtue, filial piety, and ancestral piety. For Confucius, as noted in his *Analects*, "filial duty and fraternal duty" were "fundamental to Manhood-at-its best." Such a philosophical view gave people a sense of continuity and security. A person did not feel cut off from his or her roots simply because a parent no longer walked the earth. Strength was drawn from the belief in a chain of generations. According to the *Analects*, only the wisest and most honorable men were capable of governing society; therefore moral integrity was stressed. It was incumbent upon the "gentleman" ruling China to elevate those he governed by serving as an example, rather than by exercising autocratic control. Civilization's continuity, then, depended upon the moral fiber and rules of conduct of the central authority. Confucius's finite view, resting on action, effort, benevolence, and unselfishness, was that social order rested on moral order (Confucius, 59–62).

Buddhism, founded by the Indian S'akyamuni Gautama (566–485 B.C.E.), preached the doctrine of Buddha, the enlightened One. Happiness and salvation are the product of inwardness, independent of transitory exterior phenomena. The most popular form of Chinese Buddhism, the Pure Land (Ching-t'u), based on such scriptures as the *Lotus Sutra*, taught that all people who were devoted to Amitabha (a Boddhisattva reigning in the Western Paradise), who accomplished meritorious deeds, and who possessed great faith, were capable of salvation and eternal life—not only the selected few who devoted their lives to religion (Thompson, 87; see Bary, *Sources of Chinese Tradition*, vols. 1 and 2).

The Wizened Xiao, living a contemplative but not a quiet life, is active; he is attuned to nature, and, in this regard, to Taoist principles. Restrained in his ways and uninterested in the world of appearances and in possessions, in accordance with Buddhist principles, he does not see peripherally, but *into* things and people. Because of his profound understanding of the various approaches to integrity, he meets the requirements of the Confucian canon. Li Li, on the other hand, looks down upon such spiritual notions, which he labels "superstitions," as detrimental to China's new direction. The narrator, who has been exposed through his family and his readings to traditional religious doctrine, although he does not practice its rituals, understands its import intuitively. He is a feeling person who relates to people and his surroundings. Neither swept away nor possessed by any religious or political ideology, he discerns and differentiates among them, as if reacting to dramatic leitmotifs and their variants in numerous associations and combinations (Jacobi, 8). During his sojourn in the mountain region, he is exposed to the workings of nature, learning with the passage of time to appreciate the magnitude of this universal power, this *Mana* principle: a transpersonal energetic force that creates life, form, and movement. The raw energy he confronts, living amidst the organic and inorganic world of the forest, will expand his knowledge and inculcate in him the wisdom necessary to build and structure his own world, thereby participating in the collective experience of enriching his nation.

To become a whole being, however, implies making both the physical and spiritual worlds operational. Contemplation allows the mind and psyche to unfold and reach down into the earth, responding to the vitalism it offers; as well as up into aerated climes and the spiritual values these may decant. Through contemplation one may thus become integrated into both cosmic and pragmatic worlds.

Trees and Sacredness

Mystery and awe suddenly intrude into the utilitarian world as some of the city-bred boys and girls stand in front of an enormous and most spectacular tree, wondering why this one has been left intact while others on other mountains have been cut down. The group leader informs them that "this tree has become a spirit. It will bring misfortune to the person who cuts it down," which elicits peals of laughter from the inexperienced city-bred people, and Li Li in particular, who deems such explanations retrograde and superstitious, hence counterrevolutionary. The group leader, nevertheless, reiterates his statement, adding that even "the King of the Trees" refuses to fell this particular tree: to do so might harm the "tree-spirits" living within its protective bark. Who is "the King of the Trees," the young people ask? The group leader remains silent.

For the Wizened Xiao, certain trees become hierophanies, or sacred objects. Because their leaves die yearly and are reborn each spring, they are identified with inexhaustible life and eternity; they are thought to rise from the dead and to be possessed of virtues beyond human comprehension. In that they are inhabited by tree-spirits, they are active principles, endowed with healing and/or detrimental qualities which affect human destinies.

The tree, for the primitive, is a universe, a totality of fragments. Like the boddhi tree, under which the Buddha sat when experiencing illumination, or the alchemists' Tree of Knowledge (*arbor philosophica*), symbolizing the growth and evolution of an idea, or the Tree of Paradise (Tree of Life) in the Garden of Eden, corresponding for Christians to the Cross of Redemption, *one* Tree in particular is endowed with sacredness for the Wizened Xiao. His destiny is linked with this transpersonal power.

Understandably, the narrator and his city friends encounter difficulties in their attempt to broach the mysteries inherent in the primeval forest and its inhabitants. For pragmatists such as they, trees, plants, flowers, stones, stars, and rivers are objects to be used, studied, analyzed, and approached with scientific detachment. To identify with inanimate or inorganic entities would be preposterous for them. Wood is wood, plain and simple. Not for the older generation, who consider it one of the five elements, the others being fire, earth, water, and metal. Used for both building material and fuel, wood is and always was crucial to the Chinese. When wood works in harmony with the other four elements, serenity is said to pervade both society and the cosmos. If antagonism is dominant, as it is in "The King of the Trees," crises, catastrophes, and pain overtake the world. In the *I Ching*, associated most particularly with the trigram *t'chen*, wood triggers disruptions and disturbances of all types. Agitation, however, is not always viewed as a negative quantity. The cutting of trees, or the use of a hoe or a shovel to break up soil, allows seeds or new plantings to cut through the earth's hard crust, thus paving the way, metaphorically, for the archetype of transformation to pursue its course.

The young city dwellers are, with the exception of the narrator, unaware of nature's mysteries, unaware of Tao, the life principle that infuses the world with its energy, endowing it with meaning. Climbing the mountain and carrying out the orders required of them will help the young people enlarge their understanding of both their spiritual and material needs. Trees will be viewed not only in terms of their sale value, but cosmically as well, as mirrors of eternally transforming energies. In that the roots of trees dig deeply into the earth, they may be associated with the world's navel: the center, the point of creation, that area where the primordial rhizome had its beginnings. The knowledge that trees have been here for millennia endows people with a sense of security and equilibrium. The extension of their branches toward the heavens replicates a human yearning: the need to bridge the gap between earth and celestial spheres. Their vertical trunks, extending from the earth's center to its extremities, like the human spinal column, also link disparate factors.

The narrator, an intuitive type, responding deeply to unconscious contents, is stunned as he stands directly in front of the enormous tree. He feels overpowered by its stateliness, its dense foliage, and the sound of the wind blowing through its leaves. He wonders whether its whisperings or murmurings are part of some secret language. Every now and then, as the sun's rays peep tremulously through its branches, shadows grow and lend an eerie quality to the scene, in sharp contrast to the innumerable lights falling to the ground in waves and sheets. The tension mounting in the narrator is relieved when sparse colorations of heavenly blues are glimpsed through the tree's cloaklike leaves. So dazzled is the narrator by the luminosity of this one Tree that he finds himself speechless: "The only tones I could have uttered would have been the cries of a wild beast."

The narrator notes other signs and portents that seem to emphasize the otherworldliness of the Tree as hierophany. That a barking deer appears at times in the forest is far from unusual, but that it always makes its presence known in the vicinity of this awesome natural force, as if it belonged to it, is strange. Deer in China are frequently associated with the Tree of Life and with the Buddha, whose teachings elevate and whose wisdom appeases both despair and passion. In that the deer is the single animal capable of discovering a sacred fungus (probably *Polyporus lusidus*, having the power to lengthen one's days), which grows at the roots of trees, it is associated with eternalness. Taoists believed that because the fungus was the food of spirits, it was also beneficial to humans. To this day, the Chinese eat this plant for what they believe to be its important tonic and dietetic properties.

Suddenly, as if out of nowhere, the narrator sees a barefoot child, busy digging for yams. Neither the narrator nor his friends have ever seen yams. After tasting one of them, they confess to remaining unimpressed. What does intrigue them, however, are the markings of this special child: he was born with a supplementary finger on his hand. Because of this, he tells them, he is named Six Claws. That he is the son of the Wizened Xiao draws him, for some strange reason, ever more closely to the narrator.

Six, the number of manifest heaven in the *I Ching*, is represented by a chariot pulled by six dragons through the sky, symbolizing spiritual potential in action. When something is brought into being, the *I Ching* tells us, its opposite is also established, indicating a need on the part of the participant or observer to tame the volatile and unevolved aspects of emerging elements. The intensity of the energetic power, suggested by the image of the dragons, must, when referring to humans, be stilled and meditated upon; that is, transformed into forces equipped to guide one into productive ways in an expanded universe. While Buddhism views stillness or rest as "an ebbing away of all movement in nirvana," the *I Ching* sees it as "a state of polarity that always posits movement as its complement." In keeping with Chinese views, however, these two seemingly conflicting ways are in agreement when true quietude comes into being: inactive "when the time has come to keep still, and going forward when the time has come to go forward" (Wilhelm, *I Ching*, 130, 201).

Children, generally speaking, symbolize the future, natural simplicity, and spontaneity, which can be formed and re-formed anew. As conveyed by Chuang-tzu:

> to know when to stop, and how much is enough, to leave others alone and attend to oneself, to be without cares and without knowledge,—to be in fact as a child. A child will cry all day and not become hoarse, because of the perfection of its constitutional harmony. (*Chuang-tsu*, 225)

The child need not preoccupy himself with ethics as he still has the capacity to enjoy all that is operational in the yin and yang of Tao. Because his ego has not yet been born and because he still exists in a condition of participation mystique (unconscious identification with the collective unconscious), he is truth. For him, therefore, spirit and concretion are equally real; thus will he participate in the archetypal transformation about to take place.

The Hewing of the Trees

Some of the young people sent to the mountaintop to cut, chop, and divide what Mother Nature has generated will come to realize that all situations in life may be viewed as stages of change that pave the way for individuals and societies to adapt to continuously altering needs.

Psychologically, such hacking and hewing activity may be viewed as a powerful but as yet unintegrated energy flow within the psyche. Paradigmatically, it indicates a breakthrough of unappeased instincts: anger, sexuality, spirituality, lust for power, aggressive behavior, and so on. The dismembering of the ancient natural mountain sanctuary, which for centuries has filled countryfolk and hermits with calm and serenity, and the razing of the trees in a heretofore protected area understandably generates anguish in the heart of those accustomed to the trees' inspirational quietude. The city-bred modernists, accustomed to tearing down and building in the hustle and bustle of their daily routine, are oblivious to the spiritual and psychological impact of such divestiture. Their unique goal is to end that primeval power and its uncontrolled vegetal life. The power is identified with the unconscious and with chaos, which they consider to be a waste. Li Li and his group seek, as we have seen, to order, dominate, govern, and bring to consciousness what has for centuries been obscured. To do so, they maintain, will be financially remunerative; China will grow economically and politically and again become a world power. That mystery and a sense of sacredness will be banished in the process, that rigidity, codification, and uniformity will usher in aridity and stasis, is of little concern to these slogan-conscious youths.

What Li Li and the practitioners of the new order have also not taken into consideration are the ancient shamanistic traditions practiced in this mountainous forest region. The natives believe that shamans, or holy men, have the power to communicate with a spiritual world. Sorcerers, sorceresses, mediums, exorcisers, and magicians see through the carapace of the world of appearances. Having direct access to heavenly and abysmal regions, they are in a position, through meditative disciplines, to ask advice and communicate with otherworldly spheres. Inanimate forces are active organisms for these mountain people, who have not yet come to rely on sociological, economic, political, and religious superstructures. Trees, birds, barking deers, flowers, lakes, fires: nature as a whole is alive. Whether animate or not, each entity, endowed with its own essence, follows a specific pattern of behavior that the natives understand and to which they respond. Birds, for example, suggest a soul ascending to heaven; spirits of animals and flowers are power principles identified with the earth. Chinese shamanistic views focus on a life in which cosmic rhythms are perfectly incorporated into being (Eliade, *Shamanism*, 405–7; *Patterns in Comparative Religion*, 268–305).

Since shamanism, as well as Taoism, Buddhism, and the Confucian canon, are considered by Li Li and many members of the group to be a remnant of ancient retrograde beliefs antithetical to Communist dicta, tension between the modern viewpoint and that of the Wizened Xiao runs through Cheng's novella, emphasizing the fundamental dichotomy between the two extremes in a rapidly changing culture.

The Third Day

Work for the city-bred young people is ordered to begin on the *third* day. Three, an all-inclusive male (yang) number in the *Tao-te-ching*, is said to arouse effulgence and activity: Tao produces one, one produces two, and two produces three: that is, all things. So, too, in religious concepts, do ternary forces regulate the universe: the ancient Egyptian's Trinity (Osiris, Isis, Kamu-tef), the Hindu's (Brahma, Siva, Vishnu), and the Christian's (Christ, God the Father, the Holy Spirit). In mathematics, the triangle is the third force resolving the conflicts created by duality, while in philosophy one may find syllogistic reasoning or Hegel's thesis, antithesis, and synthesis.

Three, then, is an auspicious number for starting to work. Li Li, the most energetic of the group, hacks away at the trees speedily, conscientiously, and in an organized manner. The others, tiring easily, particularly during the first days of their travail, rest a good deal of the time. It gives them the leisure to look up at the strange and perpetually altering cloud formations that hide the sun and cast eerie shadows on the mountain; to gaze at a pheasant passing by; to discover a serpent they rush to kill. Before the group eats of the plethora of strange mountain fruits, one member is elected taster. Although they have all been brought up in a strictly pragmatic manner, it is interesting to note that their cultural past was still a potent force within their psyches, accounting for the association they make between the taster and the mythical benevolent divine laborer, Shen Nong (Walls and Walls, 27). A legendary emperor, he was believed to be the one who taught agriculture to the Chinese (2737 B.C.E.) and who later became god of medicine and pharmacy.

The narrator feels a sense of shame vis-à-vis the experience in woodcutting with the Wizened Xiao and the prowess and perseverance of Li Li. Now he is determined to learn as best he can to manipulate a hatchet, wisely drawing upon his own experience: his father has taught him that a blade must be prepared prior to its use. Without the use of agents of transformation—fire (friction) and water (liquefaction of a solid)—a steel knife or hatchet cannot be given a fine edge. Moreover, "a sharp edge on a blade is the sign of a warlike soul." Armed with such knowledge, the narrator, convinced somewhat prematurely of his herohood, begins cutting every small tree and bush within range. When it is a question of hacking away at relatively large trunks, however, he succeeds in making only a dent in the wood, and in chipping his hatchet blade.

The very fact that the narrator begins questioning the reason for his failure as contrasted to the Wizened Xiao's success indicates the active presence of the archetype of transformation. Watching the mountain man using a bill-hook to sever a tree with a mere twist of the wrist, the narrator understands how much he has to learn. Experience once again opens him up to the transformation process by breaking up what had once been solid preconceived notions. To ponder and wonder, and thus to search for answers, is to invite a change of focus. The narrator is adding experience to his roster: weighing and discerning, filtering and sifting his acts and thoughts. Psychologically speaking, his ability to break up tree trunks intimates preparedness to do away with simplistic answers. Thus will he usher in a dual world of contrasts: shadows will be infused in areas bathed in blinding light. Interchange and fluidity of thought and feeling will activate what has until now lain dormant.

To sharpen a hatchet, a knife, or a bill-hook is paradigmatic of a need to shape one's world and to fashion one's destiny. Cutting tools that pierce or penetrate matter have been identified with discernment: large problems, when separated or broken down into smaller segments, may be broached in various ways and more easily solved.

The narrator, always eager to learn, observes the Wizened Xiao sharpen the blade of his bill-hook, then strike the tree and disengage the tool from the trunk without causing a dent in the blade. Again he strikes into the trunk, but this time he asks the narrator to disengage the bill-hook. He does so, both chipping and dulling the blade. The tree must be hit straight and must be disengaged in the same manner, the Wizened Xiao tells him. The narrator, realizing that it is a question of pressure and angle, follows his advice and this time neither mars nor blunts the blade.

As if intent upon conserving energy, the Wizened Xiao is a man of few words. Living inside his own walled-in, introverted realm, he is always straightforward and to the point in his utterances. But he is also generous with his knowledge and empathic; he knows when he has struck a responsive chord in another human being. The narrator is not only impressed by the Wizened Xiao's reflective ways, but relates to this man of the forest on the human and profound level of the heart.

Because the narrator feels secure and comfortable with the Wizened Xiao, he is not afraid of asking him a question that could, at first, appear indiscreet: why, when the Wizened Xiao smiles, does his upper lip form a kind of rictus (stretching his skin to such an extent that it pulls the cheek down, distorting his entire face and causing his laugh to seem eerie, almost frightening)? The woodman's answer is simple: during his participation as a soldier in a series of competitive sports, he fell from a high rock and gashed his face. The surgeon stitching him pulled the skin too tightly, accounting for his facial deformation. Despite this injury, his strength never waned and he participated in other contests held by the Chinese Army: hand-to-hand combat, shooting and dagger matches, mountain climbing, and boxing. To prove his physical strength, the Wizened Xiao now makes a fist and hits the rock he had previously used to sharpen his bill-hook. It shatters. The narrator is dumbfounded. No sign of even a scratch is visible on the old man's fist.

There is no doubt that the narrator views the Wizened Xiao as a man of mystery. Inaccessible and unfathomable, he seems at peace with himself and open and pliable in the company of those of his ilk. Jung's description of the introverted feeling type is applicable, to a great extent, to this perplexing man of the forest:

> Their outward demeanour is harmonious, inconspicuous . . . no desire to affect others, either to impress, influence, or change them in any way. . . . A superficial judgment might well be betrayed, by a rather cold and reserved demeanour, into denying all feeling to this type. (*Collected Works*, 6:439)

To conclude that the Wizened Xiao's stiff demeanor parallels a hard and steely temperament is erroneous. His feelings are *intensive* rather than *extensive*. That his libido is drawn inward gives the impression that he is cut off from normal expressive ways and therefore unapproachable, and inaccessible; in reality he is not.

The King of the Trees

Born from the Great Earth Mother, trees, identified with the phallus, are paradigms of the Great Father. So identified is the Wizened Xiao with trees that he is, as already suggested, possessed by this archetypal power. Since the group's arrival, the constellation of the archetype has caused tensions to become so aggravated as to lead to the explosion or fragmentation of the ego: the breakdown of the conscious world (Franz, *On Divination and Synchronicity*, 53).

One evening, just as Li Li is about to complete the chopping-down of a large tree, the narrator notices a man hiding in the bushes. Recognizing him as the Wizened Xiao, he tells him with pleasure of the group's great accomplishment: the rapid clearing of so many trees. Rather than rejoice, the old man turns his back to him, embarrassed perhaps by the tears filling his eyes. Later he notices that the tree Li Li believes he has successfully felled has not fallen all the way to earth; some large branches are lying precariously on creepers. Should there be a strong wind, the tree could be dislodged and fall on the unsuspecting Li Li or even on the group.

With calm and dexterity, the Wizened Xiao performs an astounding deed: he thrusts his knife into the air several times, each time severing more of the limbs and creepers that prevent the tree from hitting the ground and resting there securely. Finally, as the tree solidly comes to rest, the noise made by the branches sounds like "coughing" or "vibrating" tones, as if the entire mountain were being castrated and crying out its pain and despair for the universe to hear. Are these agonizing wails emanating from the tree? the narrator wonders. Or do they come from the Wizened Xiao's heart? Silence. As the narrator looks around, the once thriving and luxuriously green mountain has been transformed into a giant cemetery.

Some days later, Li Li decides to cut down the King of the Trees, thus doing away once and for all, he believes, with superstition and impracticality. He will substitute revolutionary slogans: "Greatness is steadfastness"; "Steadfastness is purity"; "Great undertakings form great characters." Nothing is able to dissuade Li Li from achieving his goal. As extremist in his rationally conceived utilitarian views as the Wizened Xiao is in his shamanism, Li Li is under the dominion of an autonomous complex that has for the time being divested his ego of its sovereignty. Li Li's great phantasm, an image of himself that does not correspond to any concrete external situation, is activated and directed by unconscious contents, by libido playing out through association and parallelism its own scenario (Jung, *Collected Works*, 6:439).

The narrator, on the other hand, approaching the sacred Tree, is deeply moved not only by its majesty but by the specific feeling tones it arouses in him. The noumenal or divine quality flooding his being awakens in him a terrifying awesomeness. The shock effect does not bring about a dissociation of the ego-complex, but generates a solid connection between his ego and his Self (total psyche), paving the way for increased communication between the formerly disparate and unevolved parts of his own psyche.

As if trying to take the Tree into himself, the narrator gazes at it with wonderment: the flamelike scintillae radiating from the sun's rays and touching upon its richly endowed leaves take on the configuration of a bejeweled crown. Activity is intensified by the multitude of birds plunging into the Tree's luxurious foliage, appearing and disappearing from sight, their chirpings, singly and in orchestrated melodies, reaching out in a harmony of the spheres. Like the Tree of Life or the Tree of Knowledge, this archetypal power holds the narrator in thrall. Has he stepped into a *temenos*, a sacred and protected area, that inner empty space where feelings ferment, and incubate and what is insoluble becomes soluble?

The energy packets the Tree communicates to him help him move forward and to a central point where he may concentrate on the problems at hand. As a new balance comes into being, ego unites with a nontemporal sphere (the collective unconscious). An inner order begins to prevail, establishing balance between spiritual and worldly domains. The narrator has absorbed and incorporated eternal values within himself. He has succeeded in combining traditional and contemporary ideologies, realizing that there is not one single and all-time answer to any given problem, but multiple ways; not rigidity, but a supple and pliable approach; not overidentification, but a detached and seasoned outlook with regard to human and collective needs.

Only now does the narrator realize that the Wizened Xiao is the King of the Trees called into battle to defend his empire. As Li Li approaches the Tree, his prey, walking around it as if to judge where best to strike, his antagonist rises to his feet and readies himself for war. No compromise between the two is possible because each is under the dominion of his own autonomous complex. By pointing to his chest, the Wizened Xiao has indicated that to kill the tree is to kill him; to mutilate or dismember any of its branches is to mutilate or dismember his heart. Anger flares. Li Li again rejects spiritual values as being extrahuman, outside of the rational sphere, and antithetical to utilitarian and material preoccupations. Because the Tree is useless, it must be cut down as the others have been. Who will win the contest?

The Taoist sage Chuang-tzu taught in his parable of the trees that what appears to be useless on the surface can, on another level, be profoundly useful (*Chuang-Tzu*, 22). Traveling over a mountain, he sees an enormous tree with heavy foliage and a woodsman standing before it. The sage asks why he has not cut it down. Because it is "useless," he replies. "This tree by virtue of being good for nothing succeeds in completing its allotted span." However, because nothing can avoid its mortality, there would have been "no praise, no blame" if someone *had* cut the tree down; Tao floats about, changing with the change of time. It is Tao, as vital cosmic principle, that transcends human passions and encourages people to live in harmony with their surroundings and themselves:

> for where there is completion, there is also destruction; where there is purity, there is also oppression; where there is honour, there is also disparagement; where there is doing there is also undoing; where there is openness, there is also underhandedness; and where there is no semblance, there is also deceit. (*Chuang-tzu*, 190)

Nor must one, say the Buddhists, identify too deeply with things of the manifest world. To do so is to be dominated by illusion and the sorrow that befalls the person who is possessed by anything tangible.

The contest between Li Li and the Wizened Xiao begins. Cut down all the other trees but leave this one unharmed, the old man pleads. It is and must remain a witness to the work of the God of Heaven. Li Li laughs at such "primitivism."

> Man dominates nature. Was it God that parcelled out the fields? No, man did it in order to feed himself. Did God smelt iron? No, it's man to make tools and to transform nature—including, to be sure, your own God of Heaven.

Li Li raises his arm and casts his bill-hook into the sacred trunk. Instead of impacting into the Tree trunk, it flies into the air, like a flash of lightning. The Wizened Xiao has caught it bare-handed. The Tree is unharmed. Li Li asks for the return of his instrument. The mountain man refuses. The party secretary threatens to bring the Wizened Xiao up on charges before the Public Review Committee. Tears roll down the old man's cheeks. Silently and in great pain he lets the bill-hook slip from his hands. The sound resonates. The birds are frightened. Their happy chirpings suddenly turn into lamentations.

It takes four days to cut down the tree. Identified with the quaternity, that is, the whole or completion, the old woodsman and their drastic ways win over the weaker forces of tradition. But then, does not every finite being reach a point of exhaustion? Defeated, the Wizened Xiao awaits death. Daily he weakens, and like the tree felled on the fourth day, he, too, dies.

The Cremation

It has been decreed that once the mountain is cleared, a fire should be set. So powerful are its flames, so rapidly do they spread, so thick is the smoke, that all the view of the sun is blocked. Intense crackling sounds emanate from the earth, and agonizing vibrations issue not only from the Tree but from the entire mountain.

> Suddenly, a terrible noise followed by a piercing whistling sound was heard; the fire formed like a ball had exploded. Through the flames we saw a great tree rise violently and then fly away in myriad sparks before being thrown down, and when falling, sparking innumerable live embers, the largest crushing against the earth and the lightest, flying hundreds of feet high, floating in the heavens, after which [they] whirled around for a long while. When the fire approached the top of the mountain, the summit line, seven or eight li long, was illuminated as in broad daylight.

As the narrator watches the sacred Tree blaze before him, he witnesses a virtually apocalyptic sight: a barking deer leaping to and fro suddenly stops beside the Tree, then kneels down in front of it, lowers its head and haunches, and leaps with the speed of an arrow into the fire and disappears into its flames. And "the universe was seized with terror," the narrator writes.

Other strange happenings occur. After the Wizened Xiao's body is lain to rest in a wooden coffin and buried a few meters from the great Tree, a torrential rain descend on the entire area. When it subsides, and the sun peers through the clouds, the coffin's wet surface, now above the ground, shines brilliantly. "The mountain doesn't want him!" the group leader says, his voice cracking with emotion. Cremation follows as the man of the mountain becomes one with his spiritual counterpart: that living universal spirit within the Tree.

The fire lit, black smoke issues from the coffin, rises directly heavenward, then disperses into the air, as if nothing has been. To enter fire, according to Taoist tradition, is to be liberated from the human condition. The ashes buried next to the sacred Tree, its immense trunk covered with burned hatchet-scars that look like unhealed gashes, take on the shape of "a wounded man lying on the ground." The releasing of the yang principle by the flame has generated multiple sproutings of white flowers resembling bruised and mutilated bones, the bones of one whose flesh has experienced protracted flayings.

And so the Tao of existence, the "seamless web of unbroken movement and change, filled with undulations, waves, patterns of ripples and temporary 'standing waves' like a river plate," pursues its course, every observer seeking to halt its fluidity, to possess its intangibility, and to understand its mystery.

> Vast indeed is the Ultimate Tao,
> Spontaneously itself, apparently without acting,
> End of all ages and beginning of all ages,
> Existing before Earth and existing before Heaven,
> Silently embracing the whole of time,
> Continuing uninterrupted through all eons,
> In the East it taught Father Confucius,
> In the West it converted the 'Golden man' [the Buddha]
> Taken as patterns by a hundred kings,
> Transmitted by generations of sages,
> It is the ancestor of all doctrines,
> The mystery beyond all mysteries.
>
> (Rawson and Legeza, 10)

Conclusion

Exile, whatever its form, be it chosen by or forced upon individuals or groups, be it exoteric or esoteric, has been a way of life since the end of nomadism. Enormous packets of instinctual and psychic energy have been expended in the continuous flow of peoples from one area to another, and in the efforts needed during the period of adaptation required by the new environment.

Instincts, defined as a human being's inborn and natural bodily behavior, or as an unacquired mode of response to stimuli, have always been called into play for purposes of survival and for the fulfillment of needs and desires. When instinct prevails, an individual's spontaneous reactions dominate. Under such circumstances, people are not functioning of their own volition, but are mobilized by their autonomous energy, or the autonomous energy of their group.

What are some of the factors responsible for mobilizing a human being to take the route of exile or to survive exile that is imposed? As I have suggested throughout this book, archetypes are the psychic aspects of instincts. The energy inherent in archetypes motivated Dostoevsky to survive his Siberian ordeal, and then to write his seminal work, *The House of the Dead*. First he had to come to terms with his painful displacement: the enormous move that cut him off from family and friends; then he had to create a new life for himself in prison. After his release he turned his negative experience into a positive one by transposing his ideas and his feelings into an art form. Why did Conrad's trip to the Belgian Congo and the recounting of his self-imposed exile in *Heart of Darkness*, help him to face his shadow, which he had until that time managed to expel or repress in one way or another? Here, too, it was a question of coming to grips with a corrosive aspect of his psyche. Only drastic measures, he knew instinctively, would help him through his somber moments. How can one account for the sudden burst of enormous willpower that allowed the youth Primo Levi to live through the harrowing events he depicted in *Survival in Auschwitz?* Why did Huysmans's introverted hero seek a condition of exile, cutting himself off from the mainstream of life? The protagonists in the works analyzed, so frequently projections of the authors themselves, listened to and followed the dictates of an unknown motivating dynamism—or an archetype—within their psyche.

Like instincts, archetypes are the fundaments of human nature. They have existed and exist, as far as we know, in all people since time immemorial. As patterns of behavior, they live inchoate in the collective unconscious, that is, in a suprapersonal domain, and are made available to conscious awareness in the form of archetypal images. These visualizations, which may also be experienced in the form of sonorizations and rhythmizations, are active participants in the creative process.

Archetypal exile is one yet multiple. Although their basic theme is the same, the manner in which each individual writer sees, treats, feels, and rationalizes this common motif, varies. Just as archetypal experiences have been counted and recounted in ancient and modern religious myths, fairy tales, dreams, and creative works in general, each is, nevertheless, unique: the product of an individual's inner temperament and talents, as well as his or her period, culture, and environment. We may suggest the analogy of the fingerprint: although all human beings are born with fingers, each fingerprint bears its own stamp and design. Certainly, the exilic motifs in the works of Malraux and Beckett are antipodal; as are those of Kawabata and Levi; and Garro and Cheng. Nevertheless, they have common characteristics.

When creative individuals are in touch with the archetypes available to them—those energy centers that contain the deposits of human experience since earliest days—the psychic activity these arouse has, for some, a catalytic effect. In the cases of Dostoevsky, Conrad, and Levi, the storehouse of energy within the dominant archetype helped them cope with harrowing experiences. Transmuting the explosive factors living inchoate within their psyches into words permitted these individuals to objectify chaos by projecting it outside of themselves. When properly integrated into the work of art, the energy generated by the archetypal material, led to a continuous unfolding of incredible images and dramatizations of the traumas that life had in store for the ten authors treated here and their protagonists.

Dostoevsky, Kawabata, Agnon, Conrad, Malraux, and Beckett, while molding their personifications and configurations from their archetypal depths, also articulated in their narratives their psychic backgrounds as individuals and as products of their times and cultures. As such, the behavioral patterns of the characters or noncharacters, the writers' perspectives or nonperspectives, thematics, or nonthematics exist both within and outside of time.

Personal and collective motifs, then, are interwoven into the archetype of exile. Not only are empirical anguishes and joys incised in such novels, plays, and short stories, as "Edo and Enam," *That Time*, "The King of the Trees," *Recollections of Things to Come*, or *Against the Grain*, but a transpersonal realm beyond the immediate environment is reached.

Archetypal exile is a paradigm of timely and eternal motifs, of individual and collective efforts. Archetypes, let us recall, make up the contents of the collective unconscious, that suprapersonal and nonindividual sphere within the psyche. The outcome of an author's personal need may, therefore, take on universal dimension for himself as well as for others. The ten creative artists dealt with the events, the environments in which they lived, or the relationships mushrooming about them, by developing inner aptitudes and attitudes provided for them by the archetypes constellated prior to, during, and following the creation of their novel, play, or short story.

Archetypal exile may be viewed as a code; the written work, as the decoder of the message. The images projected by the archetype, be they in the depiction of characters, landscapes, plots, colors, rhythms, figures of speech, or other stylistic devices, could be likened to palimpsests. Like these parchments that have been written upon or inscribed two or three times, the previous text or texts having been imperfectly erased and hence partially remaining, the various levels of the psyche become visible in multiple ways in the written work. The reader may interpret or react to the novel, play, or short story on a variety of levels depending upon the depth of his or her understanding and feeling. Judgments may be based on the obvious: plot, descriptions, and characterizations. Or they may be broached archetypally, that is, from the deepest levels or geological folds of the psyche. To remain open and accessible to the artist's method and message is crucial.

There is a Zen story that narrates the conversation between Nan-in, a Japanese Zen Master who lived during the Meiji period, and a university professor who had come to his home to learn more about Zen. When Nan-in started to pour the tea for his guest, he continued to do so even though the cup was filled. As the liquid kept overflowing, the professor, unable to contain his curiosity as to the meaning of the Master's actions, spoke out.

"It is overfull. No more will go in!" Nan-in replied: "Like this cup, you are full of your own opinions and speculations. How can I show you Zen unless you first empty your cup?" (Zukav, 141).

When readers experience a great work archetypally, the profoundest levels of their psyche are activated. Mobilized in this manner, they no longer approach reading mechanically as a rote activity; it becomes an exciting creative process, and frequently a healing one as well, inviting greater understanding and increased consciousness. As Jung wrote:

> The psychological rule says that when an inner situation is made conscious, it happens outside, as fate. That is to say, when the individual remains undivided and does not become conscious of his inner contradictions, the world must perforce act out the conflict and be torn into opposite halves. (*Collected Works*, 7:70–71)

When an author's theme revolves around exile, the reader may, if there is identification or projection, live out, if not a similar displacement or ejection, certainly a related psychological condition in which feelings of alienation, rejection, and exclusion have gained the upper hand. By evaluating the meanings of their reactions to the creative work, readers in certain cases also clarify their own chaotic feelings, thoughts, and impulses. When critical faculties are called into play during and following the completion of a novel, short story, or play, a better understanding of the problems and pleasures of others and of oneself may emerge. If objectification or the analytical process is not used when encountering an archetype, one runs the risk of being overwhelmed and fascinated by this energy and blinded to any kind of evolutive psychological process.

For those individuals who are highly religious, the intense power experienced as a result of an encounter with an archetype has been interpreted as a meeting with God, or, in psychological terms, a momentary eclipse of the ego. The impact of this kind of archetypal experience may have such a powerful effect upon the psyche that an individual can become identified with it and may convert as a result; or may consider himself or herself, as has happened throughout the course of history, above and beyond the laws of mortals. Messiahs or fanatics, be they religiously or politically motivated, have fallen into such traps, convinced that everyone must be compelled to live within the behavioral pattern of the archetype that dominates their lives.

To avoid such dangers—if such be possible, in view of humanity's past, fraught with destruction and intolerance—individuals and nations would do well to maintain a certain degree of detachment with regard to ideologies (political, religious, literary, or any other), thus inviting a broader-based and more balanced point of view. To prevent submersion by a particular archetype, a process that has divested so many peoples of the immense range of human experience, is to try to distance oneself from an enormous storehouse of psychic energy existing within each of us. To do so allows one to better connect with the enormous riches and powers that a spectrum of archetypes, experienced in dynamic equilibrium, continuously generates. Observing, fleshing out, and probing peoples' behavioral patterns and the happenings in which these are experienced—in our case, focusing on the motif of exile—not only expand consciousness and allow the individuation process to pursue its course; they guard against the very real dangers of becoming victimized by the explosive powers built into potentially dominating archetypes.

Fortunately, Dostoevsky, the artist, the manipulator of words, was compelled to convey his narrator's feelings of jubilation and redemption, after being freed from his Siberian prison, in thought-out sequences such as the following: "Freedom, a new life, resurrection from the dead. . . . What a glorious moment!" Had the power of the archetype not been properly decanted into words, it might have torn him to pieces.

The months Marlow spent in the Belgian Congo, as narrated in Conrad's *The Heart of Darkness*, brought him awareness, thus spelling "victory" for him. Having authentically lived out the "Great Nekyia," he felt in touch with his innermost nature. Able to objectify his feelings, he put them to work carving out a new way for himself.

Huysmans's Duke Jean des Esseintes was unable to face and live in reality. Overcome by uncontrollable ennui and hatred for society, which he saw as superficial and materialistic, he withdrew from the world. Unable to objectify his feelings of alienation, he never understood his involuted and convoluted ways. Rather than grow and evolve, he lived out the fate of the *puer aeternus*, remaining the undeveloped and callow youth about whom he fantasized in his sadomasochistic, transsexual, and homosexual encounters.

Malraux's three heroes in *The Royal Way*, exiles from Western Europe, struggled through life-threatening situations in their quest to find fulfillment, to renew lives they considered failures. As one of the heroes prepared himself for the greatest exile of them all, his exit from the land of the living, the youngest of the three realized that something within him *had* changed. For the first time he understood the real meaning of eros: relatedness. He expressed his new-found capacity to feel for someone else and to experience the meaning of camaraderie by grabbing his dying friend around the shoulders and hugging him deeply.

Agnon's tale, "Edo and Enam," narrates the irremediable sense of bereavement that fills the life of a young bride after leaving the land of her ancestors to follow her husband to Jerusalem. On a mystical and arche-typal level, Agnon's work implies another kind of crisis: that of a soul in exile. The pain endured, although tragic for the protagonists, may illumi-nate the reader's understanding of both terrestrial and spiritual matters, depending upon the depth of his or her inner vision.

Kawabata's *Master of Go* focuses on the game of Go as a paradigmatic ritual of exile into death. Going beyond the diversionary nature of contest per se, the game invites both the participants and the reader to undergo a deeply spiritual experience, so profound, indeed, as to take them out of their ego-oriented world and immerse them in the intricate patternings and interrelationships involved in the transpersonal experience.

Levi's factual account of his abduction from his native city of Turin and his ten-month exile in the Nazi death camp of Auschwitz may be viewed as a testament to his heroic capacity for endurance and, para-doxically, in view of his suicide in 1987, his will to live. No matter how harrowing his experience, it had meaning for him, and he hoped it would act as an indelible example of horror to be avoided by future generations. While Dostoevsky's *The House of the Dead* was an example of "czarist absolutism," Levi wrote, the "German camps constitute something unique in the history of humanity. . . . [T]hey set a mon-strous modern goal, that of erasing entire peoples and cultures from the world." Lest we forget!

Garro's surrealist *Recollections of Things to Come* dramatizes certain events in a cloistered small-town environment, where all the members of a family are sequestered from the rest of their country, as well as being cut off from the other members of the community and from themselves. Garro's alienated protagonists are "exiles from happiness." Unable to un-derstand the happenings they experience and incapable of relating to others, they live and die unredeemed in their own little world.

Time is Beckett's protagonist's fearful enemy; it is that which has forced him into exile and which brings about his slow deterioration in *That Time*. Eating voraciously into every moment, feeding illusions and breeding the fossilization of ideologies, dogmas, and behavioral patterns, Time is the tempter that lures limited mortal minds to hang on to deceits in their longing to arrest the nonapprehensible.

Cheng's "The King of the Trees" deals with a group of Chinese students exiled by their government to a remote forested region for reeducational purposes. Cheng's tale teaches the reader a lesson: that its protagonist is a tree suggests not only a poetic responsiveness to transpersonal powers governing the universe, but an unwillingness to reduce the tangible and intangible world to the mechanistic laws of science alone.

Dostoevsky, Conrad, Huysmans, Malraux, Agnon, Kawabata, Levi, Garro, Beckett, and Cheng attempted to come to terms with aspects of their inner turbulence by means of their verbal experiments. I have stressed certain aspects and motifs centering on archetypal exile and diminished the importance of others. Their ability to articulate unconscious pulsations and traumas in the written word helped them to achieve if not wholeness, at least the possibility of living their lives in a creative manner and in relative harmony and balance, within the framework of their temperament and culture.

Nevertheless, as Jung noted in an interview, "The world's most beautiful truths are of no use until their purport has become an original inner experience with each of us" (Jung, "On the Frontiers of Knowledge," 22). If individuals do not open themselves up to their unconscious and to their dreams, self-knowledge will not only not burgeon, but will experience a condition of stasis and eventually atrophy. Dark times may then again unfold. Jung remarked:

> Indeed, it appears, with an ever more blinding clarity, that it is not famine, nor earthquake, nor microbes, nor cancer, but man, who constitutes quite the greatest danger to man. The reason is simple, there exists as yet no protection against psychic epidemics; yet these epidemics are infinitely more devastating than the worst natural catastrophes! The supreme danger which menaces individuals as well as people . . . is a psychic danger. Against it reason has proved impotent. ("On the Frontiers of Knowledge," 12)

A dangerous river-crossing or a particularly painful fork in the road may, in some unexpected way, cast a glimmer of light on the problems at hand. It is from within the infinite reservoir of potential, the immense treasury known as the collective unconscious, that individuals and nations draw their energy: a killer instinct that breeds multiplying horrors or an imagistic world of fantasy that yields creative, healing powers capable of assuaging a spiritual famine and feeding multitudes.

Selected Bibliography

Aeschylus. *Prometheus Bound. Agamemnon. The Complete Greek Drama.* Vol. 1. Translated by E. D. A. Moorshead. New York: Random House, 1938.

Agnon, S. Y. *Two Tales by S. Y. Agnon.* Translated by Walter Lever. New York: Schocken Books, 1966.

Asmus, Walter D. "Rehearsal Notes for the German Premiere of Beckett's *That Time* and *Footfalls.*" In *On Beckett: Essays and Criticism*, edited by S. E. Gontarski. New York: Grove Press, 1986.

Awakawa, Yasuichi. *Zen Painting.* Tokyo: Kodansha International, 1970.

Baker, Joan Stanley. *Japanese Art.* London: Thames and Hudson, 1984.

Barrett, William. *Irrational Man.* New York: Doubleday Anchor, 1962.

Bary, William Theodore de, ed. *Sources of Chinese Tradition.* Vol. 1. New York: Columbia University Press, 1960.

———. *Sources of Indian Tradition.* Vols. 1 and 2. New York: Columbia University Press, 1958.

———. *Sources of Japanese Tradition.* Vol. 1. New York: Columbia University Press, 1964.

Beckett, Samuel. "Dante . . . Bruno. Vico . . . Joyce." *transition* (June 1929). From *James Joyce/Finnegans Wake: A Symposium.* New York: New Directions, 1972.

———. *Endgame.* New York: Grove Press, 1958.

———. "Le froc d'Estragon." Letter from Samuel Beckett to Roger Blin, 9 January 1953. *Magazine Littéraire*, June 1986, p. 35.

———. *Proust.* New York: Grove Press, 1957. (Originally published London: Chatto and Windus, 1931.)

———. *That Time.* London: Faber and Faber, 1976.

Bergson, Henri. *Le Rire.* Paris: Presses Universitaires de France, 1969.

Capra, Fritjof. *The Tao of Physics.* Berkeley: Shambhala, 1975.

Carr, E. H. *Dostoyevsky*. London: George Allen and Unwin, 1949.

Castedo, Leopoldo. *A History of Latin American Art and Architecture*. Translated by Phyllis Freeman. New York: Frederick A. Praeger, 1969.

Cather, Willa. *Collected Works*. Vol. 10. Boston: Houghton Mifflin, 1931.

Cheng, A. *Les Trois Rois*. Translated by Noel Dutrait. Provence: Alinéa, 1985.

Chuang-tzu. Translated by Herbert A. Giles. London: Unwin, 1980.

Confucius. *Analects*. Translated by D. C. Lau. New York: Penguin, 1979.

Conrad, Joseph. *The Heart of Darkness*. New York: Doubleday, 1983.

———. *Lord Jim*. New York: Norton Critical Edition, 1968.

Coulson, Jessie. *Dostoevsky: A Self-Portrait*. London: Oxford University Press, 1962.

Dostoyevsky, Fyodor. *The House of the Dead*. Translated and with an introduction by David McDuff. London: Penguin, 1988.

Edinger, Edward. *The Christian Archetype*. Toronto: Inner City Books, 1987.

———. *Ego and Archetype*. New York: Putnam, 1972.

———. "An Outline of Analytical Psychology." Unpublished.

Eliade, Mircea. *The Myth of Eternal Return*. Princeton: Princeton University Press, 1974.

———. *Myths, Dreams, and Mysteries*. New York: Harper Torchbooks, 1960.

———. *Patterns in Comparative Religion*. New York: New American Library, 1974.

———. *Rites and Symbols of Initiation*. New York: Harper Torchbooks, 1965.

———. *Shamanism*. Princeton: Princeton University Press, 1972.

———. *The Two and the One*. New York: Harper Torchbooks, 1969.

Ellwood, Robert S., and Pilgrim, Richard, *Japanese Religion*. Englewood Cliffs, N.J.: Prentice-Hall, 1985.

Euripides. *Ten Plays. Medea*. Translated by Moses Hadas and John McLean. New York: Penguin, 1977.

Feibleman, James. *In Praise of Comedy*. New York: Russell and Russell, 1962.

Fischer, Henry G. "Egyptian Turtles." *Metropolitan Art Bulletin* (February 1966): 193–200.

Franz, Marie Louise von. *Creation Myths*. Zurich: Spring Publications, 1972.

———. "The Dream of Descartes." In *Timeless Documents of the Soul*. Translated by Andrea Dykes and Elizabeth Welsh, 55–147. Evanston: Northwestern University Press, 1968.

———. *On Divination and Synchronicity*. Toronto: Inner City Books, 1980.

———, and James Hillman. *Lectures on Jung's Typology*. New York: Spring Publications, 1971.

Garro, Elena. *Recollections of Things to Come*. Translated by Ruth L. C. Simms. Austin: University of Texas Press, 1969.

Gontarski, S. E., ed. *On Beckett: Essays and Criticism*. New York: Schocken Books, 1965.

Harding, Esther. *The Way of All Women*. New York: Harper & Row, 1975.

———. *Woman's Mysteries*. New York: Putnam, 1971.

Herzog, Edgar. *Psyche and Death*. New York: Putnam, 1967.

Hesla, David H. *An Interpretation of the Art of Samuel Beckett.* Minneapolis: University of Minnesota Press, 1971.

Hochman, Baruch. *The Fiction of S. Y. Agnon.* Ithaca: Cornell University Press, 1970.

Homer, *Odyssey.* Translated by S. H. Butcher and Andrew Lang. New York: Airmont, 1965.

Huysmans, J.-K. *A Rebours.* Paris: Gallimard, 1977.

Izutsu, Toshihiko. "The Elimination of Colour in Far Eastern Art and Philosophy." In *Color Symbolism,* 167–95. Zurich: Spring Publications, 1977.

Jacobi, Yolande. *Complex Archetype Symbol.* Translated by Ralph Manheim. Princeton: Princeton University Press, 1959.

Juliet, Charles, *Rencontre avec Samuel Beckett.* Montpellier: Editions Fata Morgana, 1986.

Jung, C. G. *Collected Works.* Vol. 1. Translated by R. F. C. Hull. Princeton: Princeton University Press, 1975.

———. Vol. 5. Translated by R. F. C. Hull. New York: Pantheon, 1950.

———. Vol. 6. Translated by H. Godwin Baynes. London: Pantheon, 1964.

———. Vol. 8. Translated by R. F. C. Hull. Princeton: Princeton University Press, 1969.

———. Vol. 9[11]. Translated by R. F. C. Hull. Princeton: Princeton University Press, 1968.

———. Vol. 11. Translated by R. F. C. Hull. New York: Pantheon, 1963.

———. Vol. 12. Translated by R. F. C. Hull. London: Routledge and Kegan Paul, 1953.

———. *Memories, Dreams, Reflections.* New York: Pantheon, 1963.

———. "On the Frontiers of Knowledge: An Interview with C. G. Jung: 1959." *Spring,* 1960, 1961, 1962, 1973, 9–22.

———. *The Visions Seminars.* Vol. 2. Zurich: Spring Publications, 1976.

———, and C. Kerenyi. *Essays on the Science of Mythology.* Princeton: Princeton University Press, 1969.

Jung, Emma, and Marie Louise von Franz. *The Grail Legend.* New York: Putnam, 1970.

Kaplan, Aryeh. *Meditation and Kabbalah.* York Beach, Maine: Samuel Weiser, 1988.

Kawabata, Yasunari. *The Master of Go.* Translated by Edward G. Seidensticker. New York: Wideview/Perigee, 1981.

Kennedy, Sighle. *Murphy's Bed.* Lewisburg, Pa.: Bucknell University Press, 1971.

Lacouture, Jean. *André Malraux.* New York: Pantheon, 1975.

Levi, Primo. *The Reawakening.* Translated by Stuart Woolf. New York: Macmillan, 1965.

———. *Survival in Auschwitz.* Translated by Stuart Woolf. New York: Macmillan, 1959.

Malraux, André. *La Voie royale.* Paris: Bernard Grasset, 1930.

Margarschack, David. *Dostoevsky.* New York: Harcourt, Brace and World, 1962.

Marrus, Michael R. *The Holocaust in History.* Hanover: University Press of New England, 1987.

Mishima, Yukio. *Runaway Horses.* Translated by M. Gallagher. New York: Pocket Books, 1975.

Montaigne, Michel. *Complete Essays.* Translated by Donald M. Frame. Stanford: Stanford University Press, 1965.

Muehsam, Gerd. *French Painters and Paintings from the Fourteenth Century to Post-Impressionism.* New York: Ungar, 1970.

Neumann, Erich. *Depth Psychology and a New Ethic.* New York: Putnam, 1969.

———. "Dynamic Aspects of the Psyche." New York Analytical Club, 1956.

———. "Fear of the Feminine." *Spring* (1986).

———. *The Great Mothers.* New York: Pantheon, 1963.

———. *The Origins and History of Consciousness.* New York: Putnam, 1970.

Novalis. *Hymns to the Night and Other Selected Writings.* Translated by Charles E. Passage. Indianapolis: Bobbs-Merrill, 1960.

Otto, Rudolf. *Le Sacré.* Paris: Payot, 1968.

Ramayana. Translated by R. K. Narayan. New York: Penguin, 1981.

Rawson, Philip, and Laszlo Legeza. *Tao.* London: Thames and Hudson, 1979.

The Rig-Veda. Translated by Wendy O'Flaherty. New York: Penguin, 1981.

Rumi Poet and Mystic. Translated by R. A. Nicholson. London: Mandala Books, 1979.

Sarmach, Paul, ed. *An Introduction to the Medieval Mystics of Europe.* Albany: State University of New York Press, 1984.

Schimmel, AnneMarie. *Mystical Dimensions of Islam.* Chapel Hill: University of North Carolina Press, 1981.

Scholem, Gershom. *Kabbalah and Its Symbolism.* New York: Schocken Books, 1969.

———. *Major Trends in Jewish Mysticism.* New York: Schocken Books, 1961.

———. *On the Kabbalah and Its Symbolism.* Translated by Ralph Manheim. New York: Schocken Books, 1965.

Séjourné, Laurette. *Burning Water.* Berkeley: Shambhala, 1976.

Sharkey, John. *Celtic Mysteries.* London: Thames and Hudson, 1975.

Simon, Alfred, "Tout un Théâtre." *Magazine Littéraire,* June 1986.

Soustelle, Jacques. *Daily Life of the Aztecs.* Translated by Patrick O'Brian. Stanford: Stanford University Press, 1970.

Staël, Madame de. *Oeuvres Posthumes.* Geneva: Slatkine Reprints. 1967.

Suzuki, Daisets T. *An Introduction to Zen Buddhism.* Foreword by C. G. Jung. New York: Grove Press, 1977.

———. *Zen and Japanese Culture.* Princeton: Princeton University Press, 1973.

Swann, Peter C. *A Concise History of Japanese Art.* Tokyo: Kodansha International, 1958.

Thompson, Laurence G. *Chinese Religion: An Introduction.* Belmont, Calif.: Dickinson, 1969.

Underhill, Evelyn. *The Mystics of the Church.* New York: Schocken Books, 1971.

The Upanishads. Translated by Juan Mascaro. New York: Penguin, 1975.

Walls, Jan, and Yvonne Walls. *Classical Chinese Myths*. Hong Kong: Joint Publishing, 1984.

Wellek, René. "Dostoevsky and Parricide." In *Sigmund Freud: A Collection of Critical Essays*, edited by René Wellek (130–45). Englewood Cliffs: N.J.: Prentice-Hall, 1965.

Wiesenthal, Simon. *Every Day Remembrance Day: A Chronicle of Jewish Martyrdom*. New York: Holt, Rinehart & Winston, 1986.

Wilhelm, Richard. *I Ching*. Translated by Carry R. Baynes. Princeton: Princeton University Press, 1967.

———. *Lectures on the I Ching*. Translated by Irene Eber. Princeton: Princeton University Press, 1979.

Wyman, David S. *Abandonment of the Jews*. New York: Pantheon, 1984.

Yarmolinsky, Avrahm. *Dostoevsky: A Life*. New York: 1934.

The Zohar. Vol. 2. Translated by Harry Sperling and Maurice Simon. London: Soncino Press, 1933.

Zukav, Gary. *The Dancing Wu Li Masters*. New York: William Morrow, 1979.

Index